Introduction to Corrections

Introduction to Corrections

David H. McElreath • Linda Keena
Greg Etter • Ellis Stuart

CRC Press
Taylor & Francis Group
Boca Raton   London   New York

CRC Press is an imprint of the
Taylor & Francis Group, an **informa** business

CRC Press
Taylor & Francis Group
6000 Broken Sound Parkway NW, Suite 300
Boca Raton, FL 33487-2742

© 2012 by Taylor & Francis Group, LLC
CRC Press is an imprint of Taylor & Francis Group, an Informa business

No claim to original U.S. Government works

Printed in the United States of America on acid-free paper
Version Date: 20110527

International Standard Book Number: 978-1-4398-6013-7 (Hardback)

Library of Congress Cataloging-in-Publication Data

Introduction to corrections / authors, David H. McElreath ... [et al.].
    p. cm.
Includes bibliographical references and index.
ISBN 978-1-4398-6013-7 (hardcover : alk. paper)
1. Corrections--United States. I. McElreath, David.

HV9471.I65 2011
365'.973--dc23   2011021606

Visit the Taylor & Francis Web site at
http://www.taylorandfrancis.com

and the CRC Press Web site at
http://www.crcpress.com

No work of this type can be produced without the special people whose support and influence upon the lives of the authors have been significant. With this in mind, the authors dedicate this work to a series of special people, without whom this work would not have been possible. Therefore, this text is dedicated to Leisa, Michael, Bonnie, Rita, and a final individual who dedicated his life to fairness and justice in his law enforcement career that extended over four decades, Ellis Ainsworth Stuart Sr.

This book is also dedicated to Professor Columbus B. Hopper, The University of Mississippi, and Mr. Ellis Stuart, Sr. ultimate professionals in the fields of sociology, criminology, criminal justice and law enforcement.

Contents

Section II
Community Corrections

Section III
Institutional Corrections

Section IV
Issues in Corrections

The Authors

David H. McElreath, PhD, has served as professor and chair, Department of Legal Studies, the University of Mississippi; professor and chair, Department of Criminal Justice, Washburn University; associate professor, Southeast Missouri State University; assistant professor, the University of Southern Mississippi; instructor, Itawamba (Mississippi) Community College; Colonel, U.S. Marine Corps; and he has held law enforcement and corrections positions with the Oxford (Mississippi) Police and Forrest County (Mississippi) Sheriff's Departments. His education and training include PhD in adult education and criminal justice, University of Southern Mississippi; an MSS, U.S. Army War College; MCJ, the University of Mississippi; BPA, the University of Mississippi; and he is a graduate of the U.S. Army War College. He is also the author or coauthor of numerous textbooks and publications on the criminal justice and homeland security systems.

Linda Keena, PhD, obtained her BCJ (1984) and MS (1991) degrees in criminal justice from Southeast Missouri State University, and her PhD (2006) from the University of Missouri. She is a former State of Missouri adult probation and parole officer and has taught in the Department of Criminal Justice and Sociology at Southeast Missouri State University, and most recently in the Legal Studies Department at the University of Mississippi. She has established a record of scholarly publications that reflects a variety of criminal justice, restorative justice, religion, corrections, and community-based research topics. In addition, she is coauthor and project director for METH Education for Elementary Schools (MEDFELS), a nationally recognized methamphetamine program for elementary schools. Dr.

Keena is codirector of the Violence Prevention Office at the University of Mississippi, a program funded by the Office on Violence Against Women, U.S. Department of Justice, aimed at educating students and staff about the realities of sexual assault, relationship violence, and stalking.

Greg Etter, EdD, is an assistant professor of criminal justice at the University of Central Missouri. He retired as a lieutenant with the Sedgwick County Sheriff's Office in Wichita, Kansas, after 29 years of service. He is rated as a gang expert by the National Gang Crime Research Center in Chicago, Illinois. Dr. Etter's educational background includes BS and MS degrees from Wichita State University, and he earned his doctorate from Oklahoma State University. He is a member of the National Sheriff's Association, American Jail Association, American Correction's Association, Academy of Criminal Justice Sciences, and the American Society of Criminology. He is the author of a textbook on hate crimes and numerous journal articles. Dr. Etter has presented papers and conducted law enforcement and corrections training all over the United States and Canada.

Ellis Stuart Jr. has served as Director of Public Safety for the City of Hazlehurst, Mississippi; contract agent for the Mississippi Metro Narcotics Task Force; Chief of Police for the City of Greenwood, Mississippi; Director of Public Safety for the Mississippi University for Women; hearing officer for the Mississippi Parole Board; probation and parole officer for the Mississippi Department of Corrections; youth court counselor for the Mississippi Department of Youth Services; and juvenile planner for the Law Enforcement Administration Division, Mississippi Office of the Governor. Mr. Stuart's education and training include a master's degree in criminal justice from Mississippi Valley State University, a bachelor's degree in social and rehabilitation services from the University of Southern Mississippi, and he is a graduate of the Mississippi Law Enforcement Officers Academy, Mississippi State Fire Academy, and FBI National Academy. Mr. Stuart is currently serving as the Copiah County (Mississippi) Coroner.

I

Foundations of Corrections

An Overview of Corrections

Introduction

The nature of mankind, which includes the freedom to make choices, led to the development in every known society of rules of conduct, with sanctions established for those who offend. In our society, we have empowered our governmental officials to formally legislate our community rules into laws. In the legislation of these laws, prohibited conduct is defined and penalties are established for violation.

Since the arrival of the earliest European settlers in North America, the laws governing personal conduct have evolved. New offenses are continually defined and punishments established for violation. With the passage of time, punishments have also evolved. As in other parts of the world, many of the early punishments in North America were publically administered. It was expected that the administration of public punishment would serve as a deterrent to those who might feel inclined to also violate the law. Punishment options were limited. Punishments such as public whipping, stocks, or even banishment were in common use. Long-term confinement facilities did not exist, nor did formal probation, community corrections, or parole. Today, we have a wide range of punishment options available to our judicial authorities.

In this text, we will study the various aspects of what we call corrections in the United States. We will examine diverse topics, to include the concept and application of punishment, and discuss victimization and institutionalization. We will examine the functions of corrections as well as the roles of those who serve in the profession. Corrections is a dynamic profession, ever changing and constantly challenging those who call the field a profession.

Correctional Foundations

As the American colonies evolved into states and a nation, the United States grew in physical size and population. The nation's cities grew. The industrial revolution brought economic prosperity to some segments of society, but for many, economic survival was a struggle. Advancements in economic, social, and technological areas opened opportunities for crime and criminal activity. Even in these early years, gangs emerged both in our developing cities and in the West. Petty crimes dominated the attention of law enforcement and the courts.

Violent crimes were for the most part limited. Even in the West, the actual number of homicides and bank robberies that occurred was far fewer than Hollywood suggests in its movies.

For most Americans, crime was a nuisance. The North and the eastern parts of the nation responded to crime differently than the South and the West. The North and the East held the nation's major urban areas; in the South, agriculture dominated the economy typically situated around small communities with limited populations. The West proved to be the nation's frontier of the 1800s; initially wild and untamed, the rule of law and justice would emerge with time and settlement.

Accordingly, the way laws were interpreted and applied varied not only from region to region, but also within communities and social and economic segments of the society.

As we examine corrections in this text, we have to keep in mind that corrections is one part of the criminal justice system. Corrections is more than just prisons, jails, and cells. Corrections is a dynamic profession, impacting the lives of millions. Correctional leaders provide support services to those who are under some type of correctional sanction. Corrections is also the victims and their families, those whose lives have been impacted as a result of the criminal activity. Crime and corrections is also big business. Millions of dollars are expended each year in support of this part of the criminal justice system.

The Global Community

The world today is linked as never before. Socially, politically, and economically, few parts of the inhabited globe are not connected in some ways. The worldwide revolution in areas such as communications, medicine, and transportation has enhanced lives, but while doing so, it has increased opportunities for criminal activity.

The changes in society, both nationally and globally, have also changed the nature of crime and justice. This reflects the changes in established social norms. For example, slavery was once legal in most parts of the world, including the United States (never moral, but once legal). Now slavery is illegal in most of the world and has been illegal in the United States since 1865 and the passage of the 13th Amendment. But the principle of laws codifying social norms and the violation of those social norms remain with us. Thus, the need for order mandates the need for corrections, correctional institutions, and corrections professionals. Every country has a corrections system. Enforcement of the law is one of the primary responsibilities of government, and corrections is an essential part of that governmental exercise of power.

Today, corrections in the United States is directly linked to the earliest days of American colonialization. Corrections refers to the supervision of persons arrested, convicted, and sentenced for committing criminal offenses. Correctional populations fall into two general categories: institutional corrections and community corrections.

Crime

Crime and criminal activity range from local to global. Crime directly or indirectly touches everyone in the nation, as an offender, victim, family, or friend of those involved, justice professional, or taxpayer. The FBI's Uniform Crime Reports Program (UCR) collects information from local law enforcement agencies about crimes reported to police. The UCR crime index includes seven offenses: homicide, forcible rape, robbery, aggravated assault, burglary, larceny-theft, and motor vehicle theft.

Crime and criminal behavior are common. Millions in our nation are under some type of judicial sanction, with the majority of those individuals serving their sentences living and working among us in what we call the free world. These offenders are serving their sentences under some form of conditional release, and it is trusted that they will comply with the conditions under which they were released. Our population of offenders does not represent a cross section of our society. Rather, most under criminal sanctions are male and young.

How Do We View Corrections?

Most Americans have never been inside a confinement facility, nor have they witnessed the activities of the community-based correctional professions as they perform their duties assisting, supervising, and monitoring those under judicial sanctions within our communities.

The public develops its beliefs and opinions about corrections through second- and third-party sources, popular movies and television, news reports that headline rates of confinement, violence, or on rare occasions, escapes.

The public is uneducated about corrections, the number of people involved, the cost, the duties, and the responsibilities. Many in the public believe the answer to crime is tough punishment, prisons that are bleak, few opportunities for the inmate, and even fewer privileges. Most Americans do not realize that millions of those around us are under some type of judicial sanction, many working in services we encounter daily.

What Is Corrections?

Additionally, punishments evolved from public administered to formal confinement. This evolution of formal punishment is what we call today corrections.

Corrections in the United States is much more than just bars and cells; corrections and the correctional systems of the nation are composed of people and places. Many of the people are some of the most outstanding professionals to ever serve our communities. Some are in the system of corrections as a result of their conduct, which has resulted in judicial action. Others linked to the system are the families of those directly involved, the families of those serving in a professional role as well as the families of those arrested and convicted.

In the United States we do not have one system of corrections; rather, hundreds of entities form the field of corrections. Federal, military, state, local level, and privately operated confinement facilities operate across the nation. Each of these facilities is unique. Even if two facilities were constructed identically, once in operation, they would assume an identity of their own.

Corrections is a multi-million-dollar industry. It draws from public funds that could better serve to improve the educational opportunities or medical services in our communities, but rather we have clearly recognized the need for corrections.

Corrections is more than bricks and mortar; it includes functions and services, probation, community corrections, parole, juvenile justice, work release, and countless other activities. It includes medical and dental, food services, and laundry activities.

A Snapshot of Those Adults Confined and under Judicial Sanctions

Millions of people are under some type of judicial sanction in the United States today. Probation, community corrections, confinement, and parole have proven to be a revolving door of crime, conviction, sanction, release, new crime, and rearrest. Those confined and under judicial sanctions do not reflect a cross section of our nation. The majority of those under judicial sanction are male and young (Figure 1.1). Confinement is driven by both crime and public policy. The decision over thirty years ago to increase the enforcement emphasis on drugs resulted in additional arrests, prosecution, conviction, and confinement of hundreds of thousands. The wisdom of that policy decision is not suggested for debate, but the fact remains that enforcement emphasis, in any area of crime, typically results in a surge of arrests, convictions, and judicially imposed correctional penalties.

Not everyone confined is a bad person; likewise, not everyone living freely in our society is good. The vast majority of offenders committed their offenses while in the free world. For some, their arrest and conviction will be their only encounter as an offender in the system. For others, jails and prisons will become a routine part of their lives. Habitual offenders are those with extensive records of numerous convictions, serving short- and mid-term confinement, covering decades of their lives. Some offenders will never break the cycle of crime and punishment.

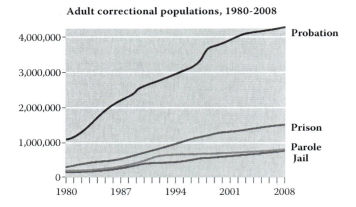

Adult correctional populations, 1980-2008

Figure 1.1 (From Bureau of Justice Statistics Correctional Surveys.)

For those who grow old within the system, one must reflect on the productive lives lost to confinement. That small percentage of long-term inmates who have become "institutionalized" view confinement as home.

In 2008, over 7.3 million people were under some form of correctional supervision, with nearly 5.1 million adults under community supervision at year-end 2008, including:

Probation: Court-ordered period of correctional supervision in the community, generally as an alternative to incarceration. In some cases probation can be a combined sentence of incarceration and a period after of community supervision. These data include adults under the jurisdiction of a probation agency, regardless of supervision status (i.e., active supervision, inactive supervision, financial conditions only, warrant status, absconder status, in a residential/other treatment program, or supervised out of jurisdiction). The most common type of offense for which probationers (29%) were under supervision was a drug offense.

Prison: Confinement in a state or federal correctional facility to serve a sentence of more than 1 year, although in some jurisdictions the length of sentence that results in prison confinement is longer. State and federal prison authorities had jurisdiction over 1,610,446 prisoners at mid-year 2008: 1,409,166 in state jurisdiction and 201,280 in federal jurisdiction.

Jail: There are approximately 3,500 jails in the United States holding people pending trial, awaiting sentencing, serving a sentence that is usually less than one year, or awaiting transfer to other facilities after conviction. In 2008, local jails held 785,556 persons awaiting trial or serving a sentence at mid-year 2008. An additional 72,852 people were serving their sentence in jails. Jail jurisdictions held more than 24,200 inmates at mid-year 2009 for U.S. Immigration and Customs Enforcement.

Parole: Period of conditional supervised release in the community following a prison term, including prisoners released to parole either by a parole board decision (discretionary parole) or according to provisions of a statute (mandatory parole). These data include adults under the jurisdiction of a parole agency, regardless of supervision status (i.e., active supervision, inactive supervision, financial conditions only, absconder status, or supervised out of state). The most common type of offense for which parolees (37%) were under supervision was a drug offense.

Juvenile Offenders

Juvenile crime and issues related to juvenile justice continually challenge our nation. About 93,000 juvenile offenders were held in residential placement facilities in our nation in 2009, with many more under judicial sanctions within their communities.

Though we can make some reasonably accurate estimates, we do not have an accurate count of the amount of crime in the nation that is committed by juveniles. Many juvenile offenses go unreported, and thus do not become a part of the national statistical picture. Indeed, many minor offenses committed by juveniles are considered part of growing up and are handled informally rather than by arrest and adjudication.

What we do see in our society is that the majority of juvenile criminal activity is committed by a same percentage of juveniles.

Professional Opportunities in Corrections

Corrections has proven to be one of the fastest growing and most challenging segments of the criminal justice system, with countless professional opportunities available to those who choose to enter the field.

For some in the justice profession, they view corrections as a stepping stone to other positions in the justice system. In private industry, it is an area in which products and services, some of which are unique to the field, can be marketed. For others, corrections is not a good fit, and they typically leave the field quickly, seeking other career opportunities. For those who choose to remain, it provides an exciting career field with daily challenges. Correctional professionals face some of the most challenging duties in the criminal justice profession. It falls to them to find ways to effectively operate safe, secure confinement facilities that house a population resistant to conformity with the established rules of society.

What Is the Goal of Corrections?

The goal of corrections is quite simple: provide services that enhance public safety and security through the supervision and management of those assigned to the custody of corrections upon their conviction. The correctional process is difficult and complex. Corrections influence those under correctional supervision, in either a positive or negative manner, because few, if any, leave the corrections experience unchanged.

Summary

Throughout this text we will examine corrections in the United States in great detail. How the corrections system developed in the United States will be examined. The changing correctional philosophies that provided the ideological basis to run the jails and prisons will be outlined and explained. New developments in correctional treatments and how the system currently works will be reviewed. We hope each reader takes away from this text an appreciation of the complexity of the system we call corrections, and the myriad aspects that affect the correctional system.

Corrections
A Historical View

The degree of civilization in a society can be judged by entering its prisons.

—Fyodor Dostoevsky, Russian novelist (1821–1881)

Introduction

Corrections in the United States is composed of numerous components, which include probation, community corrections, jails, prisons, and parole. Corrections is directly linked to judicial sentencing, and though it remains under the scrutiny of American society, it is the least known component of the criminal justice system.

Throughout most of history, punishment has been both direct and harsh. During medieval times, branding, mutilation, flogging, banishment, and death were common punishments, and frequently administered publicly to serve as a warning to others.

Though every society has found ways to punish those who have violated established rules and laws, the concept of offender confinement evolved slowly, primarily due to the costs related to incarceration and, in many cases, the desire to continue the use of public punishment as a warning to the public as to the consequences facing them if they do not adhere to established laws. As a major component of punishment and corrections in the United States today, offender confinement in itself is diverse, consisting of private, local, state, and federal facilities, ranging in size and institutional security level, with inmates typically segregated by gender, nature of the offense, and offender age.

The goal of corrections is quite simple: provide services that enhance public safety and security through the supervision and management of those assigned to their custody upon their conviction. The correctional process is difficult and complex. Corrections, unlike as implied in the name, does not correct; rather, it influences those under correctional supervision, in either a positive or negative manner, because few, if any, leave the corrections experience unchanged.

Correctional professionals face some of the most challenging duties in the criminal justice profession. It falls to them to find ways to effectively operate safe, secure confinement facilities that house a population that has demonstrated their resistance to conform to the established rules of society.

Foundation for Institutional Corrections and the Rule of Law

Humankind has maintained a constant search for ways to increase the effectiveness of punishment in an attempt to change unacceptable behavior within society. As community groups joined together to form nations, formal legal codes began to emerge. Directly linked to those legal codes were the penalties imposed upon offenders. With the evolution of legal systems, slowly the responsibility of punishment transitioned from the hands of those victimized to the legal authority of the community group.

Early legal codes, such as the Code of Hammurabi from Babylon or the Roman Law of the Twelve Tables, contributed to the evolution of law and justice. Developed about 1780 b.c., the Code of Hammurabi is one of the earliest known examples of a body of laws, arranged in orderly groups and published so that all within its jurisdiction could understand the social expectations for their personal conduct. Very straightforward and clear, it laid out both offenses and punishments.

After the Code of Hammurabi, other societies developed and then further refined their legal codes. As the Roman Empire emerged and expanded to dominate much of Europe and Northern Africa, the Roman concept of justice spread across the occupied lands, providing a degree of legal uniformity across the empire. Under Roman law, theft and assault were considered to be offenses against private individuals, and thus the victim was expected to prosecute the offender before the appropriate magistrates and the assembly of citizens.

The Roman legal system also included early prisons. Roman prisons were primarily places to hold the accused awaiting trial, rather than long-term confinement. This practice of limited use of confinement continued through the Middle Ages. As the influence of the Roman Empire declined, local populations, formerly controlled by the Romans, adopted new forms of laws and customs to more specifically meet their individual needs. The Roman system of laws and justice significantly influenced many of the legal systems that were to follow.[1]

England

With the Roman withdrawal from England and the subsequent Norman invasion, the English would see the further evolution of their laws, legal system, and punishments. By the twelfth century, the English constructed jails for the purpose of pretrial detention and limited confinement. Early English jails were as much institutions for inmate exploitation as for confinement. Food and alcohol were available for those who could pay. Inmates, males, females, old, and young were confined together. Sheriffs, who were responsible for the operation of the jails, often demanded bribes from the inmates and their families to ensure trials, visitation, and basic human needs.

By the early 1500s, urban growth, poverty, and petty crimes increased the demands placed upon the English justice system. The need to find additional punishment options became great. In 1557, the English opened Bridewell Prison in London. Bridewell employed a paid staff and operated under a philosophy of confinement with hard labor, with the intent of instilling a work ethic in the inmate. Inmates were classified as to offense and were provided basic vocational training.

Solitary confinement was intended to encourage the inmate to reflect upon his or her criminal record and repent. Bridewell proved to be an early step in the development of the modern penitentiary, but Bridewell, like so many of the prisons that would follow, soon filled with inmates. Though overcrowding and limited resources prevented Bridewell from fully meeting the early expectations of success, its influence on the penitentiary system in the United States would prove to be enormous. As increased arrests and convictions filled prisons, the English built more prisons and searched for alternatives to costly prison construction and adopted some innovative approaches to punishment.[2]

A 1678 statute of King Charles II made banishment to America the equivalent of execution as a punishment.[3] With banishment as an alternative to confinement or death, the English found a way to partially populate their colonies while ridding England of some of its criminal element. Correctional banishment would continue for England and other European nations, such as France, who shipped offenders to locations such as its penal colony Devil's Island, located in French Guiana.

Creating additional, less expensive housing for inmates, the English turned obsolete warships into floating prisons during the 1770s. These ships, known as convict hulks, were initially seen as a temporary measure when first authorized by Parliament in 1776. As the first hulks filled and others were pressed into service, these old warships proved to be an inexpensive way to confine prisoners. Never intended to serve as a place for long-term confinement, the death and disease rate among inmates was great. In spite of the unsuitability of hulks as places of confinement, the English continued to use these old warships for confinement for about 80 years.

Early Prison Reform and Reformers

As the use of confinement increased in popularity as a punishment alternative, many social reformers stepped forward, drawing the attention of the public to the deplorable conditions of the jails and prisons. In Europe, two of the most influential voices were those of Cesare Beccaria and John Howard.

In 1764, Cesare Beccaria published his pamphlet *Delitti e Delle Pene* (On Crimes and Punishments), advocating effective punishment dependent largely on the certainty of punishment rather than on its severity. He believed severe laws and punishment produced hardened criminals rather than reformed citizens. He encouraged punishment methods designed to influence inmate reform and encourage criminal deterrence. Beccaria criticized the use of torture, secret proceedings, judicial corruption, and brutal punishments during confinement and believed the death penalty to be unnecessary. He believed punishment should advance security and not exceed the amount necessary to stop individuals from committing crimes.[4]

Beccaria was not alone in this criticism of punishment. In England, John Howard took a great interest in the concept of confinement. Appointed high sheriff of Bedford in 1773, Howard's inspections of confinement facilities revealed dangerous conditions under which the inmates lived.

Howard became an advocate for confinement reform. As a result of Howard's efforts, the British Parliament passed the 1774 Gaol Act, which abolished jailer fees and recommended confinement improvements. Although Parliament passed the 1774 Gaol Act, British justices and the jailers tended to ignore these changes. In 1777 Howard published his observations in *The State of Prisons in England and Wales*, in which he shared his criticisms of confinement conditions.[5]

The immediate result of this publication was the drafting of a bill for the establishment of *penitentiary houses*, where, by means of solitary imprisonment accompanied by well-regulated labor and religious instruction, the object of reforming the prisoners and introducing them to the habits of industry could be pursued.

Development of the American Prison System

From the fifteenth century, European nations rushed to claim and colonize new territories. As European colonists settled in Asia, Africa, and North and South America, the laws, enforcement, judicial, and punishment systems under which they had lived in Europe were established in the new settlements.

In Colonial America, corporal and capital punishment were common. In the early 1680s, the Quakers in Pennsylvania worked to develop a humane approach to punishment. Influenced by the conditions in English jails, William Penn in 1682 proposed a new penal code that abolished the Duke of York's criminal code, which was in effect in Pennsylvania. Under Penn's code, only murder and treason were punishable by death, and imprisonment at hard labor and fines were the standard punishment for other serious offenses. Shortly after Penn's death many of his efforts to reform the Pennsylvania criminal code were abandoned.[6]

Over the next 100 years, confinement in Britain's American colonies was typically used for pretrial, short-term confinement, debtors, and sometimes even witnesses. Conditions in jails remained harsh. In 1776, Richard Wistar Sr., a concerned Quaker, had soup prepared in his home for distribution to the inmates in Philadelphia prisons. Wistar's social concerns led to the formation of one of the earliest organizations working for correctional improvement, the Philadelphia Society for Assisting Distressed Prisoners. The efforts of the society would be short lived due to the British occupation of Philadelphia and the society's inability to influence jail operations.[7]

With the end of the American Revolution, the new United States struggled to develop its identity as a nation. Few laws existed on the national or state levels, and as a result, crime, punishment, and the response to criminal activity remained centered on the local level. Criminal activity was unsophisticated. Sheriffs were responsible for the operation of jails, and as such, the conditions within these jails varied.

In the 1780s, the conditions within the nation's jails attracted little public attention. Soon, like in Europe, social reformers began to emerge, advocating change. In Pennsylvania, social concern led to the formation of the Philadelphia Society for Alleviating the Miseries of Public Prisons in 1787. Membership included social activists Benjamin Franklin and Benjamin Rush. Three areas attracted the interests of these early social reformers to the jails: oversight and advocacy pertaining to facility operation, inmate visitation, and assistance to those released from confinement. It was reasoned that the way a society treated those confined reflected the values of that society. This reasoning would continue to inspire social reformers.[8]

The Penitentiary in America: New-Gate, Walnut Street Jail, and the Early Efforts to Develop Prisons

The nature of confinement has changed in the United States over the last 200 years. Once used sparingly, by 2007 over 2,300,000 adult inmates were confined in the United States. Though we now see adult correctional institutions as an essential part of our system of justice, the earliest American prisons evolved as the need to hold adult offenders longer than practical in the typical jail became great.

As late as 1780, punishments such as the pillory and hanging were carried out in public in the United States. Though there is some debate over the first American prison, it is clear that both New-Gate in Connecticut and the *Walnut Street Jail* in Pennsylvania significantly influenced the correctional facilities that followed. After the Revolutionary War, as states developed strategies to punish those convicted of state offenses, it was slowly realized that longer-term confinement capabilities were needed.

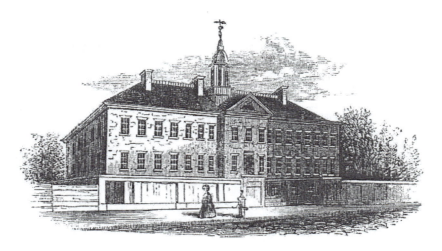

Figure 2.1 The Walnut Street Jail. (From freepages.history.)

In Philadelphia, the early 1790s brought a change in confinement that would prove sweeping. Behind the Walnut Street Jail (Figure 2.1), a small building was constructed with 16 cells to house inmates whose sentence included solitary confinement with labor for "hardened atrocious offenders."

The Walnut Street Jail became a showplace, with inmate separation and workshops providing trade instruction. The old abuse and idleness seemed eliminated. The limited capacity of the facility was congested. Inmates sentenced to solitary confinement with hard labor were soon double celled, leading to a smaller percentage of inmates productively employed and a general breakdown of the disciplinary system, as communication among inmates could no longer be controlled.[9]

Most states were reluctant to construct prisons. In the late 1700s, Thomas Jefferson proposed the construction of a "penitentiary house" in Virginia to confine and reform criminals. For more than a decade, the general assembly of Virginia debated Jefferson's proposal and continued to rely on local jails to house those convicted under state laws and sentenced to confinement. In 1796, the Virginia legislature finally authorized construction of a correctional facility outside Richmond. The facility received its first prisoners in 1800 and was completed in 1804.[10]

The general assembly of Georgia funded its first state prison in 1811, authorizing $10,000 to construct a facility that opened in 1815. Known as *Prison Square*, it was located directly across the street from the governor's mansion and confined only white inmates, housing both males and females.

As states struggled with the concept of offender confinement, New York and Pennsylvania emerged as leaders in correctional operations. From these states, two institutional philosophies emerged, the Auburn system and the Pennsylvania system. The systems were similar in that they demanded inmate silence and solitary confinement at night.

In Pennsylvania, the Eastern State Penitentiary opened in 1829. Strict rules regulating inmate behavior were established. Each inmate was confined in a cell and rarely allowed to leave. Cells were large enough to serve as a workplace. Inmates wore hoods when moved in the institutions to avoid seeing other prisoners and marched in single file.

Where the Pennsylvania system did not initially expect inmates to work, the Auburn system reduced the expense of facility operation by employing the inmates in limited manufacturing. The most common correctional occupations were nail making, shoe making, stone sawing, weaving, and processing wool. To offset the cost of the operation of the prisons, inmate labor was frequently used to manufacture their clothing and generally maintain the facilities.[11]

The Auburn system was quite similar to the Pennsylvania system, but the Auburn system allowed inmates to work together in shops. This use of inmate labor, resulting in institutional profit, stimulated the acceptance of the Auburn system over the Pennsylvania in the United States, as states sought strategies to offset the cost of inmate confinement.

Though these two systems would provide the blueprint for the prisons of the 1800s, the Auburn system became the most popular model for American prisons. The Auburn system and its use of labor influenced the emergence of reform schools and workhouses commencing in the 1820s.[12]

By the mid-1800s, to further reduce the cost of confinement, several state legislatures awarded contracts to private entrepreneurs to operate and manage state prisons. Louisiana's first state prison and Missouri State Prison were just two of the many state prisons that were "privatized." These institutions became models for entire sections of the nation where privatized prisons were the norm later in the century. Most prisons expected to turn a profit for the state, or at least offset the cost of their operations.

In the days following the War Between the States, with no money for prison construction, many states adopted the convict lease system to provide labor, in construction, manufacturing, and agriculture.

In 1869, Louisiana contracted with businessman Samuel James to take charge of the inmates of the state. For the next 31 years, James and his family used Louisiana inmate labor to operate a plantation. In 1901, responding to a public outcry to improve the conditions under which inmates lived, Louisiana reassumed responsibility for its inmates.[13]

In 1870, Tennessee began a convict leasing system, leasing inmates to the Tennessee Coal, Iron and Railroad Company. In Georgia, inmate leasing began in 1874, when Governor Ruger signed the bill authorizing state prisoners to be leased out to private individuals and companies. Each convict brought the state about $10.00 per year. Prisoners were often the labor sources for mining operations, rock quarries, and the turpentine industry.[14]

In 1897, Georgia's general assembly passed an act to end the lease system in favor of a reformed system run by a prison commission. Georgia, like many other southern states, would soon return to the use of inmate labor to offset the cost of prison operations, while a few states even eliminated their prisons and relied exclusively on the local jails to house offenders.[15]

The Reform Era

After the War Between the States, major changes occurred in the prisons across the nation. States continued to lease out inmates to private contractors. Prison conditions remained harsh. Soon, social activitists called for prison reform.

In 1866, Drs. Theodore W. Dwight and Enoch Cobb Wines toured prisons in the United States and reported their findings in 1867 to the legislature of New York. Finding conditions in the prisons across the nation to be alarming, they became a major force behind the 1870 formation of the American Prison Association, now known as the American Correctional Association. At the association's first National Prison Congress, participants developed the Declaration of Principles, and formed the foundation of correctional standards that are still in use today.[16]

Six years later, another major development in the history of American correctional institutions occurred when in 1876, the Elmira Reformatory opened in Elmira, New York, as the first reformatory built in the United States. Under the leadership of Zebulon Brockway, the reformatory pioneered programs intended to reform the offender, not just confine.

Under Zebulon Brockway's direction, inmates were classified and segregated, provided individualized treatment, including vocational training, and rewarded for good behavior, to include early release. Many of these reform efforts were aimed at youthful or first-time offenders.

Many of the methods employed in Elmira would be psychological rather than physical. Instead of corporal punishment, Elmira would encourage positive inmate behavior with rewards. Mass regimentation would yield to classification and individualized treatment. Fixed sentences would be replaced with the indeterminate sentence, designed to fit the criminal. With the indeterminate sentence, corrections officers became decision makers in influencing when inmates could be released.[17]

Emergence of the National Prison Association

As the move to create long-term confinement facilities gained momentum, many of the early leaders within the field recognized the need to organize a professional association that could serve as a major influence in the emerging field. In 1870, these visionaries formed the National Prison Association in Cincinnati, Ohio. During this period, the new members of the association developed what has become known as the *Declaration of Principles*. Those principles, though since revised, reflect an understanding of the issues and challenges those early practitioners faced.

Today, the American Correctional Association serves as a leader in correctional training and accreditation across the nation. Institutions and correctional systems point with pride to ACA accreditation.

Early Steps in Federal Confinement

On the national level, federal inmates were housed in state prisons and local jails. The conditions under which the federal inmates were confined were typically very harsh and brutal. By the late 1800s, it became clear federal confinement and the practice of housing federal inmates in state institutions was no longer practical.

Responding to the challenge, Congress enacted the Three Prisons Act of 1891, which authorized the construction of the first three federal prisons for nonmilitary offenders. The locations selected for these prisons were Leavenworth (Kansas), Atlanta (Georgia), and McNeil

Island (Washington). Each of these prisons would be constructed along the lines of an Auburn style facility, and in their own way become legendary in federal corrections. Each federal prison operated relatively independently and would serve as the foundation for the Federal Bureau of Prison, which would be formed 40 years later.[17]

By the 1920s, federal correctional institutions could no longer operate with little central control on the national level. In 1930, the federal government formalized the organization of the federal prisons with the formation of the Federal Bureau of Prisons. Sanford Bates, who had served in various leadership positions in Massachusetts corrections, was appointed as the first director. With the creation of the Federal Bureau of Prisons in 1930, Congress authorized funds to open new federal prisons. During the next decade, federal institutions were opened, to include the famous Alcatraz.

Early 1900s

By the early 1900s, correctional confinement in America had again reached a crossroads. In 1898, examining confinement costs, Tennessee estimated that the cost to house an inmate for one year was approximately $117. In spite of this low cost, many states, especially in the South, expanded the operation of agriculturally based penitentiaries to further use the labors of the inmates not only to offset the cost of confinement, but also to make a profit for the state to be returned to the general revenue.

Mississippi, which operated in the last half of the 1800s without a state prison, found that local jails could no longer house the ever-growing number of inmates. In 1901, the Mississippi legislature authorized funding to purchase a cotton plantation in the Mississippi delta for the purpose of converting it into an agricultural penitentiary. Radically different from the conventional prisons of the time, Parchman operated as a self-contained plantation, producing products that not only sustained the inmates, but when sold, returned a profit to the state treasury.

One of the very interesting aspects of the Mississippi penitentiary was discovered by the renowned sociologist Dr. Columbus B. Hopper in his institutional research in the 1960s. In his studies of Parchman, Dr. Hopper found the practice of inmate conjugal visitation had existed since at least 1918, and had unofficially evolved to a point that it was a major part of the institution's identity. Dr. Hopper was the first to study the value of conjugal visitation as a tool to assist in family stabilization and influence the conduct of those confined. Today, all state correctional facilities in Mississippi allow for inmate conjugal visitation under conditions that the visitation can only occur between the inmate and his or her spouse. Though conjugal visitation has not been accepted nationwide, a very limited number of states permit conjugal visitation in their systems.[18]

In 1903, the Georgia State Prison Board commissioners once again authorized contracts with individuals and corporations and started the *chain gang*. In this new system, counties received a share of the state inmates for public construction of highways, railroads, and other forms of public service. These prisoners were housed in camps, and by 1929, Georgia had 140 prison camps. To cut down on travel time between the camps and work sites, inmates sometimes spent the night at the sites in rolling cages.[19]

In 1901, Louisiana resumed control of state inmates. In 1916, to save money, Louisiana dismissed all correctional officers and replaced them with inmates who were armed and used to guard other inmates. This practice of inmate trustee guard was adopted by several other states and led to significant abuse within the institutions.[20]

States used inmate labor in the construction of roads and other general construction projects that were labor intensive. Inmate chain gangs quickly became infamous for their brutal conditions. There was no classification of inmates on the chain gangs. Inmates convicted on minor offenses typically served with inmates serving life sentences and even the mentally ill. Inmates survived in a harsh world.

The Industrial Era

As more states searched for ways to use their inmate population for profit, a number of state legislatures became concerned about inmate exploitation or industrial competition. Between the 1890s and 1920s legislatures in many of the industrialized states enacted laws to prohibit the sale of inmate-produced goods. As a result, the marketing opportunities of prison-produced goods declined during the first three decades of the twentieth century. By 1930, 33 states passed laws prohibiting the sale of inmate-produced goods.

From 1929, a series of federal laws limiting shipment of prison-made goods made it difficult to provide productive employment for prisoners. The Hawes-Cooper Act (1929) mandated that prison-made goods transported from one state to another be subject to the laws of the destination state. The effect was to permit a state to ban the sale of all inmate-produced goods.

In 1935, strengthening the Hawes-Cooper Act, the Ashurst-Sumners Act made shipping inmate-produced goods to a state where state law prohibited the goods a federal offense. In 1940, the Ashurst-Sumners Act was amended to make it a federal crime to knowingly transport inmate-produced goods in interstate commerce for private use. It would be the emergencies of World War II that would relax regulations on inmate labor, allowing prison industries to produce war materials. Some prisons again became self-supporting and ran surpluses.[21]

Early Twentieth-Century Correctional Leaders and the Concept of Prisonization

In the late 1920s, President Hoover called for the first in-depth study of the American system of justice. In 1931 the National Commission on Law Observance and Enforcement released its report, including recommendations for the improvement of the justice system of the United States. Its findings, which were published in 14 volumes in 1931 and 1932, covered every aspect of the justice system, including the causes of crime, police and prosecutorial procedures, and the importance of probation and parole. It addressed the issues facing the jails and prisons in the nation and reported the need for significant improvement in correctional management and operations across the nation.

As inmate populations surged early in the twentieth century, new correctional institutions opened. Correctional leaders emerged, directing their efforts to improving the professionalism of institutional confinement. Though countless individuals contributed to the growth and development of institutional corrections in the United States, three men, Sanford Bates (Figure 2.2), Lewis Lawes, and James V. Bennett, would prove essential in shaping professional corrections during the first half of the twentieth century.

On the federal level, Sanford Bates led the new Federal Bureau of Prisons during its first years. Before becoming the first director of the Federal Bureau of Prisons, Bates served as the commissioner of penal institutions in Boston from 1917 to 1919, and as commissioner of the Massachusetts Department of Corrections from 1919 to 1929. In 1929, as superintendent of prisons, U.S. Department of Justice,

Figure 2.2 Sanford Bates, first director of the Federal Bureau of Prisons. (From FBP.)

he directed the preparation of the legislation that established the Federal Bureau of Prisons in 1930. From 1930 until 1937, he directed the Federal Bureau of Prisons during its first critical years, establishing the early bureau policies and setting the tone of professionalism found in the agency today.[22]

In New York, Lewis Lawes (Figure 2.3) would emerge as the most famous warden in the nation. In 1920, he was appointed warden of Sing Sing, a position he would continually hold for almost 22 years. Under Lawes's leadership, Sing Sing would become the most progressive institution of its kind in the country, the subject of books, movies. and international study.

Lawes's innovations were decades ahead of his time. Under his direction, inmate living conditions improved, educational and

Figure 2.3 Warden Lewis Lawes of Sing Sing.

vocational opportunities were made available, and his desire that inmates maintain strong contacts with the outside world clearly assisted many as they transitioned out of the confinement world and into free society. Lawes's understanding of the challenges facing inmates and his commitment to ensure Sing Sing would be operated as safely and professionally as possible made him a leader in correctional administration during the first half of the twentieth century.[23]

James Bennett followed Sanford Bates as the second director of the Federal Bureau of Prisons. Serving as director from 1937 until 1964, he shaped the Federal Bureau of Prisons. Under Bennett's leadership, the Federal Bureau of Prisons transitioned from the depression into a continual period of expansion. By his retirement in 1964, he had established inmate educational and training programs, increased community involvement in rehabilitation programs, and opened special prisons for juveniles and some of the earliest correctional halfway houses in the nation. He continually emphasized staff professionalism and innovation in the operations of the facilities. Under his direction, federal corrections became a system with uniform systemwide policies and procedures guiding each institution.[24]

In addition to the advances in correctional administration, sociologists worked to gain a better understanding of the institutional environment in which the inmate survived. Writing in 1940, Donald Clemmer was one of the first to describe the psychological effects of prison life. When prisoners adapted to prison life, they began surrendering their self-esteem and initiative to a dependency upon the system. Clemmer originated the term *prisonization* to describe this effect. His research was based on the idea that no experience as dramatic as incarceration could occur without a significant psychological impact.[25]

Riots, Litigation, and Reform

After World War II, the nation would again experience an increase in inmate populations. Prisons filled and funding continued to fall short. Conditions within the institutions further declined. The old days of the lockstep had ended. Inmates and social reformers struggled for institutional changes. Between 1950 and 1966 over 100 prisons riots occurred in the United States as inmates struggled to force change. By the 1960s, the need to reform existing correctional confinement was clear.

Few states were willing to commit funds to improve the conditions in the nation's correctional institutions. It would take legislation and intervention by the courts to force changes in many of the nation's prison systems.

While the Eighth Amendment prohibited excessive bail, excessive fines, and cruel and unusual punishments, correctional operations had not been subjected to serious constitutional review until the enactment of the *Civil Rights Act of 1964*, under which inmates slowly began to challenge the conditions in correctional institutions through the federal court system. As the 1960s and 1970s progressed, the Supreme Court allowed 42 USC § 1983 to be used to assert prisoners' constitutional rights. By 1995, 25% of suits filed in federal district court were brought by prisoners.[26]

A New Era in Corrections

During the last part of the twentieth century, changes occurred in every aspect of correctional operations. Judicial oversight, mandated training of correctional officers, improved conditions within the institutions, changes in operational procedures, enhanced medical and food services, and movement toward American Correctional Association accreditation all served to improve the professionalism of corrections.

Innovated approaches to corrections, private facilities, and increased use of probation, parole, restitution, halfway houses, treatment programs, and community corrections relieved some of the pressure on institutional confinement. Organizations such as the American Jail Association and the American Correctional Association accreditation focused attention upon the need to improve the overall conditions of jails and correctional facilities across the nation, while academic correctional and social work programs provided the profession with a flow of college-educated personnel into the system as employees. Corrections experienced change.

Summary

The history of corrections in the United States is not only rich, but also ongoing. Every jurisdiction is served by some type of correctional service, linked to the courts and the community they serve. We know that the need for corrections will remain with us, but what we also realize is that corrections will continually be in a state of change, with the desired value gained from change being improved and a reduction of offender recidivism.

While institutional corrections play a primary role in the justice system, it is just one component of the system. Operating behind walls and closed doors, correctional institutions struggle to provide services that enhance public safety and security. Currently, with over 2,500,000 confined in the jails and prisons across the nation and the inmate population increasing, correctional professionals will continually search for ways to make the operation of the jails and prisons of the nation more safe and effective. Institutional corrections will continually face challenges as they work to provide the safest, most secure environment possible, while maintaining control over the inmate population placed into their custody.

Vocabulary

Chain gang

Civil Rights Act of 1964

Declaration of Principles

Penitentiary house

Prison Square

Solitary confinement

Walnut Street Jail

Discussion Questions

1. Explain how early legal codes, such as the Code of Hammurabi from Babylon or the Roman Law of the Twelve Tables, contributed to the evolution of law and justice.

2. Describe the condition and purpose of early English jails. Did status play a role in how a prisoner was treated?

3. Why did King Charles II make banishment to America the equivalent of execution as a punishment?

4. Who was Cesare Beccaria and what were his contributions to prison reform?

5. Explain the new penal code that William Penn proposed in 1682 and how it affected prison reform in America.

6. What is the significance of the Three Prisons Act of 1891?

7. Explain the Hawes-Cooper Act of 1929 and how it affected inmate production.

Notes

1. University of Pittsburgh School of Law. (n.d.). Ancient law. Retrieved November 15, 2007, from http://www.law.pitt.edu/hibbitts/ancientl.htm

2. Griffiths, Paul. (2003, July). Contesting London Bridewell, 1576–1580. *Journal of British Studies, 42*, 283–315.

3. The European War. (1918). *New York Times*, Vol. 16, p. 384.

4. Bridgwater, T. R. (1907). Caesar Bonesana, Marquis Di Beccaria. *Journal of the Society of Comparative Legislation, 8*, 219–228.

5. Robinson, Lewis Newton. (1992). *Penology in the United States.* Philadelphia: John C. Winston.

6. Johnston, Norman. (n.d.). Prison reform in Pennsylvania. Retrieved October 14, 2007, from http://www.prisonsociety.org/about/history.shtml

7. Johnston, Norman. (n.d.). Prison reform in Pennsylvania. Retrieved October 14, 2007, from http://www.prisonsociety.org/about/history.shtml

8. Johnston, Norman. (n.d.). Prison reform in Pennsylvania. Retrieved October 14, 2007, from http://www.prisonsociety.org/about/history.shtml

9. Teeters, Negley K. (1937). The Pennsylvania prison society: A century and a half of penal reform. *Journal of Criminal Law and Criminology, 28*, 374–379.

10. Peterson, C. E. (1953). Virginia penitentiary, 1797. *Journal of the Society of Architectural Historians, 12*, 27–28.

11. Eastern State Penitentiary. History: Timeline. Retrieved October 16, 2007, from http://www.easternstate.org/history/

12. Lewis, O. F. (2005). *The development of American prisons and prison customs 1776 to 1845.* Whitefish, MT: Kessinger.

13. Foster, Burke. (1993). Plantation days at Angola: Major James and the origins of modern corrections in Louisiana. Retrieved November 13, 2007, from http://www.burkfoster.com/plantationdays.htm

14. Crime and Punishment Museum. (n.d.). History of the prison system in Georgia. Retrieved October 14, 2007, from http://www.jailmuseum.com/About-Chain-Gangs.69.0.html

15. Crime and Punishment Museum. (n.d.). History of the prison system in Georgia. Retrieved October 14, 2007, from http://www.jailmuseum.com/About-Chain-Gangs.69.0.html

16. Virtualology. (n.d.). Virtual American biographies: Enoch Cobb Wines. Retrieved September 30, 2007, from http://www.famousamericans.net/enochcobbwines/

17. Federal Bureau of Prisons. (n.d.). Creation of the federal prison system. Retrieved September 30, 2007, from http://www.bop.gov/museum/section_b_text_version.jsp

18. Hopper, C. B. (1989). The evolution of conjugal visiting in Mississippi. *The Prison Journal, 69*, 103–109.

19. Crime and Punishment Museum. (n.d.). History of the prison system in Georgia. Retrieved October 14, 2007, from http://www.jailmuseum.com/About-Chain-Gangs.69.0.html

20. Louisiana State Penitentiary. History of Angola. Retrieved November 29, 2007, from http://www.corrections.state.la.us/LSP/history.htm

21. U.S. Supreme Court. (1937). *Kentucky Whip and Collar Co. v. Illinois Cent. R. Co.*, 299 U.S. 334. Retrieved October 22, 2007, from http://caselaw.lp.findlaw.com/cgi-bin/getcase.pl?court=us&vol=299&invol=334

22. Federal Bureau of Prisons. (n.d.). Former Bureau of Prisons directors. Retrieved November 15, 2007, from http://www.bop.gov/about/history/directors.jsp

23. Rouse, John Jay. (n.d.). Firm but fair: The life of Sing Sing warden Lewis E. Lawes. Retrieved October 18, 2007, from http://www.correctionhistory.org/html/chronicl/state/lawes/lewise-lawesnotes1.htm

24. Federal Bureau of Prisons. (n.d.). Former Bureau of Prisons directors. Retrieved November 15, 2007, from http://www.bop.gov/about/history/directors.jsp

25. Clemmer, Donald. (1958). *The prison community.* New York: Holt, Rinehart and Winston.

26. Baradaran-Robison, Shima. (2003). Kaleidoscopic consent decrees: School desegregation and prison reform consent decrees after the Prison Litigation Reform Act and Freeman-Dowell. *Brigham Young University Law Review 2003*, no. 277, p. 1334–1371.

Appendix

Declaration of Principles Adopted and Promulgated by the 1870 Congress of the National Prison Association

I. Crime is an intentional violation of duties imposed by law, which inflicts an injury upon others. Criminals are persons convicted of crime by competent courts. Punishment is suffering inflicted on the criminal for the wrong done by him, with a special view to secure his reformation.

II. The treatment of criminals by society is for the protection of society. But since such treatment is directed to the criminal rather than to the crime, its great object should be his moral regeneration. Hence the supreme aim of prison discipline is the reformation of criminals, not the infliction of vindictive suffering.

III. The progressive classification of prisoners, based on character and worked on some well-adjusted mark system, should be established in all prisons above the common jail.

IV. Since hope is a more potent agent than fear, it should be made an ever-present force in the minds of prisoners, by a well-devised and skillfully-applied system of rewards for good conduct, industry and attention to learning. Rewards, more than punishments, are essential to every good prison system.

V. The prisoner's destiny should be placed, measurably, in his own hands; he must be put into circumstances where he will be able, through his own exertions, to continually better his own condition. A regulated self-interest must be brought into play, and made constantly operative.

VI. The two master forces opposed to the reform of the prison systems of our several states are political appointments, and a consequent instability of administration. Until both are eliminated, the needed reforms are impossible.

VII. Special training, as well as high qualities of head and heart, is required to make a good prison or reformatory officer. Then only will the administration of public punishment become scientific, uniform and successful, when it is raised to the dignity of a profession, and men are specially trained for it, as they are for other pursuits.

VIII. Peremptory sentences ought to be replaced by those of indeterminate length. Sentences limited only by satisfactory proof of reformation should be substituted for those measured by mere lapse of time.

IX. Of all reformatory agencies, religion is first in importance, because most potent in its action upon the human heart and life.

X. Education is a vital force in the reformation of fallen men and women. Its tendency is to quicken the intellect, inspire self-respect, excite to higher aims, and afford a healthful substitute for low and vicious amusements. Education is, therefore, a matter of primary importance in prisons, and should be carried to the utmost extent consistent with the other purposes of such institutions.

XI. In order to [sic] the reformation of imprisoned criminals, there must be not only a sincere desire and intention to that end, but a serious conviction, in the minds of the prison officers, that they are capable of being reformed, since no man can heartily maintain a discipline at war with his inward beliefs; no man can earnestly strive to accomplish what in his heart he despairs of accomplishing.

XII. A system of prison discipline, to be truly reformatory, must gain the will of the convict. He is to be amended; but how is this possible with his mind in a state of hostility? No system can hope to succeed, which does not secure this harmony of wills, so that the prisoner shall choose for himself what his officer chooses for him. But, to this end, the officer must really choose the good of the prisoner, and the prisoner must remain in his choice long enough for virtue to become a habit. This consent of wills is an essential condition of reformation.

XIII. The interest of society and the interest of the convicted criminal are really identical, and they should be made practically so. At present there is a combat between crime and laws. Each sets the other at defiance, and, as a rule, there is little kindly feeling, and few friendly acts, on either side. It would be otherwise if criminals, on conviction, instead of being cast off, were rather made the objects of a generous parental care; that is, if they were trained to virtue, and not merely sentenced to suffering.

XIV. The prisoner's self-respect should be cultivated to the utmost, and every effort made to give back to him his manhood. There is no greater mistake in the whole compass of penal discipline, than its studied imposition of degradation as a part of punishment. Such imposition destroys every better impulse and aspiration. It crushes the weak, irritates the strong, and indisposes all to submission and reform. It is trampling where we ought to raise, and is therefore as unchristian in principle as it is unwise in policy.

XV. In prison administration, moral forces should be relied upon, with as littler admixture of physical force as possible, and organized persuasion be made to take the place of coercive restraint, the object being to make upright and industrious free men, rather than orderly and obedient prisoners. Brute force may make good prisoners; moral training alone will make good citizens. To the latter of these ends, the living soul must be won; to the former, only the inert and obedient body.

XVI. Industrial training should have both a higher development and a greater breadth than has heretofore been, or is now, commonly given to it in our prisons. Work is no less an auxiliary to virtue, than it is a means of support. Steady, active, honorable labor is the basis of all reformatory discipline. It not only aids reformation, but is essential to it. It was a maxim with Howard, "make men diligent, and they will be honest"—a maxim which his congress regards as eminently sound and practical.

XVII. While industrial labor in prisons is of the highest importance and utility to the convict, and by no means injurious to the laborer outside, we regard the contract system of prison labor, as now commonly practiced in our country, as prejudicial alike to discipline, finance and the reformation of the prisoner, and sometimes injurious to the interest of the free laborer.

XVIII. The most valuable parts of the Irish prison system—the more strictly penal stage of separate imprisonment, the reformatory stage of progressive classification, and the probationary stage of natural training—are believed to be as applicable to one country as another—to the United states as to Ireland.

XIX.   Prisons, as well as prisoners, should be classified or graded so that there shall be prisons for the untried, for the incorrigible and for other degrees of depraved character, as well as separate establishments for women, and for criminals of the younger class.

XX.   It is the judgment of this congress, that repeated short sentences for minor criminals are worse than useless; that, in fact, they rather stimulate than repress transgression. Reformation is a work of time; and a benevolent regard to the good of the criminal himself, as well as to the protection of society, requires that his sentence be long enough for reformatory processes to take effect.

XXI.   Preventive institutions, such as truant homes, industrial schools, etc., for the reception and treatment of children not yet criminal, but in danger of becoming so, constitute the true field of promise, in which to labor for the repression of crime.

XXII. More systematic and comprehensive methods should be adopted to save discharged prisoners, by providing them with work and encouraging them to redeem their character and regain their lost position in society. The state has not discharged its whole duty to the criminal when it has punished him, nor even when it has reformed him. Having raised him up, it has the further duty to aid in holding him up. And to this end it is desirable that state societies be formed, which shall co-operate with each other in this work.

XXIII. The successful prosecution of crime requires the combined action of capital and labor, just as other crafts do. There are two well defined classes engaged in criminal operations, who may be called the capitalists and the operatives. It is worthy of inquiry, whether a more effective warfare may not be carried on against crime, by striking at the capitalists as a class, than at the operatives one by one. Certainly, this double warfare should be vigorously pushed, since from it the best results, as regards repressive justice, may be reasonably hoped for.

XXIV. Since personal liberty is the rightful inheritance of every human being, it is the sentiment of this congress that the state which has deprived an innocent citizen of this right, and subjected him to penal restraint, should, on unquestionable proof of its mistake, make reasonable indemnification for such wrongful imprisonment.

XXV. Criminal lunacy is a question of vital interest to society; and facts show that our laws regarding insanity, in its relation to crime, need revision, in order to bring them to a more complete conformity to the demands of reason, justice and humanity; so that, when insanity is pleaded in bar of conviction, the investigation may be conducted with greater knowledge, dignity and fairness; criminal responsibility be more satisfactorily determined; the punishment of the same criminal be made more sure, and the restraint of the insane be rendered at once more certain and more humane.

XXVI. While this congress would not shield the convicted criminal from the just responsibility of his misdeeds, it arraigns society itself as in no slight degree accountable for the invasion of its rights and the warfare upon its interests, practiced by the criminal classes. Does society take all the steps which it easily might, to change, or at least to improve, the circumstances in our social state that lead to crime; or, when crime has been committed, to cure the proclivity to it, generated by these circumstances? It cannot be pretended. Let society, then, lay the case earnestly to its conscience, and strive to mend in both particulars. Offences, we are told by a high authority, must come; but a special woe is denounced against those through whom they come. Let us take heed that that woe fall not upon our head.

XXVII. The exercise of executive clemency in the pardon of criminals is a practical question of grave importance, and of great delicacy and difficulty. It is believed that the annual average of executive pardons from the prisons of the whole county reaches ten per cent of their population. The effect of the too free use of the pardoning power is to detract from the *certainty* of punishment for crimes, and to divert the mind of prisoners from the means supplied for their improvement. Pardons should issue for one or more of the following reasons, viz.: to release the innocent, to correct mistakes made in imposing the sentence, to relieve such suffering from ill-health as requires release from imprisonment, and to facilitate or reward the real reformation of the prisoner.

The exercise of this power should be by the executive, and should be guarded by careful examination as to the character of the prisoner and his conduct in prison. Furthermore, it is the opinion of this congress that governors of state should give to their respective legislatures the reasons, in each case, for their exercise of the pardoning power.

XXVIII. The proper duration of imprisonment for a violation of the laws of society is one of the most perplexing questions in criminal jurisprudence. The present extraordinary inequality of sentences for the same or similar crimes is a source of constant irritation among prisoners, and the discipline of our prisons suffers in consequence. The evil is one for which some remedy should be devised.

XXIX. Prison statistics, gathered from a wide field and skillfully digested, are essential to an exhibition of the true character and working of our prison systems. The collection, collation and reduction to tabulated forms of such statistics can best be effected through a national prison discipline society, with competent working committees in every state, or by the establishment of a national prison bureau, similar to the recently instituted national bureau of education.

XXX. Prison architecture is a matter of grave importance. Prisons of every class should be substantial structures, affording gratification by their design and material to a pure taste, but not costly or highly ornate. We are of the opinion that those of moderate size are best, as regards both industrial and reformatory ends.

XXXI. The construction, organization, and management of all prisons should be by the state, and they should form a graduated series of reformatory establishments, being arranged with a view to the industrial employment, intellectual education and moral training of the inmates.

XXXII. As a general rule, the maintenance of penal institutions, above the county jail, should be from the earnings of their inmates, and without cost to the state; nevertheless, the true standard of merit in their management is the rapidity and thoroughness of reformatory effect accomplished thereby.

XXXIII. A right application of the principles of sanitary science in the construction and arrangements of prisons is a point of vital importance. The apparatus for heating and ventilation should be the best that is known; sunlight, air and water should be afforded according to the abundance with which nature has provided them; the rations and clothing should be plain but wholesome, comfortable, and in sufficient but not extravagant quantity; the bedsteads, bed and bedding, including sheets and pillow cases, not costly but decent, and kept clean, well aired and free from vermin; the hospital accommodations, medical stores and surgical instruments should be all that humanity requires and science can supply; and all needed means for personal cleanliness should be without stint.

XXXIV. The principle of the responsibility of parents for the full or partial support of their criminal children in reformatory institutions has been extensively applied in Europe, and its practical working has been attended with the best results. It is worthy of inquiry whether this principle may not be advantageously introduced into the management of our American reformatory institutions.

XXXV. It is our conviction that one of the most effective agencies in the repression of crime would be the enactment of laws by which the education of all the children of the state should be made obligatory. Better to force education upon the people than to force them into prison to suffer for crimes, of which the neglect of education and consequent ignorance have been the occasion, if not the cause.

XXXVI. As a principle that crowns all, and is essential to all, it is our conviction that no prison system can be perfect, or even successful to the most desirable degree, without some central authority to sit at the helm, guiding, controlling, unifying and vitalizing the whole. We ardently hope yet to see all the departments of our preventive, reformatory and penal institutions in each state moulded into one harmonious and effective system; its parts mutually answering to and supporting each other; and the whole animated by the same spirit, aiming at the same objects and subject to the same control; yet without loss of the advantages of voluntary aid and effort, wherever they are attainable.

XXXVII. This congress is of the opinion that, both in the official administration of such a system, and in the voluntary co-operation of citizens therein, the agency of women may be employed with excellent effect.

Sentencing

Crime is an intentional violation of duties imposed by law, which inflicts an injury upon others. Criminals are persons convicted of crime by competent courts. Punishment is suffering inflicted on the criminal for the wrong done by him, with a special view to secure his reformation.

—Declaration of Principles Adopted and Promulgated by the 1870 Congress of the National Prison Association

Introduction

Imagine you are a district judge. A 19-year-old stands before you charged with operating a motor vehicle while intoxicated and damaging property. He was arrested after he sideswiped another car on the interstate. He pleaded guilty and is awaiting your sentence. This is his third conviction for an alcohol-related offense. What will be the sentence? Is it important that you make an example of him so that others will not engage in similar activities? Do you think the sentence should include incarceration to make a strong impression on the defendant? Or, do you think the defendant should be sentenced to community-based corrections to provide him with an opportunity to change his behavior to keep him in the community and expose him to positive influences?

As a judge you have an array of options: You may sentence the offender to probation with or without a requirement of community service, to a jail or prison, or to a combination of both community supervision and incarceration for varying lengths of time. Your final decision will most likely depend on your philosophy of sentencing, the types of sentencing available in your jurisdiction, and the various sentencing models designed to limit or minimize judicial discretion. *Judicial discretion* means that the judge decides the length and severity of the sentence for the convicted defendant based on relevant criteria such as severity of the crime, the defendant's character, and social ties. Sentencing is a multifaceted judgment that promotes the *social order*, a well-functioning, productive relationship among members of society. Sentencing options and rationales constantly change, reflecting society's social, economic, and political views. This chapter will emphasize the importance of understanding sentencing goals and rationales, types, models, and disparities.

Sentencing Goals and Rationales

The philosophies or goals of criminal sentencing are commonly grouped into five areas: retribution, deterrence, rehabilitation, incapacitation, and restoration. While all five goals will be presented individually in detail, sentencing goals frequently overlap.

Retribution

Retribution is defined as "giving back" and is closely associated with revenge and the *just deserts model of sentencing*, which holds that offenders are responsible for their crimes and should receive the exact punishment they deserve. Retribution is the earliest known goal or rationale for punishment. Historically, it was typically realized through acts of revenge. Victims and their family members believed they were entitled to "get even" for some perceived wrong. Death and exile were often exacted by victims, even for relatively minor offenses. The trouble with revenge, recognized by one of the children interviewed in Piaget's study of moral development, is that it is perpetual; the moment one person gains revenge, the recipient is motivated to return the favor, resulting in an endless vicious cycle.[1]

While enlightened reformers sought a system eliminating revenge as a motive for punishment, retribution remains a primary goal of criminal sentencing. Evidence of society's thirst for revenge is evident in the "get tough" approach to crime. For example, prisoners were exposed to the get tough approach with the 1996 passage of the No-Frills Prison Act, a federal law that severely curtailed the use of taxpayers' money to support certain types of prison recreation in the Federal Bureau of Prisons. The act also made prison construction and improvement money available only to states that agreed not to purchase and replace strength-enhancing weight equipment and electronic musical instruments.

Sex offenders residing in the community are also impacted by get tough policies. Most states and municipalities forbid sex offenders to live near schools or day care centers, and otherwise limit the travel of sex offenders within states and across state lines. Registered sex offenders are often required to wear ankle bracelets with global positioning units that trace their every move, while some jurisdictions mandate implanting chips for similar surveillance. In some states, counties, and cities, the residential limits are so stringent that sex offenders have great difficulty finding housing, making it virtually impossible for registered sex offenders to live there.

Finally, one of the chief arguments of death penalty advocates is that capital punishment provides a type of retribution for victims of crimes and their survivors. Death penalty advocates justify capital punishment under the principle of *lex talionis*, or "an eye for an eye," the belief that punishment should fit the crime. The Latin term *lex talionis* is formally known as the law of retaliation or revenge and prescribes retaliating, in kind, for crimes committed. Overall, supporters of retribution believe that offenders should be punished because they *deserve* to be punished, not to deter others or reduce the likelihood of future crimes by the offender.[2]

Deterrence

The goal of *deterrence* is to prevent future criminal activity through example or threat of punishment. According to the concept of deterrence, punishment is not an end per se, but a means to deter crime and protect the social order. There are two recognized types of deterrence: general and specific. *General deterrence* is defined as the impact of the threat of punishment on the general public. *Specific deterrence*, conversely, is the impact of the actual punishment on those who are convicted.

General deterrence strives to influence the behavior of people who may be tempted to commit crime, ultimately letting the community know that crime does not pay. The focus of sentencing is not on the offender or attempts at behavioral change. Instead, the focus is on the actual punishment, in order to discourage others from crime. The effectiveness of general deterrence is predicated on the court's ability to dispense fair and equitable sentences. For example, if the general public views punishment to be too lenient, it may, ironically, encourage criminal behavior. If, on the other hand, the public perceives punishment to be too harsh, then it may simply provoke resentment, reprisal, and disregard for the law. The effectiveness is also compromised by the criminal justice system's inability to swiftly apprehend, prosecute, and punish criminals. As explained in Chapter 1, most reported crime never results in an arrest, and of those arrested, most cases are dismissed or the offender is sentenced to some sort of community-based program. The likelihood of an offender being sentenced to a period of incarceration is very slight. Because the *expected punishment*, the number of days in prison that a typical offender can expect to serve for each crime committed, is low, the fear of punishment and impact of general deterrence is essentially neutralized.[3]

Specific deterrence strives to influence a specific offender to abstain from criminal offenses after experiencing punishment. The focus of sentencing is on a specific offender and how punishment can be designed to deter that particular offender from committing another crime. In order to be influential, the punishment must be significant enough to discourage future criminal activities. After suffering punishment, the offender should realize the consequences of the crime were too painful and do not justify the risk of being punished if the criminal behavior is repeated. The effectiveness of specific deterrence is difficult to measure. One reason lies in the difficulty to ascertain whether people refrain from committing crimes because they were deterred by the possibility of punishment. Another difficulty stems from the assumption that people are rational before they act. Deterrence does not account for people who commit crimes while under the influence of a controlled substance, act on impulse, or suffer from a mental illness. Supporters of deterrence believe that offenders should be punished to deter others or reduce the likelihood of the offender committing crimes in the future, not because they deserve to be punished or to reform the criminal. Noted English prison reformer and Quaker Elizabeth Frye strongly influenced new legislation in the mid-1800s that made the punishment of offenders more humane. Throughout her service, Frye recognized the significance of deterrence as a sentencing goal. She was reported to have said, "Punishment is not for revenge, but to deter crime and reform the criminal."[4]

Rehabilitation

Rehabilitation seeks to create essential changes in offenders and their behavior, thus reducing the likelihood of future criminal behavior.

Similar to specific deterrence, the goal of rehabilitation is directed toward the offender but does not imply any connection between the severity of the punishment and the seriousness of the crime. For example, offenders who commit minor crimes may receive a long prison sentence if the experts who evaluated the offender believed long-term incarceration is warranted for rehabilitation. Conversely, a murderer may receive an early parole date if officials believe the problems that led to the killing have been resolved or corrected. While retribution concentrates on revenge and deterrence focuses on the offenders' fear of punishment, rehabilitation is concerned with restoring offenders to law-abiding citizens through vocational or educational training or therapy. Offenders are "treated," not punished.

Supporters of rehabilitation believe in the *medical model theory*, which contends an offender's criminal tendencies can be identified and treated, similarly to a physical disease. Prior to sentencing, an offender submits to an evaluation. If the diagnosis indicates poor socialization, chemical dependency, and inadequate work skills as the factors leading to the criminal behavior in question, the sentence, or "prescription," may involve a combination of social skills counseling, substance abuse treatment, and vocational training.

Rehabilitation, as a goal of sentencing, has not always achieved its desired result of reforming the offender. From the 1940s through the mid-1970s, rehabilitation was the most popular goal of sentencing. During the 1970s, however, power balance between the competing goals of rehabilitation and punishment started to shift. With elevated crime rates and prison crowding, there was public and professional disillusionment toward the effectiveness of rehabilitation. Prosecutors, judges, and the public were forced to reconsider rehabilitation as a legitimate sentencing goal after the Martinson Report, or the "Nothing Works Doctrine," was released. In 1974, Robert Martinson and colleagues assessed evaluations of criminal rehabilitation programs between 1945 and 1967, concluding that "with few and isolated exceptions, the rehabilitative efforts that have been reported so far have had no appreciable effect on recidivism." While the Martinson Report negatively impacted rehabilitation as an ideal sentencing goal, there is evidence suggesting community-based and institutional treatment programs are highly effective for some offenders.[5]

Incapacitation

Incapacitation seeks to protect innocent members of society from offenders who might harm them if not prevented from doing so.

Offenders are sentenced to jail or prison to physically isolate them from society. In archaic societies, *banishment*, a common form of punishment, was imposed, which forced the offender to remain outside of that country or state. In America, offenders would sometimes volunteer to leave an area or join the military as a form of punishment. Currently, incapacitation is usually achieved through imprisonment. Incapacitation as a goal of sentencing gained momentum in the late 1970s, when public and professional cynicism toward rehabilitation grew. The get tough on crime attitude was embraced by both political liberals and conservatives.

The effectiveness of incapacitation, like the other goals of sentencing, is difficult to measure. On the surface, it appears that incapacitation effectively reduces crime. Between 1990 and 1999, after get tough policies had been in place, the overall crime rate (index crimes known to the police) dropped by 26%, violent crimes decreased by 28% (the murder rate dropped by 39%), and property crime declined by 26%. During the exact same time period, the nation's incarceration rate increased by 56%. Examination of those crime figures leads one to conclude that more people in prison equals less crime.[6]

Opponents of incapacitation quickly call attention to the 1980s, when overall incarceration went up by 114%, while the crime rate dropped by only 2% (largely from a 6% drop in property crime). During that same period, violent crime actually *increased* by 22%. Shelden and Brown extended the time frame of the research, 1971–2000, and found the overall crime rate remained virtually the same, while the national incarceration rate increased by almost 500%.[6]

Researchers have warned that increasing the number of prisoners may backfire and cause crime to increase. The term *backfire*, first used in this context by Todd Clear, implies there are "crime-enhancing effects" of increasing the use of incarceration. First, when one offender from a group, or gang, is imprisoned, another will take his place. For example, in the illegal drug business, when one dealer goes to prison, someone just assumes the vacated position. Also, social factors known to cause crime, such as broken families and unemployment, tend to increase in those communities most impacted by high incarceration rates. There is evidence that indicates the more people that are incarcerated and experience prison life, the less adverse effect incarceration has on the offender. Finally, incarceration does not reduce the chance of being a victim or limit who the victims are, e.g., other inmates or prison staff. Some of the highest crime rates are behind prison walls.[7]

Restoration

While previously identified goals of punishment focus on the offender (rehabilitation and specific deterrence) or the crime (retribution, general deterrence, and incapacitation), restoration centers on the needs of the victim and the community. The *restoration* goal of sentencing seeks to address the damage resulting from the crime by restoring the victim and the community to their precrime state. Grounded in the concept of *reparation*, the offender is required to pay or provide a service to the victim as a way to make amends for the crime.

Restorative justice has expanded the concept of reparation and has become a major goal of sentencing. Advocates for restorative justice are concerned about crime victims' needs not normally met in the traditional justice process. Because crime is defined as an act against the state, the state assumes the role of the victims. As a result, victims often feel ignored, neglected, or even abused by the justice process. Howard Zehr, one of the founders of the restorative justice movement, believes the criminal justice system must individualize sentencing by holding offenders accountable for their behavior and making them productive members of their community. Judges have the discretion to impose a number of restorative sentencing options, including victim-offender mediation, victim impact panels, community reparative boards, family group conferences, circle sentencing, and court diversion programs. Studies have suggested that victims who participated in the restorative justice programs reported lower rates of fear of revictimization than did victims in comparison groups. Both offenders and victims who participated in restorative justice also reported greater satisfaction with the process. Finally, offenders and victims reported negotiating and completing restitution agreements more often than participants from traditional court proceedings.[8]

- Victim-offender mediation (VOM) is a face-to-face meeting between the victim and the offender who committed the crime. The meeting is held in the presence of a trained mediator. VOMs are also referred to as victim-offender dialogue, victim-offender conferencing, victim-offender reconciliation, or restorative justice dialogue. Family and community members may occasionally join the meeting. In the meeting, the offender and the victim share with each other the impact of the crime on their lives and their feelings about it, and develop a plan to repair the harm caused by the crime.[9]

- *Victim impact panels* typically consist of two to four crime victims/survivors who share the details of their victimization with offenders and others. Participating victims claim speaking on a victim impact panel provides them with a forum in which to express their feelings and talk about their victimization. They have reported a sense of empowerment and healing. An additional benefit of victim impact panels is the awareness that an offender gains by hearing the devastating effects of crime from a victim, or a survivor of a victim.

- *Community reparative boards* are composed of a small group of trained citizens who conduct public, face-to-face meetings with offenders sentenced by the court to participate in the process. During a meeting, board members discuss the negative consequences associated with the crime. Board members develop a set of proposed sanctions until they are mutually agreed upon by the board and offender. A specific plan that includes a time frame to make reparation for the crime is also set. It is the offender's responsibility to document progress in complying with the plan. After the predetermined period of time has passed, the board submits a compliance report to the court.[10]

- Family group conference (FGC) is a meeting between members of a family and friends of an offender. The aim is to provide an opportunity for an offender to meet with relatives and friends to discuss how criminal behavior has impacted them. The group develops a plan to resolve the impact of criminal behavior, rather than leaving the decision making entirely in the hands of the legal authorities and service providers.

- Sentencing circles—sometimes called peacemaking circles—use a traditional circle ritual to involve the victim, victim supporters, offender, offender supporters, judge and court personnel, prosecutor, defense counsel, police, and all interested community members. Within the circle, people speak openly and secure commitments by all stakeholders to assist in healing all who have been impacted by the crime and to prevent future crimes. Sentencing circles typically involve the following steps: (1) application by the offender to participate in the circle process, (2) a healing circle for the victim, (3) a healing circle for the offender, (4) a sentencing circle to develop consensus on the elements of a sentencing plan, and (5) follow-up circles to monitor the progress of the offender.

Specifics of the circle process vary from community to community and are designed to fit community needs and culture.[8]

Types of Sentences

Once a plea of guilty has been entered or a determination of guilt has been made by a judge or a jury, the next step in the criminal justice system is to impose a sentence. The responsibility to impose a sentence may rest on a judge or a jury and may be discretional or mandatory. *Mandatory sentences* are those that are specifically required by statute for certain types of crimes, essentially removing any discretion from the sentencing authority.

Mandatory sentences do not necessarily eliminate judicial discretion. Even in cases involving a mandatory sentence, the judge must decide how to sentence an offender convicted of two or more charges. As in the example provided at the beginning of this chapter, the judge must impose a sentence for both the driving while intoxicated and property damages charges. Sentences can be concurrent or consecutive. *Concurrent sentences* are served concurrently, or simultaneously, which means that while the offender is serving the sentence for the driving while intoxicated charge, he will also serve the property damage sentence. *Consecutive sentences* are served one after another. As with the previous example, the offender would serve the sentence for the first offense. When that sentence has been served in its entirety, the offender then serves the sentence for the second offense. While concurrent sentences are the most common type of sentence, consecutive sentences are most often used for serious, violent offenders because it extends the length of time an offender will be incarcerated.

At the time of sentencing, a judge must decide whether to order the sentence to be executed, suspend imposition of the sentence (SIS), or suspend execution of the sentence (SES). Upon imposing a sentence, the judge may order the sentence to be executed. Execute refers to the process of transferring an offender to confinement. The imposition of sentence, however, may not actually involve sending the offender to confinement. The judge has the option to grant an SIS. In that event, the defendant is typically placed on probation. If the defendant violates probation and faces revocation, the judge may order any sentence within the full range of punishment for the crime convicted. If the defendant successfully completes probation, no sentence is ever actually ordered or imposed, so an SIS is not considered a conviction for anything other than law enforcement purposes.

If granted an SES, the defendant is placed on probation, yet a specific prison sentence is imposed. The judge will then suspend the execution of the sentence. The judge is limited to executing only the original sentence if the defendant is revoked. While it is possible that the offender may never be imprisoned, the SES is a conviction.

Sentencing Models

The *model of criminal sentencing* is an approach for imposing sentences that fit the seriousness of the crime and the offender's criminal history. In the past century, the act of imposing sentences has changed from a judge-focused process to an administrative-focused one. Today, judges simply have less discretion when imposing sentences because they are guided by principles established by legislative or administrative policies. The various types of sentencing models available include sentencing guidelines, indeterminate and determinate sentencing, mandatory sentences, and truth in sentencing laws.

- *Sentencing guidelines* promote fairness and reduce disparity while preserving that degree of judicial discretion necessary to issue a sentence appropriate for the offender. Disparity in sentencing and certainty of punishment are longstanding issues of concern for Congress, the criminal justice community, and the public. Historically, judges could issue a sentence that ranged anywhere from probation to the maximum penalty for the offense. In the early 1980s, Congress decided that (1) the previously unfettered sentencing discretion accorded federal trial judges needed to be structured, (2) the administration of punishment needed to be more certain, and (3) specific offenders (e.g., white collar and violent, repeat offenders) needed to be targeted for more serious penalties.

  With the enactment of the Sentencing Reform Act provisions of the Comprehensive Crime Control Act of 1984, Congress created the *U.S. Sentencing Commission* as a permanent body charged with formulating national sentencing guidelines for federal trial judges to follow in their sentencing decisions. The seven voting members on the commission are appointed by the president, confirmed by the Senate, and serve six-year terms. No more than three of the commissioners may be federal judges, and no more than four may belong to the same political party. The attorney general is an *ex officio* member of the commission, as is the chair of the U.S. Parole Commission.[11] Since the development of the U.S. Sentencing Commission, many states have created their own sentencing commission with similar state-level officials.

Typically, the guidelines are presented in a grid that indicates normal sanctions imposed for specific offenses with a range of scores for the seriousness of the offense and criminal history. Sentencing guidelines set a presumptive sentence based on the severity of the crime and also on the offender's record of prior convictions. A *presumptive sentence* is the sentence called for under the sentencing guidelines grid. The scores range from less serious to more serious. The offender's score is calculated by adding the allocated points assigned to factors such as the number of prior offenses, the number of times incarcerated, employment and educational status, and whether on probation at the time the offense was committed. Judges review the grid to ascertain what sentence should be imposed. Under specific mitigating circumstances, the judge can reduce the sentence by ordering a downward departure from the presumptive sentence. Under specific aggravating circumstances, the judge can order an upward departure from the presumptive sentence, thereby increasing the sentence. A departure from the prescribed sentence is permitted only if the judge is able to provide a written explanation of the aggravating or mitigating circumstances that justified deviating from the prescribed sentence. However, the presumptive sentence is imposed most of the time.

The guidelines generated considerable criticism. A frequent argument was that they did not allow judges to take into consideration the individual circumstances that are unique to the person being sentenced. Shortly after implementation of the guidelines, defendants began challenging the guideline's constitutionality. In January 2005, the U.S. Supreme Court changed the entire landscape of federal sentencing in the case of *United States v. Booker*. The court found that federal sentencing guidelines were unconstitutional because they violated offenders' Sixth Amendment privileges. Sentencing guidelines were ruled unconstitutional because they were based upon facts that were not proved to a jury beyond a reasonable doubt, nor conceded to by a defendant.

Since *Booker*, federal judges view the sentencing guidelines as an advisory system. According to statistics from the Sentencing Commission, the *Booker* decision has had a modest effect on sentencing outcome. The average sentence in the federal court is 56 months, the same as in 2004. The median sentence is 34 months, up from 33 months in 2004. White collar theft and fraud charges witnessed the greatest average increase. The average sentence is 21 months, up from 19 in 2004. Interestingly, since *Booker*, 61.2% of federal defendants have been sentenced within the sentencing or advisory guidelines range, a decrease from 72% in 2004. Of those that were sentenced outside of the range, the majority resulted from prosecutorial recommendation. Prosecutors had requested a departure from the range based upon the defendant's substantial assistance and to expedite deportation in immigration cases. In only 10% of the cases have judges imposed sentences below the advisory guideline ranges. Overall, the vast majority of all federal defendants have received the same, or nearly the same, sentence under the court's new decision as they would have had the sentencing guidelines been upheld. The differences have been at the low end of the sentencing scale, in cases where the sentencing guidelines mandated short prison terms, but where judges will now give a sentence of probation. Such cases typically involve minor crimes and first-time offenders.[12]

- *Indeterminate sentence* is a sentencing model in which a maximum and a minimum length of incarceration are set, within statutory limits, by a judge. A parole authority is then responsible for determining the actual date of release. For example, the offender that was introduced at the beginning of the chapter may receive a sentence of one to seven years' imprisonment for the felony driving while intoxicated offense. After he has served one year, he would be eligible for parole. Depending on parole authorities' discretion and not the sentencing judge's, the offender may not be released until he has completed seven years of confinement. An advantage to this sentencing model is that it helps reduce overcrowding and warehousing of inmates. On the other hand, critics of indeterminate sentences argue that sentencing discretion should not be transferred from a judge to the parole authority. Their concern is that political appointees may not have the expertise or training to predict recidivism accurately. Indeterminate sentencing became popular during the 1960s and 1970s, when rehabilitation was the dominant goal of sentencing. It is linked to the medical model, and when rehabilitation fell in disfavor, so did indeterminate sentencing. While judges criticized indeterminate sentencing, prison officials also thought inmates "played the game" and superficially did the things to earn early release, without adequately changing behavioral patterns.

- As another sentencing model, a *determinate sentence* is one in which the term of incarceration is predetermined, or fixed by the judge. For example, if statutes allow up to seven years for a felony driving while intoxicated charge, then the judge may sentence one offender to three years of incarceration. But, the judge may sentence another offender, who has a prior felony conviction, to the maximum sentence of seven years. If there is a reduction in the time served, it depends on the number of good time credits earned by the prisoner. Any postincarceration supervision may be part of the original sentence. Supporters of determinate sentencing dislike the lenience of parole and early release, while the critics argue that determinate sentences discourage prisoners from engaging in rehabilitation programs while incarcerated. Offenders also favor determinate sentencing. They want to know how long they are going to be locked up and when they will be released. Indeterminate is too nebulous for them.

- *Mandatory sentences* are a sentencing model that statutorily stipulates a period of incarceration for offenders convicted of a particular crime, or a specific crime with special circumstances. Mandatory prison terms are typically specified for violent crimes, drug violations, sex offenses, or crimes in which a dangerous weapon was used in commission of the crime. Mandatory minimum sentences and sentence enhancements are examples of this sentencing model.

- *Mandatory minimum sentence* is a required minimum term of punishment (typically incarceration) that is established by Congress in a statute. All 50 states have enacted one or more mandatory minimum sentencing laws, and Congress has enacted several mandatory sentencing laws for federal crimes.

When a mandatory minimum applies, the judge is forced to follow it and cannot impose a sentence below the minimum term required, regardless of the unique facts and circumstances of the defendant or the offense. In contrast, sentencing guidelines, which are now used as an advisory system, can be crafted to account for both consistency in sentencing and individual circumstances of the offense and offender. Where both statutory mandatory minimums and guidelines apply, the mandatory minimum trumps the guidelines.

In 1994 Congress created a "safety valve" that would suspend the minimum sentence mandated in drug cases, if the defendant was a low-level participant, did not use a weapon, was involved in a violence-free crime, had little or no criminal history, and told the government the truth about his or her involvement in the offense. The statutory safety valve compels courts to impose a sentence under the advisory guidelines in place of a mandatory minimum. Today, the safety valve has been used to recognize and adjust the sentences of 25 percent of all drug offenders, benefiting first-time, low-level, nonviolent offenders.[13]

- Most states have adopted *sentence enhancements*, designed to incapacitate persistent or habitual offenders through long-term incarceration. The custom of imposing longer prison sentences on repeat offenders than on first-time offenders who commit the same crime is not a new practice. Many states have had habitual offender or persistent offender statutes for years. New York, for example, has a *persistent felony offender* law that dates back to the late nineteenth century.

  Officially known in many states as habitual offender laws, "three strikes and you're out" laws mandate judges to sentence offenders who have three felony convictions to extended periods of incarceration, including the possibility of life without parole. In a two-year time frame, 1993–1995, 26 states and the federal government passed "three strikes" laws in response to public outrage over such cases as the 1993 kidnapping and murder of 12-year-old Polly Klaas by a paroled repeat offender.[14]

  Under the federal three strikes rule, now codified at 18 USC § 3559(c), the offender receives mandatory life imprisonment if convicted of a serious violent felony and has two or more prior convictions in federal or state courts, where at least one is a serious violent felony or a serious drug offense.

The State of California is noted to have the harshest three strikes laws. The law mandates that if a person has two or more previous serious or violent felony convictions, the sentence for any additional felony conviction (not just serious or violent) is 25 years to life. More than 7,000 people have been sent to California's prisons with life sentences under the state's three strikes law. In 350 of those cases, the third crime the defendant committed was a minor offense. In 2003, the U.S. Supreme Court held that such sentences do not violate the Eighth Amendment of the U.S. Constitution, which prohibits cruel and unusual punishment.[15]

- *Truth in sentencing* refers to laws that mandate offenders to serve 85% of the prison sentence before being released from confinement. In 1984, Washington became the first state to pass truth in sentencing legislation. Ten years later, as part of the effort to get tough on crime and standardize prison sentences across the states, the U.S. Congress authorized additional funding for state prison systems where truth in sentencing laws were in place and prisoners were mandated to serve at least 85% of their term, regardless of their behavior in prison. By 1998, 27 states and the District of Columbia were complying with the federal guidelines.[16]

Proponents of truth in sentencing believe crime victims have a right to know the exact sentence imposed and how long the perpetrator will be incarcerated. Paroling a prisoner after he or she has served only a small portion of the sentence undermines the extent of the victim's trauma. Critics of truth in sentencing argue the shift from rehabilitation to incapacitation has had a negative impact on inmate behavior. Before truth in sentencing laws, inmates could reduce their prison sentence by behaving well and participating in education or counseling. Truth in sentencing laws have removed that incentive as well as some of the discretion commonly held by prison authorities.[16]

Evaluations of truth in sentencing laws have revealed only short-term impacts on the volume or composition of correctional populations, but there appears to be evidence of a longer-term effect in the State of Washington. Significant effects in Washington included more growth in the state's incarceration rate and time served by prison inmates, as well as declining trends in the rates of total prison admissions and releases from prison. Prisoners appear to be spending more time behind bars, and fewer inmates are passing through the system with short stays.[17]

Sentencing Disparity

Concerns over disparity and discrimination in sentencing led to a number of sentencing model reforms that have continued for the past four decades. Many of the reforms have been implemented to address the legitimate factors that influence a judge's sentencing decision. Legitimate factors that affect sentencing include the severity of the offense, and whether the offender had a prior record or used a weapon in commission of the offense. In addition to the legitimate factors, there are other factors that influence judges when they impose sentences. Social class, gender, citizenship, and race also impact sentencing outcomes and result in *sentencing disparity*, the inconsistency in the types and lengths of sentences imposed for the same crime when no legal justification is established. If Hispanics and poor defendants receive harsher punishments than do whites and the wealthy, it may be that they commit more serious crimes. If judges, however, singled them out because of their race or social class, then that would be considered *sentencing discrimination*, the most burdensome type of unjustifiable disparity for which sentencing reform was clearly designed to eliminate.

Research revealed social class affected sentencing decision, but mainly for the very poor. For example, people who earn less than $5,000 a year receive harsher sentences than people who earn more than $5,000 a year, but there is little difference in the sentences given to offenders who earn $10,000 a year and those who earn more than $50,000. The disparity may be explained by the poor's inability to secure pretrial release and respectable legal counsel. Similarly, the offender's citizenship status impacted sentencing outcomes. Offenders who are U.S. citizens receive lower sentences by about 1.7 months, perhaps because they take advantage of their greater knowledge about the court systems and legal representation. The female-male difference is significant, especially in violent crimes. The largest differential is for bank robbery, where females receive 21.6 months less than males. Researcher David Mustard conducted a large and comprehensive evaluation of every federal sentence handed down for three consecutive years and proposed several explanations as to why gender disparity in sentencing exists. One explanation is paternalism among judges; "women are seen less as full adults, and as being less capable of being responsible for their own actions, and as a result judges depart from sentencing guidelines to give women lighter sentences."[18]

The most pronounced difference concerns racial disparity. Across the board, blacks and Hispanics incur longer prison sentences than whites. According to Mustard's study, bank robbery and drug trafficking crimes expose the largest black-white differentials. Blacks receive 9.4 and 10.5 months longer than whites in bank robbery and drug trafficking, respectively. The percentage difference is greatest for those convicted of drug trafficking, where blacks are assigned sentences 13.7% longer than those of whites. The cumulative Hispanic-white difference is mostly impacted by those convicted of drug trafficking and firearm possession/trafficking. For these two crimes, Hispanics receive 6.1 and 3.7 additional months compared to whites, or 8 and 7% longer in percentage terms.[18]

Laws concerning the possession and distribution of crack cocaine have received the most attention. Crack cocaine became widespread in the 1980s. The popularity of crack cocaine was associated with its cheap price, which for the first time made cocaine available to a lower social class. Public concern about crack cocaine addiction and its accompanying violent drug market spread quickly. Words like *crisis* and *epidemic* were used to describe the impact of crack, which was considered a social menace, more dangerous than powder. The political hysteria combined with the 1986 cocaine-induced death of Len Bias, an NBA player with the Boston Celtics, led Congress to pass the Anti-Drug Abuse Act of 1986. The law's mandatory penalties for crack cocaine offenses were the harshest ever adopted for low-level drug offenses and established drastically different penalty structures for crack and powder cocaine. For instance, the law mandated a five-year sentence with no parole for any offender who was convicted of possessing or distributing 5 grams of crack cocaine (less than two sugar packets). Yet, the punishment for the possession or distribution for powder cocaine, more popular among whites, was significantly less. For a user or seller to receive a five-year prison sentence, he would have to possess 500 grams of the powdered substance. The crack penalty equaled a 100:1 ratio.

With the passage of the law, the Bureau of Prisons experienced the largest population increase ever. By 2008, approximately 20,000 federal prisoners were serving sentences for crack cocaine offenses and 82% were black men. The racial disparity became an enormous concern, prompting the U.S. Sentencing Commission to recommended Congress to reduce the quantity disparity between crack and powder cocaine. Recommendations for an amendment to reduce the guideline sentence for crack cocaine were made by the U.S. Sentencing Commission to Congress in 1997, 2002, and 2006. Some estimated that the amendment would reduce crack sentences by 15 months on average, and reduce the size of the federal prison population by 3,800 in 15 years. Their fourth recommendation in 2007 went unchallenged by Congress and took effect on November 1, 2007. One month later, the commission voted to make its guideline reduction retroactive. The new guideline reduces the average sentence for crack cocaine from 10 years and 1 month to 8 years and 10 months. The decision, effective March 2008, made an estimated 20,000 persons in prison eligible to apply for a sentence reduction. As of December 8, 2008, approximately 12,000 people had been granted a sentence reduction averaging two years.[19]

The U.S. Commission's action to reduce the sentencing guidelines for crack offenses fueled reform momentum because a significant racial disparity in prosecutions and confinement had persisted for too long, and the hysteria that clouded the public debate on crack cocaine had done a disservice to developing responsible sentencing policy. Both have intensified the disastrous racial disparities that infect our prison system. Regional and national reporters applauded the commission's decision and await Congress to align mandatory sentences for crack cocaine.

Summary

The act of imposing a sentence is a complex judgment. Sentencing options and rationales are continuously altered, reflecting society's social, economic, and political views. This chapter highlighted the importance of understanding sentencing goals and rationales, types, models, and disparities.

The philosophies or goals of criminal sentencing are commonly grouped into five areas: retribution (deserved punishment), deterrence (punish to discourage future crime), rehabilitation (treat the offender's needs), incapacitation (remove offender from society), and restoration (repair harm to victim).

The responsibility to impose a sentence may rest on a judge or a jury and may be discretional or mandatory. Sentences can be concurrent or consecutive. A judge must decide whether to order the sentence to be executed, suspend imposition of the sentence (SIS), or suspend execution of the sentence (SES). Finally, if there are two or more charges, sentences will be concurrent (served simultaneously) or consecutive (served one after another).

Sentencing models are an approach for imposing sentences that fit the seriousness of the crime and the offender's criminal history. The various types of sentencing models available include sentencing guidelines, indeterminate and determinate sentencing, mandatory sentences (mandatory minimum and sentencing enhancements), and truth in sentencing laws.

Concerns about disparity and discrimination in sentencing led to a number of sentencing model reforms. Many of the reforms have been implemented to address the sentencing disparity and sentencing discrimination that influence judges' and juries' decisions. The U.S. Sentencing Commission's action to reduce the sentencing guidelines for crack offenses has fueled reform momentum.

Vocabulary

Backfire

Banishment

Community reparative boards

Concurrent sentences

Consecutive sentences

Determinate sentence

Deterrence

Expected punishment

General deterrence

Incapacitation

Indeterminate sentence

Judicial discretion

Just deserts model of sentencing

Lex talionis

Mandatory minimum sentence

Mandatory sentencing

Medical model theory

Model of criminal sentencing

Persistent felony offender

Presumptive sentence

Rehabilitation

Reparation

Restoration

Retribution

Sentence enhancements

Sentencing discrimination

Sentencing disparity

Sentencing guidelines

Social order

Specific deterrence

Truth in sentencing

U.S. Sentencing Commission

Victim impact panels

Discussion Questions

1. Know the difference between an indeterminate and a determinate sentence. If a judge were preparing to sentence you, which type would you prefer? Why?
2. Discuss the basic goals and philosophy of sentencing. If you were a judge preparing to sentence an offender, which goal or philosophy would you apply? Why?
3. Understand the various sentencing models. What are the strengths and weaknesses of each?
4. Discuss how social issues such as social class, gender, citizenship, and race influence sentencing.

Notes

1. Gilligan, J. (2000). Punishment and violence: Is the criminal law based on one huge mistake? *Social Justice, 67*(3), 709–744.

2. Carlson, P. M., & Garret, J. S. (2008). *Prison and jail administration: Practice and theory.* Sudbury, MA: Jones and Bartlett.

3. Reynolds, M. G. (1999). *Crime and punishment in America: 1999.* NCPA Policy Report 229. Washington, DC: National Center for Policy Analysis.

4. Goff, D. N. (2008). *A brief memoir of Elizabeth Frye.* Philadelphia: Friends United Press.

5. Anstiss, B. (2003). Just how effective is correctional treatment at reducing re-offending? *New Zealand Journal of Psychology, 32.* Retrieved from http://findarticles.com/p/articles/mi_qa3848/is_200312/ai_n9327527/?tag=content;col1

6. Shelden, R. G., & Brown, W. B. (2004). *Criminal justice in America: A critical view.* Boston, MA: Allyn and Bacon.

7. Clear, T. (1996). Backfire: When incarceration increases crime. *Journal of the Oklahoma Criminal Justice Research Consortium, 3*(2), 1–10.

8. Zehr, H. (2002). *The little handbook of restorative justice.* Intercourse, PA: Good Books.

9. Victim Offender Mediation Association. Retrieved June 4, 2010, from http://www.voma.org/

10. Community Reparative Boards, N.D. http://www.ncjrs.gov/html/ojjdp/2001_2_1/page2.html. Retrieved March 1, 2011.

11. U.S. Sentencing Commission. An overview of the U.S. Sentencing Commission. Retrieved from http://www.ussc.gov/general/USSCoverview.pdf

12. Sloan, W. H., & Levine, K. S. (2006). Booker after a year: New highs for sentences, guidelines followed. *New York Law Journal.* Retrieved from http://www.clm.com/publication.cfm/ID/88

13. Safety Valve. Federal mandatory reforms: Improve and expand the federal "safety valve." Smart on Crime. Recommendations for the Next Administration and Congress. Retrieved from http://2009transition.org/criminaljustice/index.php?option=com_content&view=article&id=43&Itemid=96

14. Law Info. (2010). Three strikes rule. Retrieved June 9, 2010, from http://www.lawinfo.com/fuseaction/Client.lawarea/categoryid/139

15. Three Strikes. Total Criminal Defense. (2010). Understanding "three strikes and you're out" laws: What are three strikes laws? Retrieved from http://www.totalcriminaldefense.com/overview/three-strikes-law.aspx

16. Curtiss, J. (2010). Truth in sentencing laws. Retrieved June 9, 2010, from http://www.ehow.com/about_5449420_truth-sentencing-laws.html

17. Chen, E. (2000). *Impacts of three strikes and truth in sentencing on the volume and composition of correctional populations.* NIJ 98-IJCX-0082. Retrieved from http://www.ncjrs.gov/pdffiles1/nij/grants/187109.pdf

18. Mustard, D. (2001). Racial, ethnic and gender disparities in sentencing: Evidence from the U.S. federal courts. *Journal of Law and Economics, 44*(1), 285–314.

19. The Sentencing Project. (2009). Federal crack cocaine sentencing. Retrieved from http://sentencingproject.org/doc/publications/dp_crack_sentencing.pdf

II

Community Corrections

History and Process of Probation and Noncustodial Supervision

Time has not been spent in getting out books, but in getting persons out of jail.

—**John Augustus**

Introduction

Although most Americans see corrections as correctional institutions, more individuals are under the supervision of some type of alternative to confinement than are confined. Probation, community corrections, correctional treatment, and parole serve to monitor the conduct of offenders living in the communities of our nation. At year-end 2008, there were an estimated 5,095,200 adults under supervision in the community either on probation or parole—the equivalent of about 1 out of every 45 adults in the United States. Of those under some type of noncustodial correctional sanction, approximately 4,270,917 (84%) were on probation, which has emerged as the most frequently used judicial alternative to confinement in the United States.[1]

Convicted offenders live in our communities; many of these people are productive members of our society, while others live on the edge of criminal and noncriminal behavior. A dedicated group of justice professionals have accepted the responsibilities of monitoring the conduct of those in our communities under judicial sanctions. Probation, community corrections, and parole officers find themselves performing a wide range of duties, to include providing transitional assistance to the offender as he or she moves from correctional oversight into the free society.

Historically, most societies have used punishments other than confinement. Nonconfinement punishments, such as corporal or capital punishment, were frequently administered in public to serve as both punishment for the offender and a warning to others. Today, nonconfinement correctional options provide the judiciary the flexibility to more effectively tailor the punishment to fit both the offender and the offense, keeping in mind that the purpose of punishment is the enhancement of public and community safety.

Overview of Noncustodial Supervision

Offenders under correctional control in the community are typically under one of three general forms of supervision: (1) *minimum*, which requires little if any formal reporting; (2) *regular*, where the offender reports to a probation, community corrections, or parole officer on a reoccurring basis; and (3) *intensive*, which requires more stringent reporting in addition to other sanctions placed on the offender as deemed necessary by the court.

It is up to the offender to conform to the rules and regulations established for his or her case. Rule violations by the offender may lead to the revocation of his or her noncustodial supervision status and subsequent confinement. While it is the responsibility of the supervising officer to ensure the offender has every reasonable opportunity to succeed, it is ultimately the offender who will succeed or fail based upon his or her willingness to comply with the conditions and sanctions placed upon him or her as a condition of his or her release.

Though there are many different types of noncustodial supervision programs, all have in common the goal of assisting the offender to become a productive member of society. Realizing no two offenders are the same, officers responsible for monitoring offenders' behavior must develop insight into the issues and challenges facing those under noncustodial correctional supervision if they are to effectively assist in the successful completion of offenders' correctional sanctions.

Probation

One of the most frequently used sentencing alternatives available to the nation's courts is probation. As an appropriate sentence for an offense, *probation* is a court-ordered term of correctional supervision of the offender in which the offender serves the sentence in the community. This community-based punishment serves as a cost-effective alternative to confinement.

Of the nonconfinement correctional alternatives, probation accounts for the majority of all persons under noncustodial correctional supervision. Probationers are required to conform to conditions ordered by the court; violations of these conditions may result in probation revocation and sentence imposition.

Probation officers perform many duties, most of which fall under two areas. First, probation officers typically conduct presentence investigations and prepare written reports for the court. These reports provide the sentencing judge detailed information about the offender, the offense, and the effects of the crime on the victim and the community. The purpose of these reports is to provide the court with greater insight in determining the most appropriate sentence for the offender.

Second, probation officers provide court-directed supervision by monitoring an offender's conduct and providing positive guidance. Offenders are expected to fully comply with the rules of their probation as well as to follow advice and guidance of the probation officer. Violations of the rules or conditions under which the offender has been released may result in revocation and confinement.

A major goal of probation and other forms of noncustodial correctional supervision is the protection of the community and its citizens. To accomplish this, the offender is expected to make positive changes in his or her life. For many offenders, change may include obtaining stable employment, participating in substance abuse treatment programs, or completing basic educational training.

For the officer supervising offenders in the community, caseload and the intensity of individual cases may range greatly. As in all other types of noncustodial supervision, offenders who pose a higher risk require more supervision and attention than low-risk offenders. Normally, probation officers who are assigned to supervise higher-risk offenders maintain a smaller caseload than those officers who supervise lower-risk offenders. Though caseloads vary by agency and jurisdiction, probation officers may supervise as few as 20 cases and as many as several hundred at a time.

History of Probation

While probation is a significant alternative to confinement today, its formal use by the court has been relatively recent. Probation had its early origin in such practices as right to clergy (privilegium clerical), dating back to the thirteenth century; securing sanctuary; judicial reprieve; and recognizance (a bond stipulating an action for a given period). The English common law practice of suspending sentences with certain restrictions is also a forerunner of probation.[2]

Modern probation owes much to Matthew Davenport Hill and John Augustus. Hill and Augustus believed confinement was not appropriate for all offenders. In England, Hill observed juvenile offenders were frequently released by the courts on the condition that they were to return home and respect the supervision of their parent or guardian. Later, as the recorder of Birmingham, a judicial post, he used a similar practice for some adult offenders who he released from confinement under the supervision of a "guardian" who would monitor and report the offender's behavior. Hill had constables visit these guardians and further monitor the offender's conduct. Hill's efforts reflected the elements found today in noncustodial correctional alternatives, the empowerment of the offender to change his or her behavior and the official monitoring of the offender's conduct to confirm compliance with the intent of the court.[3]

In the United States, John Augustus is considered the father of probation, and is recognized as the first probation officer in the nation. Born in Massachusetts in 1785, his interests in social justice led him to membership in the Washington Total Abstinence Society. His belief that abusers of alcohol could be rehabilitated through understanding and sustained positive moral influence drew his attention to the Boston Police Court, where in 1841 he accepted responsibility for and bailed out a "common drunkard."

Augustus was a positive influence on the man and the experience inspired him to continue these efforts. Keeping detailed notes on his activities, Augustus was the first to apply the term *probation* to this process of community supervision of offenders. By 1858, John Augustus was credited with the assistance of almost 2,000 offenders.[4]

Recognizing the value of community supervision of minor offenders, in 1878 Massachusetts enacted the first probation statute in the nation. Over the next several decades, probation spread across the United States as an accepted sentencing alternative to confinement.[5]

As states enacted statutes allowing for probation, each state adapted the probation process to meet its unique needs. Some states combined probation and parole, while in other states, state-administered parole systems and locally administered probation systems operate independently.

Foundations of Federal Probation and Pretrial Services

On the federal level, a dramatic increase in the federal inmate population early in the twentieth century made the need for additional sentencing options apparent. Flooding the federal system were violators whose offenses ranged from drug use and violent crimes, to include bank robbery and kidnapping, to prohibition violations. Responding to the need for additional punishment alternatives on the federal level, President Calvin Coolidge signed the Federal Probation Act of 1925, which authorized federal courts to suspend imposition of a sentence, or the execution of a sentence, in favor of probation.[6]

By the 1970s, the need to implement further means to both reduce crimes committed by persons released to the community pending trial and relieve unnecessary pretrial detention became obvious. The Pretrial Services Act of 1982 authorized implementation of pretrial services nationwide. Today, the U.S. Probation and Pretrial Services System serves as a vital part of the federal judiciary.[6]

The Probation Process

Probation and other noncustodial supervision processes operate in the following way: once the defendant is found guilty by the court, the court examines the sentencing options available that can be imposed for the specific crime for which the offender has been convicted. If the sentencing allows for probation or some other noncustodial penalty, the judge may request a presentence report to gain a better understanding of the offender to determine if a noncustodial penalty is appropriate.

This presentence report is an important document that greatly influences the sentencing decision. The officer preparing the presentence report will interview the defendant and the defendant's parent or guardian in juvenile cases, review criminal history and personal background information, contact the victim(s) if restitution is involved, and provide sentencing recommendations to the judge. In determining sentence, the judge is expected to consider all of the circumstances pertaining to the crime, the impact upon the victim, the impact upon the community, the record and remorse of the offender, and the fairness of the punishment. If, after this consideration, the judge determines probation or other noncustodial supervision is appropriate, an order is issued by the court. This order carries a set of obligatory conditions for conduct expected of the new probationer.

Offender Assessment

Proper assessment of the risks and needs of each offender is critical in the development of an effective supervision strategy. An officer conducts an intake interview to gather information regarding the offender's economic and social background after the offender has been convicted and placed on probation. This information is used to complete the risks and needs assessment tool, which provides further insight into the offender by compiling information on the offender's background, to include academic skills, employment history, financial stability, criminal record, attitude, drug and alcohol use, peer and family relations, and mental and physical health. As the supervising officer gains a better understanding of the offender's strengths and weaknesses, a plan can be developed that specifies a reporting schedule, referrals for treatment, job placement, educational needs, or any other type of service that would be beneficial to the offender.

Following the completion of the supervision plan, the officer works with the offender to ensure successful completion of the sentence. In addition to office and field visits with the offender, the supervising officer contacts family members, service agencies, and employers to assist in case management. Officers reassess cases and revise the supervision plan as needed and use a risk and needs reassessment tool to determine reporting frequency for the supervision period.

One of the major aspects of probation is its flexibility. As a vital part of the sentencing options available to the judiciary, conditions of probation can be tailored to meet the specific supervision requirements of each offender. For those that require additional supervision, intensive supervision probation (ISP) can be applied.

Electronic Monitoring

An outstanding resource that enhances the oversight of offenders on some nonconfinement supervision is electronic monitors. Electronic monitors may be used on pretrial defendants on conditional release and convicted offenders on probation, parole, house arrest, or as part of intensive supervision or work release programs.

Electronic monitoring keeps track of an offender's location through the use of an electronic device attached to the wrist or ankle and by random phone calls to the offender's residence. Electronic monitoring is intended to provide the offender with an additional influence upon his or her behavior, reduce the costs of supervision, reduce institutional populations, allow the offender to remain within the community while under supervision, and enhance the potential for rehabilitation by keeping offenders at home and in close contact with family members. The units are typically monitored on a 24-hour-a-day basis by private vendors who immediately report all curfew violations to probation staff for further investigation.

Intensive Supervision Probation (ISP)

Intensive supervision probation is similar to probation but involves more frequent surveillance and greater controls. It can also serve as an alternative to secure detention for juvenile arrestees. Intensive supervision services for both adults and juveniles attempt to reduce the danger that higher-risk offenders pose to the community while simultaneously promoting appropriate rehabilitative services.

Intensive supervision probation stresses increased surveillance and intervention. Offenders placed under intensive supervision probation are required to comply with rigorous conditions that include frequent reporting, curfews, drug testing, and community service, as well as any special conditions deemed appropriate by the court. Offenders may also be required to participate in programs, such as outpatient substance abuse programs, intensive sexual offender treatment programs, counseling services, and a life skills program designed to teach or reinforce social and family skills.

Offenders sentenced to intensive supervision probation are required to personally report to their supervising probation officer more frequently than other offenders. Additionally, many are required to participate in electronic home monitoring or other tracking services to ensure they are complying with the conditions of their sentence.

Supervision services such as breath analysis to detect alcohol use or unannounced employment or home visits are often utilized to ensure offenders comply with the terms of their release from confinement. Offenders under intensive supervision probation are also more likely to be brought before the court for a probation revocation hearing based upon technical violations of probation.

Intensive supervision probation programs have been found to be reasonably effective while reducing the danger that higher-risk offenders pose to the community. Though the operational details of intensive supervision probation often vary between jurisdictions, one characteristic of all intensive supervision probation programs is that they provide for very strict terms of probation. This increased level of control is typically achieved through reduced caseloads for the probation officers as they oversee offenders' court-ordered victim restitution, community service, employment, random urine and alcohol testing, electronic monitoring, and payment of a probation supervision fee. Intensive supervision probation can promote rehabilitative services at a cost savings to taxpayers.

Community Corrections

Community-based corrections (CBC) is a correctional option that provides an offender with sanctions, supervision, and treatment in a community setting instead of in prison. Similar to probation and intensive supervision probation, community-based corrections began to develop in the 1960s. Through the late 1960s and early 1970s, federal grants to state and local jurisdictions funded community corrections programs across the nation.

Various programs operate under the concept of community corrections. Community corrections programs include day and evening reporting centers, home confinement programs, electronic monitoring, residential reentry centers, *offender registration programs*, and offender treatment programs. Each program has a goal of increasing community safety through the reduction of crime.

Day and Evening Reporting Centers

The first day reporting center was established in England in 1974. The first American center opened in 1986, in Hampden County, Massachusetts.[7] By 1995, 114 centers were established in 22 states.

Day and evening reporting centers are nonresidential programs that require offenders to report daily activities to case managers. They allow for enhanced supervision of offenders, but differ from ISPs because they provide services such as drug treatment, job training referrals, life skills services, and general counseling.

The day reporting programs allow low-risk offenders to maintain employment while ensuring their adherence to court mandates. Many of the day reporting programs offer job skill development opportunities and resource center assistance while requiring participants to secure meaningful employment.

Day and evening reporting centers are used in juvenile corrections, providing daily supervision and structured activities for youths who need more intensive supervision. Reporting centers typically offer a wide range of services to the juvenile, including tutoring, counseling, and recreational activities.

Other day reporting services include random alcohol and drug testing, home visits, employment verifications and visits, curfew checks, and assistance with court appearances. Centers promote individual responsibility, assist the individual in developing a support system, and maintain individual accountability in the community.

Home Confinement Programs

The home confinement programs provide community-based intensive supervision, typically using electronic monitoring, for offenders who have been released on home arrest. *Home confinement* requires an offender to remain at home during nonworking hours, where they serve their sentences under strict schedules and curfew requirements. The intent of home confinement is to have the offender assume increasing levels of responsibility, while providing restrictions to promote community safety and convey the sanctioning value of the sentence.

Frequently used for juvenile offenders, home detention may also include additional conditions, such as drug testing, educational requirements, or special treatments. Violations of established conditions may result in further sanctions.

Residential Reentry Centers or Halfway Houses

Residential reentry centers or *halfway houses* provide assistance to offenders who are nearing release and are in the process of transitioning back into the community. These facilities provide a safe, structured, supervised environment, as well as employment counseling, job placement, financial management assistance, and other programs and services. *Residential reentry* centers help offenders rebuild their ties to the community and facilitate supervising offenders' activities during this readjustment phase. An important component of the residential reentry centers' program is transitional drug abuse treatment for those who have completed a residential substance abuse treatment program.

The Federal Bureau of Prisons also has the responsibility to manage the federal halfway houses. The Federal Bureau of Prisons contracts with residential reentry centers to provide assistance to inmates who are nearing release.

Offender Registration

Though not considered an alternative to custodial confinement, offender registration has become a major element in offender accountability across the nation. Driven by a series of shocking crimes and the public desire to gain information as to the location of violent offenders, legislation has been enacted on both the state and federal levels requiring sexual and violent offenders to register the location of their residence and notify local law enforcement of their presence in a community.

Washington State's 1990 Community Protection Act was the first law authorizing public notification when dangerous sex offenders were released into the community.[8] In 1994, Congress passed the Jacob Wetterling Crimes Against Children and Sexually Violent Offender Act as part of the Federal Violent Crime Control and Law Enforcement Act of 1994. This act requires state implementation of a sex offender registration program or a 10% forfeiture of federal funds for state and local law enforcement under the Byrne Grant Program of the U.S. Department of Justice.[9]

The 1994 rape and murder of seven-year-old Megan Kanka increased the public demand for broad-based community notification. On May 17, 1996, Megan's law was enacted. Included in

Megan's law are two major components: the requirement for states to register individuals convicted of sex crimes against children and, at the discretion of each state, the ability to establish criteria for disclosure.[10] Today, all 50 states and Washington, D.C., have sex offender registries.

The registration requirements of the Sex Offenders Registration Act are intended to provide the people of each state with an appropriate, comprehensive, and effective means to monitor those persons who pose such a potential danger. Combined with the rapid access to information available online, violent and sexual offenders now are required to register with local authorities as a condition of their sentence. In some states, statutory provisions require the GPS tracking of sex offenders.

Correctional Treatment

Correctional treatment specialists, also known as case managers or drug treatment specialists, assess inmates' rehabilitative development and will be discussed in more detail in Chapter 12. They work with inmates, probation officers, and agencies to develop plans for parole and release, providing case reports to the parole board when their clients are eligible for release. In addition, they arrange for offenders' attendance at education and job training programs and counsel offenders, either individually or in groups, regarding issues such as coping skills, anger management skills, and drug and sexual abuse. They usually write treatment plans and summaries for each client.

Correctional treatment specialists work in jails, prisons, community corrections, parole, or probation agencies. In jails and prisons, they evaluate the progress of inmates. They also work with inmates, probation officers, and other agencies to develop parole and release plans. Their case reports are provided to the appropriate parole board when their clients are eligible for release. In addition, they plan education and training programs to improve offenders' job skills and provide them with coping, anger management, and drug and sexual abuse counseling, either individually or in groups. They usually write treatment plans and summaries for each client. Correctional treatment specialists working in parole and probation agencies perform many of the same duties as their counterparts who work in correctional institutions.

Termination of Probation and Noncustodial Supervision

Probation and other noncustodial supervision usually end in one of three ways, early termination, expiration of sentence/term, or revocation. *Early termination* occurs when the offender's compliance with the conditions of probation and good behavior has led to a recommendation to the court, which the court may then grant, to reduce the period of supervision and end probation prior to conclusion of the original term. *Expiration of sentence/term* occurs when an offender completes his or her full probated sentence. *Revocation* occurs when the offender has not complied with the orders of the court and, in not doing so, has been recommended to the court to have his or her probated sentence revoked, and thus the original sentence reinstated.

The revocation process usually begins with the commission of a new offense by the probationer, or his or her violation of any of the other conditions of probation (these are known as technical violations). Once the violations are brought to the attention of the court by the supervising officer, the offender is entitled to a hearing. Upon the conclusion of the hearing, the court, in its discretion, may continue the offender on the original probation, add additional sanctions, extend the length of the term of supervision, or sentence the probationer to a jail or prison term.

Summary

Though probation is the single most often used criminal punishment in the United States today, several nonconfinement sentencing alternatives serve our nation's communities. The spread of crime, combined with tremendous crowding in state and local correctional facilities, has resulted in the rapid expansion of our probation and community-based correctional systems.[12]

Alternatives to confinement play an important part in corrections in the United States. Every offender that can be appropriately dealt with without confinement is a significant cost savings for the community. Confinement alternatives are only appropriate if they are a better option than incarceration. For many offenders, the second chance provided by alternatives to confinement proves to be of great benefit.

For those offenders who cannot adhere to the conditions placed upon them, revocation may well occur. The success of each noncustodial correctional option depends on the efforts and commitment of both the offender and the officer overseeing the case. Together, noncustodial correctional options provide a valuable alternative to confinement and enhance the safety of our communities across the nation.

Vocabulary

Day and evening reporting centers

Early termination

Electronic monitoring

Expiration of sentence/term

Halfway houses

Home confinement

Intensive supervision probation

Minimum supervision

Offender registration programs

Probation

Regular supervision

Residential reentry

Revocation

Discussion Questions

1. What are the three general forms of probation supervision? If you were a judge, how would you use the various forms when imposing a sentence?
2. What are the benefits of a judge imposing probation on an offender?
3. Why is the proper assessment of the risks and needs of an offender critical?
4. How do home confinement and electronic monitoring enhance the oversight of offenders?
5. What is the intended purpose of the Sex Offenders Registration Act?

Notes

1. U.S. Department of Justice. Probation and parole statistics. Retrieved June 22, 2010, from http://bjs.ojp.usdoj.gov/index. cfm?ty=tp&tid=15

2. Sutherland, E. H., & Cressey, D. R. (1970). *Criminology*, 463. New York: J.P. Lippincott.

3. New York City Department of Probation. A brief history of probation. Retrieved February 13, 2008, from http://www.nyc.gov/html/prob/html/history.html

4. Lindner, C., & Jay, J. (n.d.). John Augustus, father of probation, and the anonymous letter. *Federal probation*. Retrieved June 22, 2010, from http://www.uscourts.gov/fedprob/June_2006/augustus.html

5. Courcy, C. A. (1910). The probation system of Massachusetts. *Yale Law Journal, 19*(3), 187–192.

6. U.S. Courts. Beginnings of probation and pretrial services. Retrieved June 22, 2010, from http://www.uscourts.gov/fedprob/history/beginnings.html

7. The Senate 24th Legislature, Hawaii. (2007). A bill for an act relating to corrections. Retrieved June 22, 2010, from http://www.capitol.hawaii.gov/session2008/bills/SB910_SD1_.pdf

8. Klasskids Foundation. (n.d.). Megan's law by state. Retrieved June 22, 2010, from http://www.klaaskids.org/pg-legmeg.htm

9. Bureau of Justice. (n.d.). Jacob Wetterling crimes against children and sexually violent registration act. Retrieved June 22, 2010, from http://www.ojp.usdoj.gov/BJA/what/02ajwactcontents.html

10. Megan's law in all 50 states. (n.d.). Retrieved June 22, 2010, from http://www.angelfire.com/hi2/quickie121/Meganslaw.html

History and Process of Parole and Postconfinement Release

The exercise of executive clemency in the pardon of criminals is a practical question of grave importance, and of great delicacy and difficulty. It is believed that the annual average of executive pardons from the prisons of the whole county reaches ten per cent of their population. The effect of the too free use of the pardoning power is to detract from the *certainty* of punishment for crimes.

—Declaration of Principles Adopted and Promulgated by the 1870 Congress of the National Prison Association

Introduction

As correctional institutions continue to operate at capacity, the need to find additional ways to reduce inmate populations has become even more critical. Postconfinement release programs leading to sentence reduction, release, and postconfinement supervision operate across the nation. At year-end 2008, 5,095,200 adult men and women were under some type of federal, state, local, or privately contracted non-confinement correctional alternative. That is the equivalent of about 1 in every 45 adults in the United States. Parolees accounted for only a small percentage of offenders under community supervision, 828,169 or 16%.[1]

In 2008 parolees were more likely to have served a sentence for a drug offense (37%) than any other type of offense. Property offenders represented 23% of the parolees, while violent offenders accounted for 26%. Prior to 2002, no offense data on parolees were collected. In 2008, 88% of the nationwide parole population was male, and this percentage has remained unchanged since 2000. White parolees, in 2008, represented 41% of the parole population, an increase from 38% in 2000. Black and Hispanic parolees represented smaller shares of the population during this period. Black parolees made up 38% of the population in 2008, down from 40% in 2000. Similarly, Hispanic parolees accounted for 19% of the population, down from 21% in 2000.[1] While parole is just one of the postconfinement release programs, it is typically the best known by the public. Though this chapter will primarily focus upon parole, other postconfinement release or sentence modification programs will be examined.

Postconfinement Release Options

There are several postconfinement release options available, and states have the authority to decide what postconfinement release options they choose to use. Not only are these methods different procedurally and governed by different rules, but they also affect those to be released differently in terms of each person's obligation to report and fulfill the release conditions. The most common release options include:

1. Executive clemency, commutation, or pardon
2. Mandatory release, also called statutory release, supervised release, or conditional release
3. Release at the expiration of sentence
4. Temporary release programs
5. Parole

Executive clemency, commutation or *pardon* is the granting of a release from confinement with or without conditions or supervision under an executive order. The power to grant executive clemency, commutation, or pardon is usually vested in a chief executive, such as a governor or the president.

Executive clemency, commutation, or pardon is typically used sparingly. On the presidential level, the authority to grant a presidential pardon is included in Article II, Section 2 of the U.S. Constitution. Presidential pardons were first used by President Washington when he pardoned leaders of the Whiskey Rebellion. Other presidents also used their power to pardon, but it was President Andrew Johnson who first awarded blanket pardons, when he pardoned thousands of former Confederate soldiers at the conclusion of the American Civil War.

A pardon removes both punishment and guilt, which is why pardons are more likely to be controversial. Two of the most controversial presidential pardons occurred in the 1970s. In 1974, former president Richard M. Nixon was granted pardon by President Gerald R. Ford for his involvement in the Watergate cover-up crimes.[2] In the late 1970s, President Jimmy Carter pardoned those who had evaded service in the Vietnam War.[3]

While Article II, Section 2 of the Constitution places no limitations on the president's power to grant or deny pardons, the Justice Department's U.S. Pardon Attorney prepares a recommendation for the President on each application for presidential clemency, including pardons, commutations of sentences, remissions of fines, and reprieves.[4]

Clemency can be in the form of a pardon, the shortening of a prison sentence, a commutation of a sentence, or a reprieve. Each state's governor and the President of the United States have the power to grant clemency, though in reality, it is rarely granted.

Unlike a pardon, a commutation does not mean that there is forgiveness for the underlying offense; rather, the period of incarceration served for the offense is reduced. One of the most controversial uses of a commutation was by Governor George Ryan of Illinois. In 2003, Governor Ryan ignited national and even international debate issuing a commutation of the death sentence of all 167 prisoners off Illinois' death row. Of those receiving commutation, 164 received life sentences without the possibility of parole and 3 received reduced sentences that could allow them to be released shortly.[5]

Mandatory release, statutory release, supervised release, or *conditional release* provides for the release of offenders at or near the end of their sentences. This type of release is usually determined at the time of the sentencing, and thus there may be little flexibility in the decision to release. The basic idea behind mandatory release is that persons who are released under this system can have the benefit of supervision until the date of final discharge.

Release at the expiration of sentence or discharge involves none of the selection or supervision that characterizes the other methods of release; rather, discharge occurs after a person has completed the lawful sentence.

Temporary release programs (such as prerelease or residential community centers) include study release (particularly for juveniles), work release, and a release of the offender to his or her immediate family. Temporary release programs are often referred to as halfway houses or prerelease and work release centers. They are used for offenders who are about to be released from confinement. The programs allow offenders to seek treatment, work, or have employment opportunities in the community. Most states and the Federal Bureau of Prison (BOP) have created residential reentry centers (RRCs). In fact, the BOP currently has approximately 11,000 inmates in RRC programs. The RRCs help inmates gradually rebuild their ties to the community and facilitate supervising offenders' activities during this readjustment phase. The community and offenders benefit from RRCs. The centers provide inmates with opportunities to secure community housing, treatment and employment, emotional support to deal with the pressures of reintegration, and a low-cost housing alternative to incarceration. In addition, the BOP operates *comprehensive sanction centers* (CSCs). As collaboration with U.S. probation and contractors, a CSC offers a more structured system for granting inmates gradual access to the community. CSCs, for example, have five levels of supervision, ranging from 24-hour confinement to home confinement. *Home confinement* is used as a temporary release program. Some federal inmates are placed on home confinement for a brief period near the end of their prison term. They serve this portion of their sentences at home under strict schedules and curfew requirements. Electronic monitoring equipment is sometimes used to monitor compliance behavior. Statutory provisions limit the length of home confinement to the last six months or 10% of the sentence, whichever is less. Typically, an inmate is placed in an RRC or CSC prior to placement on home confinement.[6]

Parole is the release of an incarcerated offender to the community, under the supervision of a parole officer and with certain restrictions and requirements, after he or she has completed a portion of the sentence in a correctional institution. Generally, the offender becomes eligible for parole consideration after serving the portion of the sentence specified in the statute.

Parole is primarily concerned with helping the committed offender make the difficult transition from prison to an acceptable adjustment in society. The dual purpose of parole is the protection of society and providing the positive case supervision that may assist the offender in achieving a successful transition into lawful society. Society is protected more effectively when an offender is diverted from his or her criminal patterns, and successful diversion is more likely to occur within the community than in the prison environment.

Foundations of the Concept of Parole

The word *parole* is derived from the French expression *parole d'honneur*, which means "formal promise" or "a word of honor given or pledged." In the French military, the promise was given by a prisoner of war, whereby he agreed not to escape or, if freed, would not again take up arms again against his captors for a stated period of time.[7] During the American Civil War, the parole of captured soldiers on both sides of the conflict was not uncommon, though many of those "paroled" did return to the conflict.

In the sixteenth and seventeenth centuries, the British used a form of parole as they transported convicted offenders from England to the American and Australian colonies. As envisioned by the British, convicted offenders were expected to remain in the colony and work until given a reprieve or pardon, releasing them from their sentence. Though many of these transported offenders successfully completed their sentence, some returned to England without permission before their sentence expired. British authorities responded by placing additional conditions upon the exiled offenders, to include a requirement that upon successful completion of the term of their sentence, they be awarded a "ticket of leave," which was an official declaration of release from the imposed sentence. The English Penal Servitude Act of 1853 related this practice to conditional release and gave legal status to the system of ticket of leave.

Overview of Parole in the United States

Similar in many respects to the evolution of probation, parole began as an informal process, historically linked to the concept of the pardon and mercy. Early in our nation's history, there was little need for postconfinement parole. Small inmate populations and the extensive use of inmate labor made the inmate a valuable commodity to the confining authorities. With the adoption and increased popularity of indeterminate sentencing, combined with an increasing prison population, the need to develop and utilize a program of selective postconfinement early release under supervision became apparent.

An early notion underlying the development of parole was the incentive it presented inmates to conform to the rules of the penal institution, and thus earn the opportunity to be considered for early release. Thus, the dynamics resulting from the desire to find ways to improve inmate behavior while confined without resorting to measures such as corporal punishment, and the need to have a viable option to reduce inmate populations when the institutions face overcrowding, led to the need and use of parole. Therefore, parole as we know it today, in many states, serves a role as a release valve for highly crowded institutions. It, like probation, must absorb a large number of offenders, as prison bed space is limited.

Today, parole is the discretionary release of an inmate from confinement after he or she has served a portion of a prison sentence. Each state has its own laws regarding the selection of those to be paroled and the administration of the supervision process. As a condition of their release, parolees remain under parole supervision and must adhere to designated parole conditions that, if violated, can be grounds for parole revocation and a return to custody.

History of Parole in the United States

The idea of an offender "earning" his way out of prison as a result of "good behavior" is not new. In the United States, sentence reduction earned as a result of good behavior was first formalized in 1817 by New York's "good time" law. It was reasoned that once inmates recognized their conduct while confined would have a direct bearing on their confinement release date, their conduct while confined would improve. Today every state and the federal jurisdiction have some type of reduction of sentence as recognition of positive inmate behavior while confined.

Directly in line with the concept of sentence reduction resulting from good behavior is parole. The concept of parole as related to supervision first began with the use of volunteers, who worked closely with those confined in the effort to socially and spiritually redeem them. Though much of the early work was performed by volunteers, the value of their efforts was recognized when, in 1837, Massachusetts enacted the first legislation in the nation authorizing parole.

The duties of the first Massachusetts parole officers included assisting released prisoners in finding employment and housing. Supervision by a paid public employee was first provided in Massachusetts in

1845, when the state appointed an agent to help released prisoners successfully transition into free society.

As early as 1851 the Quakers' Society for Alleviating the Miseries of Public Prisons appointed two agents to work with discharged prisoners from the Philadelphia county prison and the penitentiary.

A major advancement in correctional reform and parole occurred with the opening of the Elmira Reformatory in New York in 1876. Wardened by Zebulon Reed Brockway, Elmira proved to be the center of correction reform and innovation in the late 1800s. Within the institution, educational, training, and inmate-focused incentives were implemented, all designed to positively influence inmate behavior. One of the most valuable incentives found in Elmira was the indeterminate sentence and early release as a form of parole.

Indeterminate sentences were pioneered in the reformatory movement of the last quarter of the nineteenth century. Release was determined by progress made under the program of training rather than by a judicially established sentence. In current practice, release on parole from an indeterminate sentence is initiated by the recommendation of prison staff personnel, field parole officers, and the parole authorities. Evaluation of the offender's conduct in prison, the nature of his offense, his life history, his prospects in the community, his general personality, and his attitude determine his suitability for parole.

This early attempt to institutionally apply parole at the Elmira Reformatory proved successful. Other states adopted the model, and by 1900, 20 states had provisions for parole. By 1944, all states had parole laws.

The first statute providing for the reduction of sentences of federal prisoners resulting from good conduct was enacted in 1867. This statute authorized a deduction of one month in each year from the term of sentence of federal prisoners confined in state jails or penitentiaries, upon certification of the warden with the approval of the secretary of the interior, who at the time was responsible for federal inmates (Peter B. Hoffman, *History of the Federal Parole System*, United States Parole Commission, 1997).

Parole of federal prisoners began after enactment of legislation on June 25, 1910. During this period, the federal penitentiaries operated with relative independence. At each of the three federal penitentiaries, parole was granted by an institutionally based parole board. The membership of each parole board consisted of the warden of the institution, the physician of the institution, and the superintendent of prisons of the Department of Justice in Washington, D.C.

By legislation of May 13, 1930, a single board of parole was established and operated in Washington, D.C. This board consisted of three members, serving full-time, appointed by the attorney general. The Bureau of Prisons performed the administrative functions of the board.[8]

Parole Differs from Probation

Many Americans cannot distinguish between probation and parole. Parole differs from probation in two major aspects: Parole involves the early release of an offender from imprisonment, depending upon his or her acceptance of and compliance with a set of conditions; while this sounds similar to probation, the key difference is that the offender has already served some time in a jail or prison. Contrast this with probation, where usually no imprisonment has occurred for the current offense, but looms as future punishment should the individual choose not to comply with his or her conditions of supervision.[9]

The parole process does not function under the authority of the judiciary (courts); it is an administrative responsibility of the state (or federal) government. Only the court can grant or revoke probation, but the court usually has no authority in parole. Since the parolee is still under sentence of the state (or federal government), an executive, as opposed to judicial, agency is responsible for the supervision function.[7]

Parole Boards and Parole Selection

Parole is not a right, but a privilege, a privilege in the perfect setting that should be earned. The decision to grant or withhold parole is up to the discretion of a paroling authority, frequently called a parole board. Parole boards have the statutory authority to grant parole, set conditions of parole, monitor parole supervision, and terminate parole by successfully discharging a parolee or revoking an offender's parole. While each state varies in the composition of its parole board, most are administered by either an autonomous model (independent agency) or a consolidated model (part of a large department that operates all state correctional programs).[10] Parole board members are typically appointed by the governor and are normally assisted by a paid staff who gather information concerning inmates eligible for parole consideration.

The process of parole selection, which is an executive function, differs greatly from probation, which is a judicial sentence. Whereas the court remains the only body to grant or revoke probation, in most states a parole board, commission, or panel decides which inmates will be released early to parole. Parole guidelines, or specific standards, are established by some states to assist in the parole decision-making process. Parole guidelines are instruments that predict inmates' risk of recidivism. Most guidelines are based on the U.S. Parole Commission's *salient factor score* (SFS). The SFS, for example, is a scale used to screen offenders and predict parole success. The SFS scores the inmates in one of four categories of risk: very good, good, fair, or poor. While the actual practice of determining parole eligibility differs from state to state, the mechanics are typically similar. In some states the prisoner may initiate the process by applying to the parole board, while in other states the parole board may make a parole investigation when the inmate approaches the predetermined eligibility date.

Once a decision is made that the inmate will be considered for parole, a hearing is held, with or without the inmate, in which the merits/risk factors of his release are reviewed and considered. State rules typically dictate the manner of the hearing, who is present, disclosure of nonconfidential information, what evidence can be introduced, and representation. It is not uncommon for inmates to have several parole eligibility hearings before they are released.

Decisions by a parole board vary significantly. In 1976, Vincent O'Leary and Katrine Hanrahan developed a typology of decisions made by parole boards. Each of the six categories represents a parole board's particular value system. The *jurist value system* regards parole decisions as a natural process. Fair and equitable decisions are made because the parole board members strive to be sensitive to the offenders' rights. The *sanctioner value system* strives to balance the amount of time served with the seriousness of the crime. The more serious the crime, the longer the offender will need to serve before parole is granted. The *treater value system* connects rehabilitation with the offenders' participation in correctional programming. If the offender is able to provide evidence of rehabilitation, then parole is more likely to be granted. The *controller value system* is primarily concerned with community safety. If parole is granted, the board will set strict conditions that are designed to control the offenders' behaviors in the community. The *citizen value system* considers the interests and expectations for the community and is concerned with deterring recidivism. Finally, the *regulator value system* is focused on the effect of the board's decision on the prison, field supervisors, and offenders' reactions. Board members are cognizant of the powerful influence of their decisions on how inmates and parolees are treated.[10]

After the parole hearing, the parole board will respond with the decision. The parole board has three options in deciding each case: deferment, serve-out, and parole. By imposing a deferment, the board denies parole and establishes another eligibility date for the individual to meet with the board some time in the future. Deferments are given when the board does not believe the offender is a good risk for parole at the time of the hearing, but thinks the inmate should not have to serve the entire sentence without further review. Cases are also deferred for short periods of time when additional information is needed to reach a decision.

By ordering a serve-out, the board is requiring the offender to serve the remainder of the sentence incarcerated, with no additional review, and hence no additional opportunity for parole.

If parole is recommended, the board permits the offender to be released from the institution to continue serving his or her sentence in the community. Following the decision to grant release, the inmate will be informed and conditions for supervision will be set. If the decision is to not grant parole, some states require a summary of the reasons for the parole board's decision and access to the review of its decision by the convict.

Parole decisions are based on a number of factors that weigh the need for punishment, successful community reintegration, and victim and community restoration. These factors include the nature of the crime; the offender's criminal history, behavior in prison, social background, and risk posed to the community; and information from crime victims and affected communities. Other factors considered include the inmate's attitude toward authority (before and during incarceration), history of alcohol and substance abuse, educational and job skills, employment history, emotional stability, and health.

Parole decisions enhance public safety by working to keep dangerous offenders incarcerated and ensuring that other offenders carefully selected for release receive the necessary structure and assistance to become law-abiding citizens in the community in which they reside.[11]

Other Factors Influencing the Awarding of Parole

During periods when there are an inadequate number of correctional beds, parole boards apply a rational process, targeting for release those inmates who pose the least risk to community safety. Parole boards are the only component of the criminal justice system that can weigh all of the factors and release only those offenders who can be best managed under community supervision, thus providing a powerful enhancement to public safety.[7]

It is important to note that in addition to persons released at the choice of the parole board, parole departments may also be responsible for supervising persons on *mandatory/statutory release* from a penal institution. These are offenders who must, according to the law, be released from prison early due to the accumulation of good time. Simply put, good time is time credited to the fulfillment of a sentence that hasn't actually been served by the inmate. Many states have been forced to implement very liberal good time credits as a result of crowding and the need to make room in the penitentiary for new prisoners.

The core services offered by parole—investigations, victim advocacy, release planning, community supervision, immediate response to violations, and treatment services—provide optimum public protection.

Parole is a powerful partner to both the courts and victims. Parole boards ensure that the victim's voice is both heard and heeded, creating a natural and valuable ally for victims and victim advocacy groups.[10]

Process of Parole and Postconfinement Supervision

Parole officers perform many of the same duties that probation officers perform. Parole officers supervise offenders who have been released from prison on parole to ensure that they comply with the conditions of their parole. Probation and parole officers supervise offenders on probation or parole through personal contact with the offender and his or her family.

Some offenders are required to wear an electronic device so that probation officers can monitor their activities. Officers may arrange for offenders to get substance abuse rehabilitation or job training. They also attend court hearings to update the court on the offender's compliance with the terms of his or her sentence and on the offender's efforts at rehabilitation.

In 2008, 85% of parolees were on active parole supervision. The parolees were required to report on regular bases to a parole officer. They are required to report in person, by mail, or by telephone. Absconders, those parolees who could not be located, accounted for 6% of the 2008 parole population, and 4% were on inactive supervision, not required to regularly report to a parole officer.[12]

Though there has been a movement in some states to abolish parole, where the process continues to be employed, parole serves as a postprison supervision program where eligible inmates must meet specific terms and conditions of conduct to remain in the community. At the end of 2008, there were 828,169 adults on parole.[13] Prisoners may be released to parole either by a parole board decision or by mandatory conditional release.[14] Parole supervision is typically provided by the state department of corrections. While nationally the future of parole is uncertain, the need to employ alternatives to traditional confinement remains critical.

There are basic conditions that every parolee must adhere to, and there are special conditions that the parole board imposes based on criminal history, mental health, record of substance abuse, and other risk factors. Basic conditions include notifying the parole officer in advance of any changes in employment or residence, making an honest effort to find and maintain legitimate employment, and paying a monthly supervision fee. Special conditions may include drug testing, electronic monitoring, a curfew, mandatory counseling, sex offender counseling, and polygraph exams.

Termination of Parole or Postconfinement Release

Expiration of sentence: The period of parole supervision usually runs as long as the offender's original calendar sentence or ends upon reaching a statutory date. Therefore, a parolee is discharged when this date is reached. *Revocation*: If a parolee violates the conditions of his or her release, the parole officer informs a section of the parole department, at which time a decision is made whether or not to issue an arrest warrant for violation of parole. Once a warrant has been served and the parolee arrested, he or she is entitled to a hearing before a representative of the parole board (usually known as a hearing officer). Parole may be continued or it may be revoked. If parole is revoked, the offender is returned to the custody of an institution. The parole cycle may not stop there, however, for eventually the revoked parolee will probably again become eligible for parole consideration.

Of the estimated 543,600 parolees discharged from supervision in 2007, 46% had met the conditions of their supervision and served their full-term sentence or received an early discharge. The rate of successful parole completion increased to almost half (49%) of the estimated 574,000 parolees who were discharged during 2008.

Summary

Although parole began in Europe, it is now more fully developed and used in the United States. Today all but 16 states have parole agencies. The Comprehensive Crime Control Act of 1984 provides for the abolishment of parole at the federal level.

The provisions for parole vary considerably from state to state, and no one statement applies generally to the administration of parole. There is considerable variation in the extent to which the different states use parole and the efficiency with which the parole functions are carried out.

Parole, like probation, has witnessed explosive growth during the last decade, owing primarily to prison crowding. There also have been political positions taken that advocate the abolishment of parole altogether. But until society is willing to commit the vast resources necessary to incarcerate most offenders for long periods of time, parole boards and officers will continue to try to fulfill their obligations of public safety and the successful reintegration of offenders within society.

Alternatives to confinement play an important part in corrections in the United States. Every offender that can be appropriately dealt with without confinement is a significant cost savings for the community. Confinement alternatives are only appropriate if they are a better option than incarceration. For many offenders, the second chance provided by alternatives to confinement proves to be of great benefit. For those offenders who cannot adhere to the conditions placed upon them, revocation may well occur. The success of each noncustodial correctional option depends on the efforts and commitment of both the offender and the officer overseeing the case. Together, noncustodial correctional options provide a valuable alternative to confinement and enhance the safety of our communities across the nation.

Vocabulary

Citizen value system

Comprehensive sanction centers

Conditional release

Controller value system

Executive clemency

Executive commutation

Executive pardon

Expiration of sentence

Home confinement

Jurist value system

Mandatory/statutory release

Parole

Regulator value system

Release at the expiration of sentence or discharge

Revocation

Salient factor score (SFS)

Sanctioner value system

Statutory release

Supervised release

Temporary release programs

Treater value system

Discussion Questions

1. How do the mechanisms that are used to release offenders from correctional facilities differ?
2. Understand temporary release programs. What steps are taken to ease the offender's reentry into the community?

3. Discuss the origins and evolution of parole in the United States.

4. Identify the six categories of a parole board's value system.

5. What factors should a parole authority use to release an offender from confinement?

Notes

1. Glaze, L. E., & Bonczar, T. P. (2009, December). Probation and parole in the United States, 2008 (NCJ 228230). Retrieved March 7, 2010, from Bureau of Justice Statistics website: http://bjs.ojp.usdoj.gov/content/pub/pdf/ppus08.pdf

2. President Gerald R. Ford's Proclamation 4311, granting a pardon to Richard Nixon. (1974, September 8). Retrieved February 11, 2008, from http://www.ford.utexas.edu/LIBRARY/speeches/740061.htm

3. The MacNeil/Lehrer Report. (1977, January 21). Carter's pardon. Retrieved March 11, 2008, from http://www.pbs.org/newshour/bb/asia/vietnam/vietnam_1-21-77.html

4. Title 28 Code of Federal Regulations. Presidential pardons: Legal guidelines. (2000, July 1). Retrieved March 11, 2008, from http://usgovinfo.about.com/blpresardons.htm

5. Illinois Governor Ryan commutes all death sentences. (2003, January 11). Retrieved February 21, 2008, from http://www.ccadp.org/news-ryan2003.htm

6. U.S. Bureau of Prisons. Community corrections. Retrieved March 7, 2010, from http://www.bop.gov/locations/cc/index.jsp

7. History of the federal parole system. (n.d.). Retrieved March 11, 2008, from http://www.usdoj.gov/uspc/history.htm

8. Gottfredson, M., & Gottfredson, D. (1998). *Decision making in criminal justice: Toward the rational exercise of discretion.* New York, NY: Plenum Press.

9. Carter, R. M., & Wilkins, L. T. (1970). *Probation and parole.* New York, NY: John Wiley.

10. Clear, T., & Dammer, H. (2003). *The offender in the community* (2nd ed.). Belmont, CA: Wadsworth/Thomas Learning.

11. Discretionary parole. (2002). Retrieved March 14, 2008, from http://www.appa-net.org/about/ps/discretionaryparole.htm

12. Glaze, L. E., & Bonczar, T. P. (2009, December). Probation and parole in the United States, 2008 (NCJ 228230). Retrieved March 7, 2010, from Bureau of Justice Statistics website: http://bjs.ojp.usdoj.gov/content/pub/pdf/ppus08.pdf

13. Glaze, L. E., & Palla, S. (2003). Probation and parole in the United States. Retrieved February 21, 2008, from http://www.csdp.org/research/ppus03.pdf

14. U.S. Parole Commission. (2004). *History of the federal parole system.* New York, NY: Wm. S. Hein.

III

Institutional Corrections

Jails

I submit that an individual who breaks the law that conscience tells him is unjust and willingly accepts the penalty by staying in jail to arouse the conscience of the community over its injustice, is in reality expressing the very highest respect for law.

—Martin Luther King Jr.

Introduction

In the beginning, there was the dungeon. It was a temporary holding facility for accused offenders awaiting trial and convicted offenders awaiting punishment. In ancient Rome the first dungeons were underground, often beneath the sewers. An early reform demanded the inmates could be able to see the light of day. Long-term confinement was not an issue. Punishment (either corporal or capital) was meted out to those convicted on site by the dungeon personnel and was public. Most castles and cities had a dungeon.

Today, jails operate across the United States. Estimates place the number of jails at over 3,500, with most operating under the authority of local jurisdiction, typically under the control of a county sheriff. Jails are a doorway into prisons. Jails are also a revolving door with many inmates passing through jail in processing on a regular basis due to the life decisions they have made (drugs, petty crime, etc.).

Jails have long been overlooked as a critical element in the justice system, with many states requiring the minimum in training for personnel. One of the major leaders in the advancement of jails in the United States is the American Jail Association. The American Jail

Association was formed in 1981 as a result of a merger between the National Jail Association and the National Jail Managers' Association and now plays a function similar to that of the American Correctional Association. The American Jail Association performs a vital role in the advancement of jail-related knowledge to the practitioners in the field.

As we move into the twenty-first century, all of criminal justice remains a dynamic element within our society, not the least of which is the jail. The jail has a long and rich history in both the United States and Europe.

The British Gaol

The *gaol* was designed as a temporary holding facility to house accused offenders awaiting trial, convicted offenders awaiting punishments, and debtors until they could pay what they owed. Although shelter was provided, food was not a rule. The inmates had to either depend on friends and relatives to bring food or beg food from passersby. These facilities were not the cleanest and generally did not have running water or toilet facilities beyond a bucket. Men, women, and children were all housed together in large cells and left to fend for themselves. You can imagine what kind of conditions prevailed. The gaol was run by officials of the crown. Disease was rampant. While in custody many inmates died from disease, were killed by other inmates, or committed suicide. Local confinement facilities in the United Kingdom are still called gaols, although conditions have improved tremendously over the years.

The Advent of the American Jail

The advent of a jail, run by a sheriff, was considered to be a reform by many. In the United States, most state constitutions mandate that each county maintain a jail run by a sheriff. Prisoners were incarcerated in the county in which they committed their offense and were tried there in a public trial, a right guaranteed by the Sixth Amendment of the U.S. Constitution. The new jails ranged from a single exposed cell to multistoried brick structures that housed hundreds of inmates. Jails often had apartments for the sheriff to live in. The sheriff's wife acted as the jail cook and saw to any female inmates. Some cities had their own jails too. Jails were placed in locations as a matter of the availability of accommodations and as a convenience to authorities. For example, prisoners in one of the first Sacramento County, California, jails were held in the hulls of old ships called hulks.[1]

Czarnecki found that most early new jail construction was driven by specific needs or reform measures. Citing the example of this that was stated in a report of a county board of supervisors for a new jail in Westchester County, New York, in 1854, he found that they said:

> The present condition of the courthouse, jail, county clerk's and surrogate's offices ... call for immediate measures.... The condition of our jail has been repeatedly made the subject of complaint to former boards of supervisors, a grand jury of the county having represented it as unfit for the purposes to which it is devoted, and it has been forcibly impressed upon the minds of your committee, that humanity add a proper regard for the unfortunates confined therein, demand a radical and speedy alteration in the position and appointments of this portion of the public buildings included in this resolution.[2]

The new Westchester County jail was built and opened in 1856. Although updated, it served until 1932, when the "new" jail was opened. Parts of this jail are still operational, as the "new, new" jail was attached to it in 1992. The county now operates several jails within the county to hold all of its prisoners, with a total capacity of 1,600 prisoners. The operation of multiple jails within a unified sheriff's correctional system is common in large metropolitan counties. For example, the Sedgwick County Sheriff's Office in Wichita, Kansas, operates a main jail and a work release facility with a total capacity of 1,500 inmates.

Coming to Jail

A crime occurs. After determining probable cause, the police arrest a suspect. Where do they go now? Jail of course! Arrested offenders are taken to jail by the arresting agency and processed into custody. Booking forms detail what specific offenses the accused was alleged to have committed. The accused is then searched, identified, fingerprinted, photographed, and assigned to a housing unit during the booking process. The length of an inmate's stay is determined by his or her offense, the result of his or her trial, or his or her ability to make bail. Offenders are often under the influence of drugs or alcohol and are combative to their captors. These inmates have to be subdued and isolated from the rest of the inmate population for their own safety and the safety of others. Remember, everyone that has ever gone to death row went to county jail first!

The Garage Sally Port

Arriving at jail, the officer often drives into a *sally port* located in the jail building or on the jail grounds. This is where the arresting agency can park their vehicles when bringing an arrestee to jail. The Sedgwick County Jail garage sally port can hold up to eight vehicles. This is a security measure that protects both the officers and the suspect from escape attempts or attack by angry citizens. The garage sally port leads directly into the detention facility and the arresting officer's work area. There are gun lockers where the officers can lock up their weapons before entering the facility. If the suspect is a fighter, jail deputies assist the officer in moving the suspect into the facility.

Booking/Intake

The incoming inmate is taken into the arresting officer's work area. In the arresting officer's work area, the arrestee's personal property is taken by the arresting officer and inventoried along with his or her money and a description of his or her clothing. The arresting officer also completes the booking form, which includes the arrestee's identification and personal information, and charges. After completion of the booking paperwork, the arresting officer brings the handcuffed suspect to the booking desk to be processed. The booking sergeant or corporal examines the paperwork for accuracy and legality.

You can't just throw someone in jail. The arresting officer must list specific charges violating a specific law, statute, resolution, or ordinance. In most states, the arresting officer must swear to an affidavit of probable cause used in making the arrest. An inmate may be brought to jail upon an order of the court (remand or warrant). A *remand* is an order from the court, usually after a court hearing remanding the inmate into the custody of authorities; a specific charge is listed along with a specific sentence or instructions by the court. The amount of bail may also be listed.[3] An inmate may also be booked "in transit." In this type of booking the inmate is legally in the custody of an agency, and that agency is en route elsewhere. They require secure housing for their inmate so the deputies can sleep, eat, and so on. Determining the legality of the arrest is required by the Fourth Amendment of the Constitution.

Booking and intake are critical times in the in-possessing of a new inmate into the jail. Failure to identify the inmate can cause critical booking errors that affect security. Failure to properly search the inmate can cause contraband to enter the institution with fatal results. Upon acceptance of the booking paperwork, the suspect is searched again by jail deputies. The suspect is then administered an intake medical questionnaire by the detention staff. Inmates with obvious medical problems are not admitted into the facility without a medical release from a hospital. This prevents inmates that were injured during capture or who have overdosed on drugs from encountering serious medical problems or even dying while in jail.

Once accepted into custody, the inmate is then placed into a holding area for processing. While people are usually not happy about going to jail, most do not physically fight. However, some do. When they struggle, they must be separated from the general population at booking. For those individuals that would choose to make a "goal line stand" at the cell door, there is usually a safety cell. The activities are videotaped for evidence and to answer questions about police use of force later. For those who continue to fight, there is the *restraint chair*. The restraint chair is a control measure, not punishment. When the inmate agrees to behave, he or she is taken out of the chair and placed back into the safety cell. Inmates are videotaped and checked every 15 minutes while restrained. The chair is designed to limit the possibility of positional asphyxia and inmates causing harm to themselves or others.

Two of the primary goals of the booking process are identification of who is being arrested and the documentation of the arrest.[4] This is considered part of the due process required by the Fifth and Sixth Amendments of the Constitution. The inmate has already been asked a series of questions as to who he or she is, as well as other identifying information. Next, the inmate is photographed and fingerprinted for identification purposes. Mug shots are identification photographs that are taken of each inmate during the booking process. In more modern jails, they are digital photographs that transfer directly into the sheriff's office records section and into the inmate's booking file.

Fingerprints are taken from each inmate for identification during the booking process. In more modern jails, a Print-Track machine makes digital fingerprint cards. The fingerprints are then electronically transferred to the sheriff's office records section and to AFIS. AFIS is the Automated Fingerprint Identification System. AFIS compares the suspect's fingerprints against the entire known national database for matches. This helps ID the suspect, solve open cases, and so on. In less modern sheriff's departments, fingerprints are taken by the traditional wheel and ink methods. The fingerprint cards are then physically transferred to sheriff's records, the state police, and the Federal Bureau of Investigation.

Booking can be a lengthy process. In the Sedgwick County Sheriff's Office in Wichita, Kansas, 36,000 inmates are booked and released each year. As a practical matter, this means that an incoming inmate might have to wait two to four hours to get booked on a slow day. On a busy day it could take up to 24 hours. Most states have a specific time that an inmate may be held in custody without seeing a magistrate. After inmates have been booked into jail, they are allowed to make a phone call to someone to let them know that they are in jail. They are then placed into a holding cell to determine whether they will be released or sent to inmate housing. Most inmates make bail and are released until their court appearances. Bail is set by a magistrate and is a monetary pledge to insure the appearance in court by the inmate at a time and place set by the judge. If the inmate fails to show up for court as required, the money can be forfeited to the court. Bondsmen are licensed by the courts to "post" money for an inmate's release for a fee. An inmate may post bond using a bondsman, post a cash bond, or in some instances authorized by the courts, sign an ROR (release on own recognizance) bond promising to appear as required by the courts. Inmates not released on bail or administratively (the prosecutor or judge declined charges) are sent to inmate housing.

An inmate who did not make bond is assigned to a housing unit. The inmate's clothing is taken and placed into his or her personal property. In most jails, in order to limit the spread of disease, fleas, and lice, the inmates are required to shower before they are allowed to proceed any further. The inmate is then given clean bedding, a clean jail jumpsuit in the color of his or her security classification, and a pair of flip-flops or other jail footwear to wear on his or her feet. In most cases, inmates are allowed to retain their socks and underwear from the street after they have been searched. When the inmate is released from custody or transferred to another penal facility, the process is reversed.

Inmate Classification

The incoming inmate is assigned a security classification upon booking (Table 6.1). According to Omodt et al. and the National Sheriff's Association: "The primary purpose of the classification system is to assign inmates to appropriate cells within the jail in order to achieve maximum compatibility and safety within each cell."[5] There are two major schools of thought on jail classification of inmates. The American Correction's Association advocates a system of classification that is based on the seriousness of the offense charged. The American Jail Association advocates a system of classification that is based on the inmate's behavior within the institution. Both systems are in use at various jails across the United States. Thus, the security classification of an inmate is usually based on current charges, prior inmate behavior in the institution, gang or security threat affiliation, or other considerations (such as prior suicide or escape attempts).

The *security classification* affects the inmate's housing assignment and privileges within the jail. In most jails, inmates wear color-coded jump suits so deputies can readily recognize each inmate's security classification. Another security measure is the identification of inmates by wristbands or, in more modern jails, by picture identification cards that must be displayed on the inmate's jumpsuit. No movement in the facility is allowed without these identification items being checked. This is not only to control movement, but also to prevent false releases or escapes.

Inmate classification is an important procedure in determining inmate housing. Inmate housing is based on security levels. Jail administrators are responsible for the safety and security of the inmates, the public, and the facility.

TABLE 6.1: CATEGORIES OF INMATES HELD IN COUNTY JAILS

Category	Status	Presumption of Guilt	Release on Bail Available
Pretrial detainees	Not convicted	Innocent until proven guilty	Yes, except in capital cases
Convicted felons awaiting transport	Convicted	Guilty	No, except on appeal
Convicted misdemeanants	Convicted	Guilty	No, except on appeal

TABLE 6.2: SGSO INMATE CLASSIFICATION CODES

Color Code	What This Means	Restrictions
Red	Maximum security	May have attacked an inmate or staff, escape risk; may not be moved without being leg ironed and with officer close escort
Green	Flagged	The inmate cannot be with somebody because of gang affiliation, witness/victim in jail, and so on; the jailer has to check every time these inmates are moved to make sure they are not in the same place or within reach of the inmate that they are flagged against; the other inmate is in green also
Orange	General custody	No restrictions
Tan	Trustee	Don't trust them too much; trustees perform work details in the facility

How Inmate Classification Works

How does this really work? The 1,500 inmates at the Sedgwick County Sheriff's Office Jail, for example, are classified according to behavior within the jail and color coded (Table 6.2). Inmates are classified as maximum, medium, or minimum security risks. For example, a highly aggressive inmate would be housed in a single cell away from the general population as a max. He would be put into a red jumpsuit. He would have fewer privileges than the general inmate population. Everything is a privilege and must be earned through good behavior: TV, commissary, visitation, and so on. When he decides to behave, his classification can be upgraded. An inmate who misbehaves can have his security classification downgraded.

Inmate Housing

One of the key factors in the construction of a jail is security. The inmates cannot be allowed to escape. Thus, *first-generation jails* (1776–1970s) were generally built in a linear arrangement, where prisoners were housed in side-by-side cells arranged in a row. While making his rounds, the guard walked the run outside the cell block and directly observed what was going on inside the cell. Many older first-generation jails are still in operation and using this method of confinement. The advantages of this system are that it uses existing resources. Prisoners were confined to individual cells either singly or in small groups (usually one to six inmates per cell). This arrangement achieved the correctional objective of incapacitation. The disadvantages of this system include: Contraband can be (and often is) passed from cell to cell. The guard's span of control ends when he passes the cell. Inmates have been assaulted or committed suicide while the guard was making rounds elsewhere in the cell block. Escapes are sometimes attempted when the cell door is opened by the guard, to put in or remove an inmate.

The need for security led to some interesting experiments in jail construction. During the late 1800s some jail designers advocated a rotating jail cell block that actually moved the cells around a central spindle to preset openings in the jail wall in order to gain access to the cell. Emmanuel and Moynahan observed: "The original idea was to rotate the floor constantly during the night, making it very difficult for prisoners to escape."[6] Other advantages were cited, including:

1. The cells were completely enclosed thus making it difficult for communications between prisoners.
2. Escape from the facility would be difficult because the cells are completely enclosed.
3. The jail keeper was much safer as only one prisoner at a time can be released from the cell.
4. A central shaft provided superior ventilation in both the summer and winter months.
5. There was a toilet flushed from the central shaft which was available in each cell.

This unique design was employed in Montgomery County, Indiana (1882–1973), and in 15 other states (although not in Mississippi). The Sedgwick County Sheriff's Office actually operated a squirrel cage jail (1888–1920s). Inmates often suffered broken arms or legs as the cells rotated. The jails were described in most inspection reports as firetraps, and the sanitary conditions were wanting. It was a unique experiment that did not catch on in most places. However, examples still exist as museums in Council Bluff, Iowa; Crawfordsville, Indiana; and Gallatin, Missouri.[6]

In *second-generation jails* (1980–present), the officer sits in an armored control booth and the inmates do not have direct physical contact with the deputy. If a deputy needs to enter the direct housing area, a second deputy comes and does this duty. In a second-generation jail a housing unit is divided into pods. Each pod is controlled separately from the enclosed control booth. The pod is divided into separate sections containing separate cells. Each pod contains about 50 inmates. Inmates are housed in single cells. The cells open into an enclosed day room. Inmates may be allowed time in the day room at the discretion of the deputy, depending on inmate behavior. The deputy controls how many inmates are allowed out at once. The guard is able to observe behavior in the day room through the booth window. Behavior in the cells is monitored through cameras.

The guard controls inmate behavior by use of a structured environment where everything is a privilege. For example, the inmate cells must be cleaned daily by the inmates. The cells are inspected daily, and if an inmate fails to clean his or her cell, he or she is not allowed out of the cell for 24 hours. Deputies must search the cells frequently to prevent weapons or contraband. Television and access to the day room are privileges that are earned through good behavior. The inmates must ask permission to do anything. For example, all pods have inmate shower facilities. Access to the showers is controlled by the deputies. Only a few prisoners are allowed in the shower at one time for security reasons. Deputies need to maintain vigilance to make sure the showers are not used as a place for assaults or sexual misconduct by the inmates. Hours and inmate movement are strictly controlled.

In a *third-generation jail*, the concept of inmate supervision shifts from indirect to direct. The indirect housing pods are still present but only used (space permitting) for max and administrative segregation (disciplinary) inmates. The other inmates are allowed to live in direct supervision pods and in dormitories. The direct pods revolve around the concept of an open type of construction. In a direct pod, the deputy sits in a control workstation that is located in the center of the day room. Deputies control the doors, phones, TVs, and so on, from the station. There is no glass booth. The deputy is in the open, inside with the inmates. Inmates are not allowed to cross the red line on the floor. The deputy is monitored with cameras from a master control area for safety, and interacts directly with inmates in day-to-day activities.

General custody inmates are allowed to live in a direct supervision pod. A direct pod holds about 48 inmates. Each inmate has his or her own cell. Inmates are required to stand for head count and clean their cells; otherwise, they are free to roam around their assigned pod. Good behavior is rewarded by access to television and phone calls. Poor behavior is punished by lockdowns or a reclassification of custody status to a higher level of custody.

Inmates who have behaved can come to the day room for TV, telephones, playing games, and so on. The dayroom contains televisions, tables for the inmates to eat or play games at, and chairs for the tables. The chairs are plastic to prevent injury in case of inmate fights. The pod is monitored from a computerized master control center by camera and voice mike. In a third-generation jail, everything is a privilege. Conduct within the facility determines custody status. While you might not see an accused murderer living in a dorm pod, the possibility of seeing one living in a direct pod is reasonably high.

The dorm is for minimum security inmates and is the least restrictive type of housing. Each inmate has a secured area for his or her personnel effects. The deputy's workstation is located within the pod and is similar to the ones in direct pods. In Maricopa County, Arizona, the dormitory concept has been expanded to include a tent city in Phoenix. This has reduced jail overcrowding.

Inmate Supervision

In the twenty-first century, due to overcrowding, the nature of offenders, and inmate rights litigation, the older, more traditional methods of inmate management have proved to be ineffective in the long run. New styles of inmate supervision and inmate programs are needed.

Deputies working a third-generation, direct supervision jail require the highest levels of training. Interpersonal communication and discipline are their only weapons. There are, of course, response teams that can come to their rescue if needed. However, the goal is not to have to use them. In this type of inmate supervision, minimum staffing is critical.[7]

Inmate supervision takes a great deal of training and skills in a direct supervision jail. Correctional officers are outnumbered 48 to 1. You have no bars to protect them from the inmates. The challenge of inmate management in a direct pod is maintaining order. This is done by establishing a routine for activities. Every cop knows that you can talk your way into a fight or you can talk your way out of it. This is interpersonal communications. A deputy must be able to motivate the inmates to act in an orderly fashion and do what the deputy needs them to do in order to maintain a stable environment in the pod. Order is also accomplished by the deputy's usage of interpersonal communication with the inmates.

Clean living equals clean minds. It sounds simplistic, but it has proven to be true in a jail setting.

A key point in direct supervision is keeping the jail spotlessly clean. A dirty jail reduces morale in both prisoners and deputies. It also allows for the outbreak of disease in very close living quarters.[8] Most third-generation jails look more like a hospital setting than a jail. Inmates quickly learn that participation in jail programs is a privilege that is earned by good behavior, and good behavior begins with cleaning your cell.

In order to do this, inmate labor is utilized. The female trustees usually do the laundry. The male trustees clean the pods and the floors. You cannot let the trustees (male and female) mix on work details. Wherever two shall walk together, three will surely follow! Inmates are required to clean their cells daily, and they are inspected by the pod deputy before the inmates are allowed into the day room of the pod. Inmates are required to change their clothing and bedding several times a week.

Work Release Programs

Some jails in coordination with the courts maintain *work release programs*. In this type of program, an inmate is released from custody for the hours that he or she works and returns to the jail for the rest of the day. This allows some nonviolent offenders to keep their jobs and support their families while they are serving their sentence. Inmates must be convicted of a misdemeanor, not be awaiting trial for another offense, have no behavior problems in the institution, and have permission from the court. If an inmate fails to return to jail as required, he or she is charged with escape in most states.

Inmate Healthcare

Like any other people, inmates require healthcare. Frankly, the inmate population is largely considered to be a high-risk healthcare group because of the large number that abuse drugs and other lifestyle issues. Many of the inmates have mental health issues. Since jails vary so widely in size and staff, you will find anything from a contracted healthcare nurse who visits on an as needed basis to full-blown healthcare clinics with dentists, mental healthcare professionals, and so on, that are staffed 24 hours a day.[9,10]

Inmate Programs

One inmate program that almost every jail has is family visitation. Visits by an inmate's family are an important part of inmate morale. The length, frequency, and scheduling of family visitation is a matter of jail policy. Visits are supervised by a deputy to ensure proper behavior by both inmates and visitors. Visitation is a privilege that is earned by good inmate behavior. In order to limit contraband (weapons, drugs, etc.), family visits in most jails are noncontact. This also limits the need for the jailers to extensively search the family members before each visit, although in most jails the visitors are required to walk through a metal detector upon entry to the jail.

Professional visitation with attorneys is a constitutional right. Defense attorneys can visit their clients anytime. The visitation rooms cannot be listened to because of attorney-client confidentiality. However, visual observation of the attorney-client visit is usually maintained for security reasons (clients have attacked attorneys, attorney misconduct has occurred).

Most jails have a chaplain available. The position may be paid or volunteer. The role of the chaplain in jail is an important one. Larger jails appoint and pay a chaplain to oversee the religious activities in their jail. Smaller jails use volunteers. Failure to act or provide a chaplain can be a violation of the Religious Freedom Restoration Act under federal law. Religion is protected under the First Amendment of the Constitution. A chaplain can provide for the spiritual needs of the inmates, including finding and vetting visiting clergy in whatever flavor the inmate needs to satisfy his or her religious needs, if possible. The chaplain acts as a stress relief valve and thus reduces violence within the facility. The inmates can confide in the chaplain without fear that what they say is going to the jail staff. Chaplains are excellent at teaching anger management and reducing violence. They are an excellent resource in suicide prevention. Chaplains are also excellent at identifying inmates that are at risk and helping to counsel them to have more productive thoughts. The chaplains also often work on charitable needs of inmate welfare, such as providing approved "goody" bags for new inmates with soap, toothpaste, a comb, and so forth, to help them transition into custody.

Many jails provide educational programs for their inmates. These are usually staffed with volunteers or may be on contract from the local school system. These are adult basic education (ABE) classes where inmates are taught to read (yes, there is still illiteracy in

America), and GED classes to help the inmate complete high school. Inmates without basic skills are most likely to reoffend.[11]

Depending upon the size of the jail, other inmate programs may be offered. These programs are usually staffed by volunteers and are often funded by grants rather than by tax dollars. Typical inmate programs often include anger management, Alcoholics Anonymous, Narcotics Anonymous, and sex offender's treatment.

Managing a Jail

Jails vary in size widely, but one thing remains the same: Someone has to be in charge. The inmates have to be fed and protected. The jail building must be secure and no escapes allowed. The jail staff has to be supervised. In smaller jails this is accomplished by the supervisor at the booking desk. In larger jails, it is a little more complicated. Take the Sedgwick County Sheriff's Office jail as an example, with 1,500 inmates and 312 employees. There are three shifts of employees.

The watch commander commands a shift (at Sedgwick County Sheriff's Office about 100 deputies). The watch commander is a lieutenant and has several sergeants and corporals that work for him or her. The watch commander can monitor all radio traffic, hear inside any area of the jail, and see anywhere in the jail at any time. He or she is responsible for all deputies and inmates on his or her shift. Inside the jail, all doors and movement throughout the jail are controlled by a master control. The master control deputies are specialists and are responsible for monitoring all inmate movements and activities in their area. Deputies are briefed before each shift in the squad room by a supervisor. Roll is taken, assignments are made, and any happenings on the pervious shifts are discussed. Larger jails are run in this fashion.

Jail Overcrowding

Jail overcrowding has been an issue since there were jails. This has often been the motivating factor in building new jails. It has also been a factor in many inmate lawsuits. One way that many larger jurisdictions attempt to solve this problem is by renting empty jail beds from those jurisdictions that have them available. This has grown into an industry in some smaller cash-strapped counties, providing much needed funds and renovations to the local jail that otherwise could not be supported by the local tax base. The jail that is farming out the inmates is responsible for inmate transport and healthcare expenses.[12]

The Jail as a Place of Execution

Until the end of the nineteenth century, jails were the place that you were executed if you were sentenced to the death penalty. Executions were public and the responsibility of the sheriff of that county. The last public execution was in 1935.[13] Mississippi even had a portable electric chair that it took around the state from 1940 to 1954.[14] By the mid-1950s executions had been moved to the prison system in all states.

Summary

The modern jail has different inmate control techniques, different inmate programs, and increased training for jail staff. The modern jail is a far cry from the dungeons of old. It is staffed with a professional and well-trained staff. Computer literacy is a required job skill. The modern jail is a part of American corrections.

Vocabulary

First-generation jails

Gaol

Inmate classification

Remand

Restraint chair

Sally port

Second-generation jails

Security classification

Third-generation jails

Work release programs

Discussion Questions

1. Compare the three generational jails. What are the advantages and disadvantages of each?

2. What are the various ways in which an inmate can secure pretrial release? Discuss the main problems associated with bail.

3. What type of programs do you believe a jail should provide to inmates?

4. Understand the diverse categories of inmates held in jails.

Notes

1. Moynahan, J., & Deitrich, V. (1999, July/August). Prisoners on ships: Sacramento County Jail hulks (1850–1859), *American Jails, XIII*(3).

2. Czarnecki, A. (2006, September/October). "A proper regard for the unfortunates": Origins of the jail system in Westchester County, New York. *American Jails, XX*(4).

3. *Ex parte Chalfant*, 81 W.Va. 93.

4. Cornelius, G. (2008). *The American jail: Cornerstone of modern corrections*. Upper Saddle River, NJ: Pearson/Prentice Hall.

5. Omodt, D., et al. (1974). *Jail security, classification and discipline*. Washington, DC: National Sheriff's Association.

6. Moynahan, J., & Emmanuel, E. (2001, May/June). America's squirrel cage jails. *American Jails, XV*(2).

7. Dawe, B., & Kirby, J. (1995, March/April). Direct supervision jails and minimum staffing. *American Jails, IX*(1).

8. Frey, R. (2007, October). Cost-effective methods for managing contagious diseases in the jail setting. *Corrections Today, 69*(5).

9. Torrey, E. F. (1999, November/December). How did so many mentally ill persons get into America's jails and prisons? *American Jails, XIII*(5).

10. Goldstein, P., Lurigio, A., Lyons, T., & Chosy, J. (2006). Health care needs of jail detainees with substance abuse problems: A work in progress. *American Jails, XX*(3).

11. Albers, J. (2006, November/December). Inmate education program at Harris County Sheriff's Office. *Sheriff, 58*(6).

12. Etter, G. (1996, July/August). The shell game. *American Jails, X*(3).

13. Woods, J. (2001). *The silver shield II: The Sedgwick County, Kansas Sheriff's Department.* Paducah, KY: Turner.

14. Cabana, D. (2000). The history of capital punishment in Mississippi: An overview. Mississippi Historical Society. Retrieved May 9, 2009, from http://mshistory.k12.ms.us/index.php?id=84

Correctional Systems and Institutions

Our mission is to protect society by confining offenders in the controlled environments of prisons and community-based facilities that are safe, humane, cost-efficient, and appropriately secure, and that provide work and other self-improvement opportunities to assist offenders in becoming law-abiding citizens.

—Juan D. Castillo, Warden, FCI Memphis

Introduction

After conviction and sentencing, the offender is typically subjected to court-designated judicial sanctions. In many cases, the judicial sanctions include institutional confinement or some type of noncustodial correctional supervision. In 2008, over 7 million people were under some form of correctional supervision in the United States, of whom over 2,300,000 were confined in the nation's jails and prisons.[1]

There are multiple correctional systems in the United States, and each struggles to supervise convicted offenders in the community or house them in a safe environment. The cost of correctional supervision and the conditions under which offenders are confined vary greatly, as do the size and identity of each institution or intensity of the supervision program. Though correctional programs vary in size and operation, each works to enhance public safety and community security.

Types of Correctional Systems and Institutions

Correctional systems and institutions may be classified in many ways. Correctional systems and institutions may be classified by the level of government in which they operate: federal, state, local, or private. Institutions may be classified by the security level of the facility: maximum, medium, or minimum; by gender: male or female; or by the age of those confined: adult or juvenile. Though correctional systems and institutions have much in common, each has its own identity.

Some correctional systems have proven to be leaders in the profession, while others have been subjected to underfunding, abuse, and judicial oversight. Some institutions have become legendary (Leavenworth, Alcatraz, and Sing Sing) and part of our nation's historical identity, while others operate virtually unknown outside the jurisdiction they serve. Whether large or small, adult or juvenile, each correctional system and institution operates as a closed community, attracting little public attention and less public concern.

Local Corrections

Almost as quickly as Europeans established colonies in America, it became clear that communities needed some ability to confine those arrested for violating laws. In 1625, Fort Amsterdam, which would later become New York, constructed "dungeon-like" facilities to hold prisoners.[2] Other early settlements soon followed, constructing limited stockades as temporary confinement resources.

Over the next 350 years, jails served communities across the nation, providing confinement resources, holding short-term offenders and those awaiting trial. Today, approximately 3,500 jails serve as the institutional element of local corrections and most frequently operate under the authority of the local sheriff.[3] Jails range in capacity from small facilities that confine less than 100 inmates to the largest jails in the nation, such as the New York, Los Angeles, and Chicago jails that confined thousands on any given day.

Jails serve as the door to corrections. The majority of offenders eventually convicted and sent to prison are initially confined in jails after their arrest. By 2006, the nation's jails confined approximately 750,000 inmates on any given day.

Jails normally confine three types of offenders: those arrested awaiting trial, those convicted and serving a short-term sentence that is appropriate for jail confinement, and those convicted of a serious offense and are being held in the jail until they can be transported to a more appropriate facility. Other types of inmates are also confined in jails. As an example, many local jails contract with state and federal agencies to hold federal or state inmates for a predetermined cost per day. Many of the jails that contract to house state and federal inmates rely on those contracted funds to offset the cost of annual jail operations.

Jails typically provide only the basic of inmate services. Medical, dental, drug or alcohol counseling, and education or training opportunities are limited by both lack of resources and the short duration of inmate confinement. Though many inmate services found in prisons are absent from jails, jails continue to play a vital role in the justice system.

Jail conditions and jail standards have significantly increased in the last two decades. Professional organizations such as the American Correctional Association and the American Jail Association have proven to be major advocates for jail standards to include professional training and institutional standards, and have proven to be leaders in the advancement of jail operations across the nation.

State Corrections

Of those confined in prisons across the nation, the majority are held in state-level facilities. Every state operates some correctional system to handle those convicted and sentenced under state jurisdiction. As of 2008, there were more than 1,700 public and private adult correctional facilities housing state offenders across the country.

There is no typical state correctional system, as each has developed its own identity. Some state systems are large and operate extensive probation, community corrections, confinement, and parole programs, while others operate with small offender populations. As an example, North Dakota and Maine confine less than 3,000 inmates, while Texas and California confined approximately 170,000 offenders.[4]

States have been traditionally reluctant to build and operate prisons, often seeing them as an unfortunate drain of public funds. The fact that most offenders commit and are convicted of state crimes forces states to develop and implement strategies to respond to judicial sentencing.

Throughout the early 1800s, as the use of offender incarceration increased, states struggled to respond. As most early prisons served as little more than human warehouses, work in Pennsylvania and New York advanced the knowledge of institutional confinement and correctional operations. The early work in both Pennsylvania and New York influenced both the design and operational strategies that would shape the future of corrections.

Over the next 200 years, state prison populations increased. Additional prisons were constructed, and as new prisons opened, many states searched for ways to offset the cost of inmate confinement. As a result, even the most reluctant states faced the reality of confinement.

The history of institutional corrections in America has affected the growth and construction of prisons in this country. The prison systems in the United States have evolved from several different models: the penitentiary, the prison, the reformatory, and the prison farm. Each model had its own correctional philosophy to begin with, and this philosophy affected the conditions of prison life within the walls for the inmates inside. Interestingly enough, each was considered a penal reform in its time. In their own ways, each attempted to accomplish the correctional objectives of retribution, deterrence, incapacitation, and rehabilitation.

The idea behind the penitentiary was that the offender was "out of touch with God" and needed to repent.[5] Thus, the new *Eastern Penitentiary* in Pennsylvania that opened in 1829 was considered a model of penal reform and incorporated ideas that became known as the *Pennsylvania system*. Prisoners were kept in solitary confinement. They were given work to do in their cells and a Bible to read. There, they were to learn the errors of their ways and be penitent. In New York, the *Auburn system* took hold. The congregate system practiced at Auburn called for strict discipline and inmate work in organized groups. Many American state correctional facilities were built around either philosophy. This era lasted from the early 1800s to the 1860s.[6] Many of these facilities are still in operation today.

The idea behind the prison was that offenders were "evil, and evil must be destroyed."[5] The philosophy of "lock 'em up and throw away the key" was expressed in long sentences by courts. Inmate labor was often punitive (i.e., breaking rocks) and meaningless. However, this began to be seen as a waste and prison industries arose. The industrial era of prisons was in its zenith from the early 1900s to the 1930s. In the 1930s the Medical model attempted to treat crime as a disease and find a "cure." By the 1970s, this method was seen as not working. Prisons returned to what has been referred to as the retribution era (lock 'em up and throw away the key) and a great expansion of prisons that continues today.[6]

The idea behind the reformatory was that offenders were "uneducated and ill trained to function in modern society."[5] Originally *reformatories* were designed for younger offenders (typically 16 to 30). The thought was that by being taught job skills and proper work habits, the inmate could be reformed. The first reformatory was opened in Elmira, New York, in 1876. The reformatory era lasted from the 1860s to the early 1900s. The movement fell out of favor after World War I; however, there are still some reformatories in operation.[7]

The idea behind the prison farm was that prison inmates and the overall penal operation should be self-supporting. The prison farm was the sucessor to the disastrous *contract system* of inmate labor. Although developed in Massachusetts in 1798, the contract system of leasing the labor of convicted inmates to private famers, builders, and miners took hold after the Civil War in Alabama and spread quickly through most of the south.[5-8] The contract system was so brutal and abusive that it was banned in Mississippi by a state constitutional amendment that took effect in 1894.[8] Prison farms sprang up in Arkansas, Louisiana, Mississippi, Texas, and many other states. They were even present in the north and the rest of the United States. Although they are not as popular as they once were, prison farms continue in many correctional systems.

As the United States developed as a nation and witnessed an ever-increasing population and subsequent urbanization, judicially mandated punishment increased its reliance on confinement and community-based correctional programs. By 2008, many state-level corrections systems were operating at near capacity. Institutions filled as enforcement efforts focused upon violent offenders and drug offenses. Enhanced sentencing led to longer sentences, which in turn further pushed the capacity of correctional facilities and their resources.

Realizing that state size and population directly impact statistically the number of inmates one would expect to find confined in any state, the dramatic growth of the inmate population in California is the best example in the nation of an inmate population on the state level increasing at a rate much greater than would be expected. In 1980, California confined fewer than 24,000 inmates. By 2008, the inmate population had increased to over 170,000.[9]

Within institutions across the nation, gangs and gang violence often became commonplace. Personnel recruitment and retention continually proved challenging. Budgeting for corrections competed with other state services for funding, such as education, public health, and various social services. Despite overcrowding and limited resources, many state correctional systems worked to improve institutional conditions and increase the services provided to those confined and their families.

To respond to the correctional demands of the twenty-first century, many state systems continually search for alternatives to confinement. Many states developed prerelease centers, from which the inmates are required to work in the community and return to the facility at the end of their work shift. Offenders participating in this type of program are required to contribute to a controlled savings plan, contribute to family and child support, pay court-ordered restitution, pay room and board expenses to the state, and pay state and federal income taxes, and they are responsible for their medical and dental expenses.

Other states have developed offender treatment and support programs, such as vocational training, educational, drug, sexual offender, and parenting programs in the hope that assistance provided to the offenders while confined will reduce the chances of their return to the system as offenders.

No matter the size of the state correctional operation, each will continue to operate with the ultimate goal of the enhancement of public safety.

Federal Corrections

For years, the federal government did not operate correctional institutions, but rather confined federal prisoners in state prisons at federal expense. By the late 1800s, federal authorities recognized that continued state confinement of federal inmates was no longer practical. Federal inmates under state control were subjected to the same abuses as were state inmates. Inmate abuse included the leasing of federal prisoners to private contractors and the use of federal inmate labor for public works projects where the health and safety of the inmate were frequently in jeopardy as a result of dangerous working conditions.

In 1887, Congress prohibited states from including federal inmates in their inmate leasing programs. Responding to the legislation, many states refused to accept additional federal prisoners. Recognizing state confinement of federal inmates was no longer practical, Congress passed the *Three Prisons Act* in 1891.[10] The Three Prisons Act authorized the construction of the first three federal prisons, which were to be located in Leavenworth, Atlanta, and McNeil Island. These three institutions laid the foundation of the federal system of corrections that we have serving our nation today.

These three new federal prisons would take years to complete. As a short-term solution, the federal government transferred the *U.S. Disciplinary Barracks* (USDB) at Fort Leavenworth from use as a military confinement facility to civilian use for the confinement of the growing federal inmate population. Civilian federal inmates confined in Fort Leavenworth were used as a labor source in the construction of the new federal penitentiary, which was located nearby. Inmates marched from the Disciplinary Barracks to the site of the new penitentiary, where, over the next two decades, they completed one of the most famous prisons in the United States, the U.S. penitentiary at Leavenworth, which has now been in operation almost a century.

Upon completion of the first three federal prisons, it was soon realized that additional federal confinement facilities would quickly be needed. New federal prisons opened over the next several decades as the inmate population increased. In 1927, the first federal prison for female inmates opened in Alderson, West Virginia.[11]

By the late 1920s, the need to bring federal prisons under the control of one agency became clear to ensure efficient management. In 1930, Congress established the Federal Bureau of Prisons as a component of the Department of Justice and charged it with the "management and regulation of all federal penal and correctional institutions."[12] At the time, the federal prison system included 11 correctional institutions, confining about 10,000 inmates.

Sanford Bates, an experienced correctional administrator, was selected to head the Federal Bureau of Prisons. Before becoming the first director of the Federal Bureau of Prisons, Bates served as the commissioner of Penal Institutions in Boston from 1917 to 1919 and as commissioner of the Massachusetts Department of Corrections from 1919 to 1929. In 1929, he was appointed superintendent of prisons, U.S. Department of Justice, where he assisted in developing the legislation establishing the Federal Bureau of Prisons in 1930. Under his direction, the new Federal Bureau of Prisons established a legacy of professional service to the nation.[13]

By 1931, the Federal Bureau of Prisons operated 14 facilities confining about 13,000 inmates. Over the next decade, the federal inmate population increased to 24 institutions confining about 25,000 inmates.[14] From 1940 until 1980, the federal inmate population remained stable. With the increased emphasis upon federal drug enforcement and prosecution in the early 1980s, the federal inmate population dramatically increased. By 2008, the federal inmate population reached 200,000, with over 50% of the confined adults convicted of at least one drug-related offense.

Legislative changes continually influenced federal correctional operations. The Sentencing Reform Act of 1984 established federal determinate sentencing,[15] abolished federal parole, and reduced good time for federal offenders. These changes further stretched the capability of federal correctional institutions. By 2008, the Federal Bureau of Prisons operated 114 institutions, 27 of which confined female inmates, and 28 community corrections offices that coordinate federal community corrections centers and home confinement programs.[16] Each federal institution offers programs and services that vary based on the needs of the institution's specific inmate population.

In addition to adult offenders, the Federal Bureau of Prisons is also responsible for juveniles adjudicated for federal offenses. Federal juveniles are placed in a facility that is appropriate for their security and programming needs.

Throughout its history, the Federal Bureau of Prisons has been a leader in the advancement of innovations and professionalism in the field of corrections and is one of the earliest correctional systems to appoint, assign, and advance correctional personnel without regard to their race or gender. In 1992, Dr. Kathleen Hawk Sawyer was appointed the first female director of the Federal Bureau of Prisons. A career correctional professional, she began her career in the Federal Bureau of Prisons in 1976 as a psychologist at the Federal Correctional Institution in Morgantown, West Virginia, and advanced to lead the agency for 11 years as its director.[17]

The current director of the Federal Bureau of Prisons is Harley G. Lappin. Director Lappin, like the directors that preceded him, is a career member of the Federal Bureau of Prisons who moved up the ranks to the directorship. The service of correctional professionals as directors for the Federal Bureau of Prisons has ensured the Federal Bureau of Prisons some of the most outstanding leadership in the field of corrections. As the Federal Bureau of Prisons moves into the second decade of the twenty-first century, it can look back with pride at its service to the nation.

Private Corrections

With the nation experiencing a dramatic growth in the prison populations during the last part of the twentieth century, state and federal authorities sought additional options in dealing with the increasing numbers of inmates and the cost of providing inmate services. Rather than investing public funds in the construction of new facilities, many states and the federal authorities explored partnerships with the private sector.

Privatization of correctional operations or services has a history reaching back to the inmate lease system and the private operation of facilities seen during the last two centuries. As all aspects of corrections struggled to keep up with the increasing number of those placed in their custody, it was just a matter of time until private enterprise would enter a new era as an operational partner with corrections.

The first new era, *private prison-for-profit*, was established in 1975 when RCA contracted with the state of Pennsylvania to open a training school for juveniles. Since that time, other corporations have entered the correctional service market, providing services ranging from full institutional management to specific support services, such as medical or food management. Privatization of these services can serve as a way to reduce the cost of institutional operations.

By 2005, over 107,000 federal and state prisoners were held in private facilities, with an additional 73,000 inmates held in privately run local jails.[18] While many corporations have entered the field of private correctional services, several leaders have emerged in the field. The *Correctional Corporation of America* and GEO have grown to become international in the scope of their operations. In 2008, the Correctional Corporation of America established itself as a leader in the field of contract correctional services, managing about 75,000 inmates in 60 facilities in 21 states and the District of Columbia. The Correctional Corporation of America represents the fifth largest corrections system in the United States, following behind the correctional systems of the Federal Bureau of Prisons, California, Texas, New York, and Florida.[19]

Military Corrections

While all branches of the military maintain a judicial, enforcement, and confinement capability, each branch of service works closely with the other branches to avoid the unnecessary duplication of justice services. Historically, military punishment relied on corporal punishment, such as flogging, forfeiture of pay and allowances, branding, short-term confinement, and for more serious offenses, the death penalty or confinement in a state or territorial prison. Military stockades, which were comparable to civilian jails, were in poor physical condition and were designed to be punitive and not rehabilitative.

Concern for the safety of military prisoners after their confinement in state prisons led the military to establish a formal military correctional system. Alcatraz Island, as an example, was originally planned as an army defense site, but as early as 1859, 11 enlisted men were incarcerated in its guardhouse. Other army bases in the West sent their deserters, escapees, thieves, and drunkards to Alcatraz, which was more secure than their garrison stockades. In 1861, Alcatraz was officially designated the military prison for the Department of the Pacific.

In 1907, the military base on Alcatraz Island was redesignated the Pacific Branch, U.S. Military Prison, Alcatraz Island. The army finally acknowledged that the future of Alcatraz was as a prison and not a defense site.[20]

In 1871, the military evaluated the treatment of military inmates in civilian jails and confirmed inmate abuse, lack of uniform treatment, and limited army control of inmates in state penitentiaries. Realizing the confinement of military prisoners in state or territorial prisons was no longer practical, the military correctional system was established by Congress in 1873. In May 1875, the U.S. Disciplinary Barracks (USDB) at Fort Leavenworth, Kansas, was opened. This facility would serve as the military prison for officers and longer-term enlisted personnel convicted of military offenses.[21]

The mission of the USDB is to incarcerate U.S. military prisoners sentenced to long terms of confinement; conduct correctional and treatment programs to maintain good order and discipline and reduce recidivism upon release; and, on order, provide trained and ready soldiers to conduct worldwide deployments in support of contingency operations.

The USDB is the only maximum security prison within the Department of Defense. Of the approximately 500 male inmates confined in the institution, 9 are currently on death row and 10 are serving life without parole.[22]

The Navy also operates an extensive disciplinary system, which was revised in 1985. As part of the Navy's disciplinary reorganization, offenders were grouped into three classifications, based upon the severity of their crimes, sentences, and potential return to duty or society. Level I offenders faced 30 days or less upon sentencing and are considered minor in status and are typically confined in base brigs (jails) located at Naval and Marine bases; Level II offenders are those serving terms 31 days to 7 years; and Level III offenders are the most serious offenders, with sentences of more than 7 years. Male Level III offenders are typically confined in the U.S. Army

Disciplinary Barracks at Fort Leavenworth. In 1999, a Department of Defense (DoD) decision was made to consolidate all DoD women prisoners in California, including Level III.[23]

The military's 59 confinement facilities have a design capacity of 4,166 and an operational capacity of 3,249. The total population in military facilities at year-end 2002 was 2,377.[24]

There were 2,322 prisoners under military jurisdiction at year-end 2005. Within the Department of Defense, the Army operates six confinement facilities, confining the most military inmates, approximately 41%, while the Navy operates 11 facilities confining approximately 34% of the military inmate population. The U.S. Marine Corps operates six facilities, confining approximately 20% of the inmate population, and the Air Force operates 36 facilities, confining approximately 5% of the military inmate population.

One of the most striking differences between military and civilian corrections is the offender recidivism rates. Most military personnel convicted of serious offenses are discharged from service effective the date of their release from confinement. As a result, few of these offenders remain in service, and thus have no opportunity to reoffend and return to the military correctional system.

Juvenile Corrections

The juvenile court movement contributed greatly to the development of juvenile corrections, to include juvenile confinement and juvenile correctional alternatives to confinement. While the desire in dealing with juvenile offenders is to provide every opportunity possible to refocus juvenile behavior away from criminal activity, the reality that juvenile crime is a continuing problem is faced by every community in the nation.

With the establishment of the first juvenile court in the nation in Chicago in 1899,[25] the trend to separate the adjudication of juveniles from adults began. Over the next several decades, other states created juvenile courts and commenced the separation of juvenile punishment from adult corrections.

Though the intent of the juvenile justice system is to protect the due process of law rights of youth and avoid, where possible, juvenile confinement, the public concern over the increase in juvenile crime and the demand for action have resulted in tougher sanctions for juvenile offenders. Rehabilitation became a lesser priority to public safety in the aggressive campaign against crime of the 1990s. As an example, the 1974 Juvenile Justice and Delinquency Prevention Act was amended to include provisions that would allow states to try juveniles as adults for some violent crime and weapons violations. Minimum detention standards were also put into place in some states, making the juvenile justice system more similar to the adult criminal justice system. By 2008, over 100,000 juveniles were confined in the nation's institutions.[26]

Across the nation, juvenile sanctions reflect significant diversity in both strategy and approach. Traditional confinement facilities exist and are used to house the most serious of juvenile offenders. Juvenile probation, youth ranches, and camps and juvenile boot camps reflect some of the variety in juvenile corrections.

Juvenile correctional authorities must concern themselves with and provide for the medical, educational, cognitive behavioral, and residential rehabilitative needs of those assigned to their custody. Specialized programs for adjudicated sex offenders, female offenders, juveniles with mental health needs, juveniles with serious chemical dependency needs, and serious juvenile offenders must be provided. The special nature of juvenile corrections, to include the requirement to provide services typically not required for adult offenders, results in significantly higher costs related to juvenile justice than to adult corrections.

Summary

The evolution of corrections in the United States has spanned three centuries and has moved from an origin of basic community-based confinement to an extensive system of corrections that includes federal, state, local, private, and military facilities and programs. By 2011, corrections in the United States faced a crisis. As both adult and juvenile inmate populations dramatically increased, federal, state, and local correctional systems struggled to find ways to house the influx of inmates and to pay for those services necessary to safely operate correctional facilities and systems. Though innovative alternatives to traditional corrections have proved promising, the need for traditional confinement remains strong.

As we remind ourselves that the vast majority of those convicted or adjudicated for a criminal offense return to society, the need to develop effective correctional strategies and programs designed to reduce the chances of inmates returning for new convictions after initial release becomes great.

Vocabulary

Auburn system

Contract system

Correctional Corporation of America

Eastern Penitentiary

Pennsylvania system

Private prison-for-profit

Reformatories

Three Prisons Act

U.S. Disciplinary Barracks

Discussion Questions

1. What are the similarities and differences between the Auburn system and the Eastern Penitentiary?

2. Understand private prison-for-profit. What is the scope of the private institution? Discuss whether there is agreement on the effectiveness of these facilities.

3. Explain the historical development of federal and military corrections. What forced the federal government and the military to establish formal correctional systems?

Notes

1. Couture, H., Harrison, P. M., Sabol, W. J., Bonczar, T. P., & Glaze, L. E. Bureau of Justice Statistics. Retrieved June 21, 2010, from http://www.ojp.usdoj.gov/bjs/abstract/p06.htm and http://www.ojp.usdoj.gov/bjs/abstract/ppus06.htm

2. New York Corrections Timeline I. (n.d.). Retrieved February 12, 2008, from http://www.correctionhistory.org/html/timeline/html/timeline.html

3. Arnold and Port Law Firm. (n.d.). Retrieved December 17, 2007, from http://law.wustl.edu/prisoncommission/PDF/Accreditation.pdf

4. Pomfret, J. (2006, June 11). Crisis in prison systems a threat to public: Longer sentences and less emphasis on rehabilitation create problems. Retrieved November 13, 2007, from http://www. washingtonpost.com/wp-dyn/content/article/2006/06/10/ AR2006061000719.html

5. Allen, B., Simonsen, C., & Latessa, E. (2004). *Correction in America: An introduction* (10th ed.). Upper Saddle River, NJ: Pearson/Prentice Hall.

6. Reichel, P. (1997). *Corrections.* St. Paul, MN: West.

7. Clear, T., Cole, G., and Reisig, M. (2006). *American corrections* (7th ed.). Belmont, CA: Thompson/Wadsworth.

8. Oshinsky, D. (1996). *Worse than slavery: Parchman Farm and the ordeal of Jim Crow justice.* New York, NY: The Free Press.

9. Thomson, D. (2007, December 26). 2008 looms as year of reckoning on California's prison crowding. Retrieved February 2, 2008, from http://www.sfgate.com/cgi/article.cgi?f=/ n/a/2007/12/26/state/n140555S79.DTL&type=politics

10. Federal Bureau of Prisons Museum. Retrieved September 9, 2007, from http://www.bop.gov/museum/text_version.jsp

11. Hanrahan, C. (2003, March). Reclaiming the vision. Retrieved October 3, 2007, from http://prisonmemoir.com/AldersonAlumnae.aspx

12. Federal Bureau of Prisons. Former directors. Retrieved December 17, 2007, from http://www.bop.gov/about/history/directors.jsp

13. Federal Bureau of Prisons. Former directors. Retrieved December 17, 2007, from http://www.bop.gov/about/history/directors.jsp

14. Federal Bureau of Prisons. A brief history. Retrieved December 17, 2007, from http://www.bop.gov/about/history.jsp

15. Seghetti, L. M., & Smith, A. M. (2007, June 30). CRS report for Congress. Retrieved December 21, 2007, from http://www.fas. org/sgp/crs/misc/RL32766.pdf

16. Federal Bureau of Prisons. Former directors. Retrieved December 17, 2007, from http://www.bop.gov/about/history/directors.jsp

17. Federal Bureau of Prisons. Former directors. Retrieved December 17, 2007, from http://www.bop.gov/about/history/directors.jsp

18. Benefield, N. A. (2007, October 24). Testimony to the House Labor Relations Committee: Private prisons increase capacity, save money, improve service. Retrieved January 7, 2008, from http://www.commonwealthfoundation.org/commentary/private-prisons-increase-capacity-save-money-improve-service

19. About Correctional Corporation of America. (n.d.). Retrieved April 10, 2010, from http://www.correctionscorp.com/aboutcca.html

20. Federal Bureau of Prisons. A brief history. Retrieved December 17, 2007, from http://www.bop.gov/about/history.jsp

21. Hassenritter, D. (2004, October 10). The military correctional system: An overview. Retrieved from http://www.prisontalk.com/forums/archive/index.php/t-82683.html

22. Death Penalty Information Center. (n.d.). The US military death penalty. Retrieved October 24, 2007, from http://www.death-penaltyinfo.org/article.php?did=180&scid=32

23. Setting the standards for military corrections. (n.d.). Retrieved October 24, 2007, from http://www.brigmiramar.navy.mil/brief.htm

24. Haasenritter, D. (2003). The military correctional system: An overview. Retrieved December 18, 2008, from http://www.aca.org/publications/ctarchivespdf/dec03/haasenritter.pdf

25. Clapp, E. J. (1995, March 17). The Chicago juvenile court movement in the 1890s. Retrieved January 18, 2008, from http://www.le.ac.uk/hi/teaching/papers/clapp1.html

26. Bureau of Justice Statistics. (2008, November 7). Retrieved from http://www.ojp.usdoj.gov/bjs/pub/press/p03pr.htm

Prison Life

America is the land of the second chance—and when the gates of the prison open, the path ahead should lead to a better life.

—George W. Bush

Introduction

Life in prison has been described as restrictive, regimented, and confining. All of these are true whether you are a worker in a prison or an inmate in a prison; you are all doing time together. It takes a special kind of person to work in a prison. Prison workers are usually dedicated, well trained, and committed to protecting society from those that society has chosen to isolate itself from. On the other hand, prison workers exhibit coping skills, communications and social skills in working with inmates that are superior to many other types of workers. Let us begin our examination of prison life by taking a look at the prison staff.

Staff: Managing the Prisoners

Being the warden of a prison or the commander of a jail involves many skills that could be found in any large organization. A correctional administrator needs to have leadership, management, and budgeting skills that would be useful in any Fortune 500 corporation. The problem faced by most correctional administrators can be summed up thusly: We run the only hotel in the world where we don't control the front door (that is done by the courts or the arresting officers), we don't control the back door (that is controlled by the courts or the parole boards), and we have to persuade our honored dinner guests to continue to stay with us in spite of their expressed wishes to leave.

In order to properly run things, a warden must have a well-trained and well-managed staff. Leading this staff is a primary responsibility of management. Most prison correctional officers are unionized. Thus, labor negotiations are another skill that must be developed for correctional managers.

While most governmental organizations enjoy a certain amount of "qualified immunity" from civil actions under state and federal constitutions, there are several areas that if management fails, the governmental unit and the correctional administrators acquire a great deal of liability. These areas are:

- Wrongful hiring of personnel
- Wrongful retention of personnel who fail to meet standards
- Wrongful discharge of personnel
- Failure to train personnel
- Failure to supervise personnel

The responsibilities of a prison warden include hiring and firing personnel, implementing new correctional policies, insuring the safety of prisoners and staff, and establishing regulations to deal effectively with rule infractions by staff or inmates. Limited correctional budgets impose serious constraints that prevent wardens from being fully effective in the performance of their tasks. The very nature of the warden's job requires being a combination of politician and correctional professional.

Wardens are most often evaluated in their job performance by the absence of riots and other disturbances, and the warden's job is supposed to involve keeping the prison at a low profile in the public eye. Prison riots such as those at Attica, Atlanta, and Santa Fe have forcibly demonstrated what can occur if the prison administration loses control. Control of the institution must be maintained at all costs. Deadly force has been legally used to maintain control. Security is the primary directive.

Most wardens have advanced through the system, and this is the pinnacle of a long corrections career (unlike secretaries of corrections who are politically appointed by the governor).[1] Wardens are usually a very educated (many have graduate and postgraduate degrees) and professional lot. The skills and abilities of the warden combined with the correctional philosophy adopted by the warden determine the direction that the correctional institution is headed.

In addition to leading their employees, the correctional manager has to manage the physical facility of the correctional institution (you lead people, you manage things). The buildings tend to remain in use for hundreds of years and often are of various stages of penal design. In addition, depending on how well maintained these facilities have been, they may be in various states of repair. The plumbing and light fixtures still have to be fixed, when they are not working. The modern prison is like a small city. It is complex in its structure and organization. Skilled administrators leading highly trained individuals make for a successful operation. Unfortunately, limited budgets and overcrowding often diminish or even nullify the best programs.[2]

Correctional Officers

The correctional officer is the backbone of the prison system. His or her role is that of both a follower and a leader. The correctional officer supervises inmates and is in turn supervised by other, higher correctional supervisors (corporals, sergeants, etc.). In most prisons, the correctional officer structure is organized in a paramilitary fashion with defined ranks and duties. The correctional officers provide both services to inmates and security for the facility.

According to Silverman, correctional officers have traditionally been viewed as the lowest rung in the criminal justice hierarchy, but this is changing, as the job has acquired better training, pay, and benefits over the years.[3] As the professionalism of the correctional staff increases, the job satisfaction of the employees also increases. This has resulted in lower employee turnover in the corrections field than was experienced in the past. Organizations like the American Corrections Association and the American Jail Association strive to improve professionalism among officers.

The Role of the Corrections Officer

Corrections officers serve many different functions within the institution. However, many of these functions are common to all assignments. The primary need of a correctional institution was and is security. The bad guys can't get out until someone (a court or a parole board) says they can. Preventing escapes is a primary institutional goal. In addition, no one from the outside should be able to get in without permission. The physical security of the staff and the institution as a whole is a primary consideration.

Another primary function of all corrections officers is the control of inmates and contraband inside the institution. Inmates are violent people. Contraband control becomes a major issue. Weapons, drugs, and other items that could be used for escape have been smuggled into correctional institutions by visitors, attorneys, and even corrupt correctional staff. Security threats to the institution can come from within the institution (prison gangs, unruly inmates, corrupt staff) or external sources (fellow gang members on the outside, relatives, etc.). The diligence by staff to control contraband must be unceasing.

Staff safety is another primary concern for correctional officers. They must be observant of inmate behavior and perceived threats to themselves, other officers, and the prison at all times. Other threats include prison gangs. The traditional prison gangs (Aryan Brotherhood, Black Gangster Family, Mexican Mafia, Texas Syndicate, etc.) have been supplemented (but not replaced) by street gangs and extremist groups (both white and black) operating inside the walls of the institution. Often these groups hide behind various religions to conduct their business because religion is a protected activity by the First Amendment of the Constitution of the United States. The correctional officer must be observant of the activities of these groups and aware of the implications of their group activities and the effect on institution security or staff safety.

Correctional Officer Assignments

Corrections officers may be assigned to various duties within the institution. Most of these duties are functional assignments. Institutional security is a primary function of all corrections officers. However, other duties vary and sometimes are specialized.

1. *Intake/release*: These are officers who process inmates into and out of the institution. They process the inmate into the institution, record the inmate's property, identify the inmate as the person who is listed on the court order, issue the inmate clothing or other items (bedding, toiletries, etc.), and

after classification, assign the inmate to a housing unit. The process is reversed upon release. Care has to be taken as to just who is being released and when.

2. *Housing*: Officers who are assigned to work in the housing units are often called block officers or pod officers, depending on whether the housing unit is called a cell block or a housing pod. These COs supervise inmate activities in the housing units where the inmates live. They provide security, make sure the inmates go to assignments, and provide for inmate welfare. "Dormitory officer" provides a similar function in that type of housing unit.

3. *Perimeter security officers*: These officers man the watch towers on the prison walls, patrol the perimeter of the institution, and provide security to the facility by controlling access to it. They are alert for any attempts by inmates to escape or attempt by those on the outside to break in and permit inmates to escape.

4. *Administrative officers*: These officers control movement within the facility (from a computerized master control station in most facilities), perform administrative duties, and may have little actual contact with inmates.

5. *Work detail supervisors*: These are COs who are assigned to supervise inmate work crews and details. They may supervise an inmate shop, kitchen, farm detail, or chain gang.

6. *Yard or compound officers*: These COs provide security and maintain order in the prison yard during inmate activities. They watch for fights, contraband, and gang activity.

7. *Rovers or relief officers*: These officers travel over the institution, giving other COs breaks and assisting or filling in where needed. They provide an extra measure of security to the institution, because while they are wandering around from place to place to perform their duties, their movements are hard to predict by inmates watching for a guard routine.[3]

Gender

For decades the idea of staffing a correctional facility focused on large men who could force inmate compliance, if necessary. Today, correctional officers are both male and female. They supervise both male and female inmates. This is called *cross-gender supervision*. This is a substantial cultural change from 40 or 50 years ago, when men worked in the men's prison and females only worked in the women's prison. Men and women now work at all levels of the prison system. It is not uncommon to see a female warden in a male prison or a male warden in a female prison.

Though it is not a prison, the Shelby County jail located in Memphis, Tennessee, for years had a reputation of being one of the most violent facilities in the southeast part of the nation. Today, with much credit due to Sheriff Mark Luttrell, the facility has been reorganized, accredited by the American Correctional Association, and is now one of the safest in the nation. The personnel serving in this all-male facility are over 70% female officers and staff members. Shelby County is an outstanding example of how successfully a male facility can operate with a majority female staff.

Correctional Officer Power

While they have a great deal of power over the inmates, a corrections officer has to make use of interpersonal skills to manage inmates. You can't beat every inmate into submission. Even if it were legal to do so (which it isn't), it is not physically possible. Even when it *was* legal, it was not an effective measure of inmate control and only raised the levels of violence within the institution.[4,5] A typical correctional officer in a direct supervision housing unit will probably be supervising about 48 inmates. Thus, over the years, correctional officers have had to develop other ways of inmate control. However, they must be prepared to use physical force if needed. Officers who fail to respond in a proper manner lose all moral authority with the inmates and with other officers.

Training of Correctional Personnel

Training of correctional personnel is divided into three basic categories: initial or basic training (aimed at new employees), in-service training (aimed at current employees), and management training (aimed at future leaders and managers). Training can come from either internal (academy, field training officers, etc.) or external sources

(American Correctional Association, American Jail Association, National Institute of Corrections, etc.). Courses of instruction include security, inmate management skills, ethics, combatives, and other related subjects.

Administering Inmate Rehabilitation Programs

Depending on budgets and policy, many of the staff that conduct inmate programs within the prison are volunteers. Some may be paid correctional officers acting in these positions. This leads to different problems. The volunteers must be vetted for security and trained in the rules of the institution. Paid staff have a similar problem in that they often must be trained in how to conduct or administer the inmate program. Paid staff are not usually inmate program experts unless they were hired specifically for that position. Therefore, they must be trained in how to do the job. Conflicts of interest may arise between the good of the inmate and the needs of the institution.

Inmate World: Living behind Bars

Inmates that come to a correctional institution are not rule followers by nature (that's how they got there in the first place!). Many are violent. Most have drug or alcohol abuse in their histories, leading to health problems induced by withdrawal symptoms. Many of the inmates are mentally ill. Many inmates are either illiterate or functionally illiterate. Because of their lifestyle choices, many of the incoming inmates have severe or chronic health problems that must be addressed by staff. The needs and welfare of the inmate population are a responsibility of correctional supervisors.

The inmates' lives are heavily regulated. They are told when to get up in the morning. They are fed whatever is being served at times regulated by prison staff. They are assigned jobs that they must perform or face prison discipline. Their movements are restricted within the institution. Then, finally, they are told when to go to bed. It is a very stressful lifestyle, especially for those who do not like to follow rules anyway. The inmates have reacted to the prison environment by developing an inmate subculture.

The Inmate Subculture

The majority of inmates in custody are males. Penologists have observed that male inmates in custody have evolved into a prison-based *subculture* with its own values, roles, language, and customs. As a subculture they have adopted social norms that vary widely from those of mainstream society. Traditions and oral history reinforce these social norms, and an inmate pecking order evolves based upon cunning and fear. The rise in gang activity within the prison culture is modifying this subculture somewhat.

Social Structure

At the top of the pecking order in the inmate social structure are the murderers (based on fear), the gang leaders (based on fear), and the con artists (based on cunning). On the bottom of the inmate social structure are child molesters (known as baby bangers), informants (snitches), and former law enforcement personnel who have been convicted of a crime and are now in custody. It is an ultra-violent and dominant culture that contains both the exploiters and the exploited.

As a group, males are more violent than females. Over half of the male inmates are either serving time or have served time for a crime of violence. Thus, a culture of dominance abounds within the existing cultural suppression that is inherent to a detention environment. Social Darwinism prevails inside the walls. The predators and the prey are often housed in the same cell blocks together. Many inmates exhibit the same types of violent or antisocial behavior that got them locked up in the first place. The prevailing attitude among the inmates is "Whata ya gonna do? Put me in prison?"

Much of the control exerted by inmates over other inmates is based on fear. Fear of violence. Fear of rape. Fear of being left without the support or protection of your fellow inmates against the rest of the wolves out there in the prison yard. Fear causes paranoia and other reactive behaviors.

How Does It Form? Prison Social Structure and the Inmate Code

The values and norms within the prison system are reflected in an informal inmate code that often develops within the walls. While not exactly in the inmate handbook, given to "new fish" by prison authorities, the *inmate code* is quickly absorbed and adhered to by most inmates. Those that choose to violate it do so at their own peril. The code is based on the usage of hostility and manipulation. The resulting atmosphere created by the inmate code is ripe for the formation of prison gangs. The inmate code has several aspects, including:

- Do your own time (don't butt into another inmate's affairs unless asked to).
- Be a stand up guy (don't snitch even if it means you take the rap alone).
- Don't suck up to the bulls (solidarity of all inmates against staff).
- Don't snitch (a code of silence prevails).

Silverman has observed perceived changes to the traditional inmate code that have been caused by prison gang influences within many institutions. Among these he cites:

- Toughness has become a central focus of inmate identity.
- Loyalty has shifted from the inmate population as a whole to one's group (usually ethnic or racial group).
- Violence, once an administrative tool of control, is now being used by inmates to send the prison hurling out of control.[3]

Clear, Cole, and Reisig point out that the inmate code results in several social adaptations by inmates in serving their sentences, including:

- *Doing time*: Men "doing time" view their prison term as a brief inevitable break in their criminal career, a cost of doing business.
- *Gleaning*: These inmates take advantage of prison programs to better themselves and improve their minds and prospects for release. Some inmates engage in the underground economy of the institution by running either goods or services for other inmates.
- *Jailing*: The choice of those who cut themselves off from the outside and try and construct a life within the prison.

- *Disorganized criminal*: This describes inmates who are unable to develop any of the other three role orientations; these inmates are often of low intelligence or afflicted with disabilities, have difficulty functioning within prison society, and are human cattle to be manipulated by others.[6]

In a prison society that is composed of predators, it is almost natural to assume that there will be a higher level of violence than is the societal norm in the "outside world." Clear et al. observed that each year there are over 34,000 inmates attacked, and that 51 inmates died as a result of prison violence in 2001. There are several types of violence in prison:

- *Prisoner-to-prisoner violence*: This is the most common type of violence. This is influenced by gangs. Homemade weapons are common and are most often used against other prisoners (either for protection or to intimidate).
- *Prisoner-to-officer violence*: Usually verbal. However, violent threats can turn into violent acts very quickly. Inmates will throw feces and urine at officers. They will physically resist officers who attempt to place them into cuffs or leg irons. Sometimes they will physically attack officers with the intent to injure or kill the officer (this frequently happens during prison riots).
- *Officer-to-prisoner violence*: This type of violence usually revolves around the officers trying either to get the inmate under control or to prevent escape.[6]

Male Prison Sexuality

Again, prison society is heavily populated by predators. Among these predators are sexual predators. Thus, you face the phenomenon of prison rape. While a certain percentage of the population is homosexual, prison rape is most often committed forcibly by those who profess to be heterosexual on the "outside." Rape is a crime of violence. Most victims are coerced, bribed, tricked, or trapped into a rape encounter by "lone wolves" who have chosen rape as the way they express their masculinity within the prison environment. The prison rapist usually has a strong self-concept and no mental health problems, but the rape victim usually develops mental health problems or has preexisting ones. Victims are sought out who appear weak. Prostitution (male) and sexual slavery often flourish behind the walls, especially as a result of gang activity. Once an inmate has been raped, he is exploited by other inmates in a variety of ways. Prison officials who fail to render protection from rape can be sued for monetary damages.[7]

Only seven states allow conjugal visits for prisoners (California, Connecticut, Mississippi, New Mexico, New York, Washington, and Wyoming). Not all prisoners are allowed access to this program in the states that participate in it. Usually only married inmates are allowed to participate in a conjugal visit as a privilege of good behavior. Perhaps if more states participated in this program sexual violence would lessen in our prison systems.[8]

Of course, some inmates engage in homosexual sex within the prison. Some of the inmates are homosexuals, and some voluntarily participate while incarcerated and return to the "straight life" upon release. Sexual abuse by the staff is rare, but a few cases of male inmates having sex with guards (usually female) have occurred. Correctional officers having sex with an inmate is a felony in most states.[8]

Inmate Suicide and Prison

Although the rate of suicide among prison inmates is lower than that of inmates in jails, it is still a problem for prison officials. Inmate suicide or attempted suicide is a major problem within the institution. Officers receive training on how to spot at-risk inmates, steps to prevent inmate suicides, and what to do if there is an attempt by an inmate. However, sometimes, in spite of the best efforts by staff, the inmate succeeds in either injuring himself (self-mutilation) or in actually killing himself. Inmates in danger of or who have threatened suicide are placed on a suicide watch. Objects that could be used by inmates to injure themselves are removed. Often the inmate's clothes are taken and the inmate is given a paper gown to wear. Officers maintain an observation log of the inmate that is on suicide watch that mandates that the inmate is observed frequently during each shift. The inmate is often moved to a special observation cell for this suicide watch. The most dangerous times for an inmate and the most likely times that an inmate will attempt suicide are:

- Shortly after intake into the institution (within the first eight hours)
- After being placed in administrative segregation, solitary, or isolation
- Upon losing an appeal
- After being sexually assaulted
- After receiving bad news from home

Mentally Ill Inmates

Another problem is the high number of mentally ill inmates within the institution. Since the closing or downsizing of most of the mental institutions in the United States beginning in the mid-1960s, the number of mentally ill inmates has risen dramatically. While some treatment programs are available in most institutions, many are woefully inadequate. The prison was not designed as a mental hospital. However, prisons usually have better and more available mental health treatment programs than jails because the inmates are there for a longer stay and the programs have the potential to be more effective (however, this is not always the case). Mentally ill inmates often are discipline problems. Many become violent predators; however, even more become victims.

Aging Offenders

The general aging of the baby boomer generation has made the median age in the U.S. population rise slightly. Combined with longer sentences and repeat offenders, this has resulted in an inmate population that is older than experienced previously. The larger numbers of older inmates has resulted in increased needs for healthcare by these inmates. The Alabama DOC went so far as to buy a nursing home for its older inmates that required that level of medical care. Older inmates also are at greater risk for victimization by younger predator inmates.[9]

In his study of the aging inmate population, Williams observed:

Other factors that contribute to an accelerated aging of inmates include lifestyle choices that are common among prisoners, both before and after incarceration. These include drug and alcohol abuse; risky sexual behavior; lack of preventive healthcare; and other causes that also can be associated with poverty and lack of education. In fact, the combination of these patterns is unique to this group and can be used to forecast patterns of physical deterioration for elderly inmates.[10]

A Society of Violent Males

The society of the male inmate is a dominant and often violent one.[9] Close inmate management by correctional officials must be maintained in order to prevent inmate suicide, rape, or other violence.[2] The problem with criminals is that they are in many ways like alcoholics. In spite of the best programs available to "cure" them, they will reform when they are good and ready to do so. Hence, we find ourselves doing a lot of human warehousing and precious little reforming when it comes to inmates.

The Radicalization of Male Prison Inmates

There have always been racial divides among male prison inmates. The addition of prison gangs operating within the prison system, and carrying over to the streets, has been disruptive for the prison environment and further polarized the inmate population.[9] This has been further complicated by the adaptation of types of radical religions by some prison inmates. Inmates have a right to practice their chosen religion under the First Amendment of the Constitution. Not all inmates that participate in radical religions have become security threats or joined security threat groups; however, many have.[11]

Female Inmates

The problem with females is that they are different than typical prisoners—males. They have different needs (medical, housing, programs). They respond differently to programs designed to "reform" convicted inmates (actually, females respond better to programs than males). The culture of the female inmate is different from that of the male inmate. What is known is that the number of female inmates is increasing rapidly.

What happened? Two things basically: The first was the rapid expansion of drug usage and the resulting war on drugs. Approximately half of females in prison were using mind-altering substances at the time of their most recent offense. Drug usage before incarceration is higher for females than males. Curry observed:

> The 1990's have shown a significant increase in the amount of women being charged for drug and alcohol use as well as an increase in incarcerated repeat drug offenders. Although most sentences can be traced to substance abuse, violent crime is also on the rise.[12]

The second reason is that with the onset of the feminist movement in the 1960s there has been an overall change in women's criminality. Traditionally, the crimes committed by women were economic crimes (fraud, credit card fraud, bad checks, embezzlement, prostitution, etc.) or crimes of passion (assault/killing of a lover or rival). Crime has become a more equal opportunity employer, and you now see women charged with burglary, robbery, and even as sex offenders. As a group, females are being convicted of more violent crimes and are being sentenced to prison rather than probation, as was the previous correctional norm. Curry noted:

> There has been a shift in the gender composition of the nation's correctional population, for more than 950,000 females are under correctional supervision. This shift has been caused by tougher substance abuse sentencing guidelines, economic hardships and rising violence levels among women. Although the male inmate population remains significantly larger, the escalating numbers of women in prison are causing a tilt in the U.S. population.[12]

The state and federal institutions that house female inmates are different from those that house males. Clear et al. observed that:

1. Female facilities are smaller.
2. Female institutions have looser security and are less structured in terms of inmate-staff relationships.
3. The underground economy is not as developed in female facilities.
4. Female inmates are less committed to the inmate code.

5. Female institutions lack the high walls, guard towers, and cyclone fences that characterize male institutions.

6. There is less pressure to design effective treatment programs for women than for men.

7. Successful programs relate to the social realities from which women come and to which they will return.

8. The regime of women's prisons tends to treat women like children and "domesticate" them.[6]

When you look at who goes to prison among the female population, certain characteristics are prevalent:

- The majority of female inmates are either Hispanic or African American (63%).
- A large percentage is undereducated and has not finished high school (44%).
- Most female inmates are mothers (65%).
- Many (30%) were receiving welfare prior to their incarceration.
- Women receive shorter sentences than men for the same offense.
- Most female inmates are serving sentences for substance abuse-related crimes.
- However, 32% were serving sentences for violent crimes.

While incarcerated, women behave differently than men. The female inmate subculture is a group, rather than an individual way of doing time. DeBell observed:

Females possess different social needs than males. Cognitively, women process the need for belonging more strongly than men. It is quite common to see male offenders segregate themselves for a time alone. Female offenders need the closeness of others to such a degree that while incarcerated, females will develop and foster "fictive families"—congregate units of other offenders who assume family roles. There is a mother, a father, aunts, uncles and siblings. We can associate this with the development of a learned "sex role trait" behavior ingrained in children at a young age. There is something "acceptable" for females in society to hold hands, dance and physically touch one another in a nonsexual manner; it is learned behavior. However staff will often observe what is learned sex trait behavior in the female offender and associate it with homosexual behavior. This is not typically the case.[13]

Other differences between male and female inmates include communication skills.

Cranford and Williams found:

One critical difference between male and female inmates is the manner in which they communicate. Social-behavioral scientists during the last two decades have consistently researched this concept. Not unlike their free-world counterparts, women offenders are generally more verbal, more open, more willing to share the intimacies of their lives, and more emotional. Men, especially men in prison, do not communicate in the same ways. Men are more guarded about the information they share, the manner in which they share it, and the reason for sharing it in the first place. Men share information on a "need to know" basis; for men, information is power. For women, talking helps establish a common ground, a way to relate to others. For women, especially those in the offender population, talking, communicating and sharing are methods by which they stay connected.[14]

Critical Needs in Dealing with Female Inmates

Female inmates have certain needs that are critical in dealing with them in a correctional setting. Among these needs are:

- *Specialized healthcare*: Women have a high number of STDs, including HIV. Many women are substance abusers. About 25% of women are pregnant when they enter custody.

- *Specialized mental healthcare*: Many women suffer from depression, anxiety, or other treatable mental illnesses.

- *Vocational training programs*: Most women need vocational training if they are to succeed in legitimate occupations outside the walls.

- *Social or family counseling*: Most female inmates are mothers. Many have co-dependent relationships with abusers or co-defendants. Incarcerated women are most concerned with the fate of their children. Teaching coping skills would go a long way to ensure success on the outside.[1]

The needs of the female offender are different than those of the typical male offender. However, the correctional systems have to adapt to those needs either by choice or under court order (lawsuits filed under the 14th Amendment). The fact is that female inmates are increasing, and correctional administrators are going to have to train their staffs and build facilities to deal with this increased need.

Female Prison Sexuality

Many female inmates enter the correctional system as a victim of previous sexual abuse. As noted previously, most correctional systems do not allow conjugal visits in prison. Female inmates tend to form into pseudofamily groups for social reasons within the correctional institution. In some of these groups homosexual behavior is practiced that is incidental to the inmate's incarceration. When the inmate returns to heterosexual society, she returns to heterosexual behavior. One female Missouri correctional officer called this phenomenon "gay for the stay." Of course, other inmates are homosexual, and this represents no difference in their sexual activity (if any is participated in). Female inmates have been the target of sexual abuse by staff. Staff having sex with an inmate is a felony in most states.[8,15]

Female Inmate Suicide and Self-Mutilation

Female inmates seem to successfully commit suicide in custody at about the same rate as male inmates. However, female inmates have a higher rate of attempted suicides than the males. The female inmates also self-mutilate at a higher rate than the male inmates.[15,16]

Summary

Prisons, prisoners, and prison staff have been with us since the founding of the United States. Prison staff have been assigned the difficult task of maintaining order, maintaining security, and trying to rehabilitate a group of individuals that by their very nature are not rule followers. They have done so with professionalism and imagination. The education and quality of prison staff has improved over the years, developing into a professional corrections force that is capable of dealing with the ever-changing needs of our incarcerated population.

The inmates have developed into a subculture of captivity. They have an inmate code that is adapting to the realities of modern imprisonment. Inmates are often self-divided along racial, gang affiliation, and now in some cases, religious lines. While different, male and female inmates have both adapted to the inmate subculture in their own ways. Until someone actually figures out a "cure" for criminality, there will always be prisoners and those who watch them for the rest of society.

Vocabulary

Administrative officers

Cross-gender supervision

Doing time

Gleaning

Inmate code

Inmate subculture

Jailing

Officer-to-prisoner violence

Perimeter security officers

Prisoner-to-officer violence

Prisoner-to-prisoner violence

Rovers or relief officers

Work detail supervisors

Yard or compound officers

Discussion Questions

1. Describe the responsibilities of a prison warden and how his or her effectiveness is evaluated.

2. What are the primary roles and assignments of the corrections officer?

3. What is the inmate subculture? How is it central to understanding prison life?

4. Compare prisoner-to-prisoner, prisoner-to-officer, and officer-to-prisoner violence.

5. Understand how female and male inmates differ regarding criminal histories, needs, and prison social structure.

Notes

1. Allen, H., Latessa, E., Ponder, B., & Simonsen, C. (2007). *Corrections in America: An introduction* (11th ed.). Upper Saddle River, NJ: Prentice Hall.

2. Johnson, R. (1996). *Hard time: Understanding and reforming the prison.* Belmont, CA: Wadsworth.

3. Silverman, I. (2001). *Corrections: A comprehensive view* (2nd ed.). Belmont, CA: Wadsworth/Thompson Learning.

4. Lawes, L. (1932). *Twenty thousand years in Sing Sing.* New York, NY: The New Home Library.

5. Oshinsky, D. (1996). *"Worse than slavery": Parchman Farm and the ordeal of Jim Crow justice.* New York, NY: The Free Press.

6. Clear, T., Cole, G., & Reisig, M. (2006). *American corrections* (7th ed.). Belmont, CA: Wadsworth/Thompson Learning.

7. *Farmer v. Brennan,* 511 U.S. 825, 1994.

8. Reichel, P. (1997). *Corrections.* Minneapolis/St. Paul, MN: West.

9. Seiter, R. (2005). *Corrections.* Upper Saddle River, NJ: Prentice Hall.

10. Williams, J. (2006). The aging inmate population: Southern states outlook. Southern Legislative Conference. Retrieved June 16, 2010, from http://www.slcatlanta.org/Publications/HSPS/aging_inmates_2006_lo.pdf

11. Bohn, L. (2008, May/June). A homeland security issue: The radicalization of Muslim inmates in American correctional facilities. *American Jails, XXII*(2).

12. Curry, L. (2001, February). Tougher sentencing, economic hardships and rising violence. *Corrections Today, 63*(1).

13. Debell, J. (2001, February). The female offender: Different ... not difficult. *Corrections Today, 63*(1).

14. Cranford, S., & Williams, R. (1998, December). Critical issues in managing female offenders. *Corrections Today, 60*(7).

15. Banks, C. (2003). *Women in prison.* Santa Barbara, CA: ABC-CLIO.

16. Pollock-Byrne, J. (1990). *Women, prison & crime.* Pacific Grove, CA: Brooks/Cole.

IV

Issues in Corrections

Current Issues and Problems Facing Corrections

About all this—the causes of crime—we need more information, more research, more experimental data. Even our present prisons, bad as many of them are, could be extensively used as laboratories for the study of many of the unsolved problems.

—**Dr. Karl Menninger, in *The Crime of Punishment***

Introduction

Correctional professionals constantly face challenges as they strive to provide effective and safe operations of the institutions and programs they supervise. In this chapter, we will examine the major challenges facing correctional professionals as they struggle to provide cost-effective, safe, and secure correctional services.

As the correctional population continues to increase across the nation, correctional services must also expand. The cost of expansion of correctional services is significant, and funding drives or limits all correctional operations. Institutional costs directly in support of inmate *confinement* include, but are not limited to, housing, medical, support services, facilities, and staff. To provide confinement and supervision services for the ever-increasing offender population, funding must continually increase to support the cost of institutional operation. Every correctional function is thus dependent upon funding. Solutions to the many issues we will examine in this chapter often require creativity on the part of the correctional administrator.

Funding

As stated in the introduction, funding impacts all aspects of corrections. The cost of the correctional supervision varies greatly. Probation, parole, and community corrections are less costly than confinement. Basic institutional confinement is less expensive than offender hospitalization and treatment. Confinement costs range greatly between juvenile and adult confinement. When confinement is combined with treatment programs, costs may range well over $100 per day, per inmate.

Thus, funding remains the most significant challenge in all aspects of corrections. There is no single source of correctional funding supporting all of the correctional facilities and programs across the nation; rather, funding sources include local, state, and federal funds. The majority of correctional budgets are drawn from public taxes, and therefore, local, state, and federal correctional systems compete with other public services in the struggle for funding. Funding supporting corrections is funds that cannot be used for other public services, such as education, health, or support of the community infrastructure.

It is clear that correctional funding will never be adequate to support the desired offender programs. It is critical for correctional professionals to work closely with funding sources to determine funding priorities to ensure the operation of the safest, most professional facility possible. With correctional funding flowing from public funds, difficult decisions are continually made as to how funds will be divided among those functions that are the responsibility of government.

For most states, corrections funding represents a relatively small portion of the annual budget, but those funds cannot be used to support other public services. On average, states spend about 6% of their general funds on corrections. During FY 2006, states spent nearly $35.6 billion on corrections and budgeted $37.6 billion for FY 2007.

Correctional facilities are *closed communities*, and as a result, many of the costs related to providing inmate and institutional services are expensive. Escalating inmate healthcare costs, overcrowded prisons, and rising personnel expenses are principal drivers on correctional budgets. Inmate healthcare costs have caused many jurisdictions to contract for these services in an attempt to reduce or limit the increase in these costs.

As states feel the fiscal pressures of high incarceration rates on their budgets, they are making policy changes to help ease the situation, in some cases loosening the mandatory sentencing requirements because they have become too expensive.

Personnel Recruitment, Training, and Accreditation

Across the nation new correctional facilities are under construction to house the growing inmate population. It is expensive to build and staff prisons and costly to operate these facilities. Officials face ongoing costs to recruit, train, and staff the facilities and offer programming. As demonstrated in recent years, one of the top concerns is recruiting and retaining high-quality correctional personnel.

Corrections is a highly stressful profession, and not everyone can be successful working within a correctional facility. Correctional professionals face many challenges as they recruit quality personnel. The need to provide a competitive salary and benefits package is just one of the problems facing recruitment. Job stress, working hours, and conditions drive many out of the profession early in their careers. Additionally, the need to find mature employees, without criminal records or affiliation, is critical in maintaining staff integrity. Across the nation, much of the contraband that enters correctional facilities enters as a result of staff misconduct.

Personnel training is an important component of the correctional process. Staff members have to understand correctional law, constitutional rights, psychology, first aid, and human relations. They must quickly gain an understanding of the inmate mentality and recognize the culture of the institution itself to be able to successfully manage and supervise an adversarial inmate population.

The correctional environment is not representative of society in general, but rather, it is unique, and to be successful, the correctional professional must not only understand, but also be able to function in the dramatically different environment of corrections. As important as training of correctional personnel remains, it has not kept pace with law enforcement training. In most states, the training required for correctional personnel is far less than that of other public safety personnel. The future of corrections requires constant assessment of the training needs of the staff.

Institutional accreditation by the American Correctional Association has proven to be a great benefit to correctional administrators who have for years sought resources to improve the operations within their facilities. To be awarded accreditation, the institution must meet the professional guidelines for the operation of the facility. Rigorous standards touching all aspects of the correctional operations must be met and maintained to receive accreditation.

Overcrowding of Institutions

Over the last two decades, the inmate population across the nation has outpaced institutional capacities. This increased rate of growth has occurred despite a prolonged reduction in property crime and relatively stable rates of violent crime. The dramatic growth of adult and juvenile correctional populations is only partially explained by trends in crime and changing patterns of offending. Changes in criminal justice policies at the federal and state levels, including mandatory penalties regarding drug offenses, new laws increasing the severity and certainty of punishment, mandatory minimum sentences, and sentencing enhancements for certain offenses and offenders, have all contributed to our growing inmate population. Combined with sentencing guidelines that limit the discretion of judges and parole boards, inmate populations have reached unprecedented levels.

Overcrowding creates dangerous situations in terms of facility management. Overcrowded institutions are typically more dangerous. Concerns for personal safety of both inmate and staff have a negative impact upon the ability to provide appropriate programs to the inmate, such as drug or alcohol treatment.

Concerns about institutional overcrowding have caused many states to explore programs intended to reduce inmate populations or reduce recidivism. Some states are reviewing and modifying probation and parole policies to limit the number of violators who return to the prison system for technical violations. Other states, like California and Maryland, are allocating additional funds for education, counseling, community-based services, and other programs to further reduce the number of offenders from returning to confinement. No matter the program or approach, what is clear is that the growth in inmate population has exceeded that nation's ability to build and staff correctional facilities.

Health, Medical, Mental Health, and Substance Abuse Treatment

The reduction of institutionally and community-based mental health programs across the nation has also unintentionally affected corrections. Many believe America's jails and prisons currently house more mentally ill individuals than all of the nation's psychiatric hospitals combined. Many of these inmates have suspected or diagnosed mental illness, and unfortunately, rather than being committed to mental institutions, the justice process has led them to correctional institutional confinement.

Many more under correctional custody struggle with difficulties, to include addictions, mental illness, cognitive limitations, drug and alcohol dependency, and personality or learning disorders, and are found in institutions across the nation. Many of these challenged offenders have been placed under community-based correctional supervision and failed to abide by the required conditions, and are eventually incarcerated.

Mentally ill offenders reported high rates of homelessness, unemployment, alcohol and drug use, and physical and sexual abuse prior to their current incarceration. Inmates with mental illness are also at an increased risk of sexual or other physical victimization, to include assault. Female inmates report higher rates of mental health or substance abuse problems than male inmates.

In addition to the concern related to the mental health of those under correctional supervision, other significant medical issues are continually addressed in corrections.

Health Issues: HIV/AIDS, Tuberculosis, and Hepatitis

Physical health issues and their related costs are another major concern for correctional administrators. Medical services for inmates, to include screening for tuberculosis, treatment for prisoners with HIV/AIDS, tuberculosis, hepatitis B and C, access for women to gynecological and obstetric care, and dental, are just a few of the issues that face correctional administrators.

Access to healthcare in the correctional setting is deemed a constitutional right for inmates. In 1976, the Supreme Court case of *Estelle v. Gamble* determined that "deliberate indifference to serious medical needs" constitutes cruel and unusual punishment and violates an inmate's Eighth Amendment rights. As a result, correctional administrators struggle to provide appropriate health and treatment services.

HIV, AIDS, tuberculosis, and hepatitis B and C are major public health problems within America's correctional facilities. In 2000, 25,088 inmates in federal and state prisons were known to be infected with HIV/AIDS. In 2000, HIV/AIDS accounted for more than 6% of all deaths in federal and state prisons. Infection rates for other sexually transmitted diseases, tuberculosis, and hepatitis B and C are also far greater for prisoners than for the American population as a whole.

Drug and Alcohol Treatment

Substance abuse and dependency within the offender population is significant. Methamphetamine, cocaine, and alcohol abuse is very common in the offender populations. In a 2004 survey, Bureau of Justice Statistics reported nearly a third of state and a quarter of federal prisoners committed their offense under the influence of drugs. Over half of those offenders used drugs in the month before the offense, and more than two-thirds had used drugs regularly at some time in their lives. Marijuana remained the most common drug used by offenders. Forty percent of state prisoners reported using marijuana in the month before their offense, and 15% said they had used marijuana at the time of the offense.[1]

Progress has been made in institutional substance abuse treatment programs. When conducted properly and linked with education, job skills, and reintegration services, the treatment programs provide a valuable service to the offender.

Sexual Offender Treatment Programs

Among the most controversial treatment programs in corrections are the sexual offender treatment programs being presented in an effort to reduce recidivism in the sexual offender population. Few correctional issues capture the public's attention more than the dangers posed by sexual offenders. As a nation, sexual offender registration is required, but within the institution, correctional administrators struggle to ensure the majority of sexual offenders can live without undue threat within the institution's general population while also providing sexual treatment programs.

Sexual offender treatment programs and subsequent evaluations of those programs are very difficult to design and conduct. Most programs and their evaluations suffer from methodological deficiencies, such as lack of a controlled comparison to untreated offenders, inadequate measures of reoffense or recidivism, small samples, or inadequate follow-up periods. Many treatment professionals believe that treatment can help some offenders manage and control their sexual behaviors, even if deviant sexual arousal patterns such as attraction to children cannot be totally eliminated.

Initial estimates of a cost-benefit analysis of child sex offender treatment programs for male offenders in correctional services suggest that, within plausible parameters, the costs of such programs are likely to be more than compensated by the benefits that they produce.

Aging Offender Population

The National Institute of Corrections defines elderly inmates as those with a chronological age of 50 years or older. The tendency of inmates to engage in risky behaviors such as drug and alcohol abuse, combined with their lack of preventive healthcare, leads to an "early aging" of inmates. It is therefore not unusual to find inmates with health problems that are more common in persons 10 years older in the general population.

Like the general population, the inmate population is growing older. This demographic development is exacerbated by stiffer sentencing laws that keep inmates in prison longer. For the correctional administrator, the impact of an aging inmate population can be seen in the rising health-related costs. The health costs alone for housing an inmate age 50 or older are estimated as being almost four times that of a younger inmate.[2]

Geriatric inmates, many of whom are in poorer health to begin with, will continue to generate significant increases in healthcare costs. In addition to the costs for basic healthcare, states face rising expenses for dental health and mental health services. As corrections professionals begin to assess and address the unique needs of older inmates, it is expected that more comprehensive approaches will begin to emerge. Of the concepts being proposed by correctional professionals to policy makers in an effort to reduce the medical costs upon institutions of aging inmates, one is to identify ways to release terminally ill inmates who are low-security risks to hospice facilities. Another suggestion is the release of geriatric, special needs, and severely disabled inmates to secure private facilities.

Violence and Sexual Assault in Institutions

Correctional institutions can be dangerous for both the inmate and staff. The threat of physical or sexual assault and homicide are ever present. Prison rape undermines the public health by contributing to the spread of sexually transmitted diseases, and often giving a potential death sentence to its victims. A study of seven men's prisons in four midwestern states indicated that 21% of the surveyed inmates indicated they had experienced at least one episode of pressured or forced sexual contact since being incarcerated.

The high incidence of sexual assault within prisons involves actual and potential violations of the U.S. Constitution. In *Farmer v. Brennan*, 511 U.S. 825 (1994), the Supreme Court ruled that deliberate indifference to the substantial risk of sexual assault violates prisoners' rights under the Cruel and Unusual Punishments Clause of the Eighth Amendment. The Eighth Amendment rights of state and local prisoners are protected through the Due Process Clause of the 14th Amendment. Pursuant to the power of Congress under Section 5 of the 14th Amendment, Congress may take action to enforce those rights in states where officials have demonstrated such indifference. States that do not take basic steps to abate prison rape by adopting standards that do not generate significant additional expenditures demonstrate such indifference. Therefore, such states are not entitled to the same level of federal benefits as other states.

On September 4, 2003, President Bush signed the Prison Rape Elimination Act of 2003 that was enacted by Congress to address the problem of sexual abuse of persons in the custody of U.S. correctional agencies. The predominant concern of the supporters of the law was a focus on violent male-on-male inmate rape, primarily in the adult prison and jail settings. The addition of staff sexual misconduct with offenders as a component of the legislation placed correctional personnel on notice that sexual exploitation within the correctional setting could well result in criminal sanctions.

Prison Gangs

All correctional facilities deal to some degree with gang problems. Over the last several decades, the formation and growth of prison gangs have forced correctional administrators to reexamine security within their institutions. To a great extent, many of the prison gangs are extensions of criminal gangs that operate in the community. With arrest and incarceration, the gang member transitions from one element of the gang to another. For other gangs, especially gangs such as the Aryan Nations, the prison community provides a rich area for membership recruitment. Prison gangs are responsible for much of the crime and rule violations that occur within the facilities, to include violence and the black marketing of contraband. Operating on a foundation of inmate and staff intimidation, prison gangs remain a major concern for the correctional professional.

Women in Prison

Since 1995, the male inmate population has grown 32% while the female inmate population has increased 53%.

In 2004, there were 104,848 women incarcerated in U.S. prisons, according to the Bureau of Justice Statistic's prisoners in 2004 report. This represents about 7% of the total incarcerated population, up from 6.1% in 1995 and 5.7% in 1990.

The female inmate population faces challenges within the correctional setting unique to their male counterparts. Most incarcerated women are low income and frequently suffer drug addiction. Many have been convicted of drug-related offenses or for aiding in the support of a male, such as a boyfriend or husband, in their criminal activities.

Women and girls represent the largest growing population under correctional supervision. Studies report that between 40 and 88% of incarcerated women have been the victims of domestic violence and sexual or physical abuse prior to incarceration.[3]

National surveys of women prisoners find that three-fourths of them were mothers, with two-thirds having children under the age of 18. An estimated 4 to 9% of women come to prison pregnant. Women who give birth while incarcerated are rarely allowed to spend time with their child after birth. Women offenders are very likely to have an extensive history of drug and alcohol use. Women offenders often have specific health needs related to their risky sexual and drug using behavior prior to imprisonment.

Women in prison are also at risk for infectious diseases, including HIV, tuberculosis, sexually transmitted diseases, and hepatitis B and C infections. Pregnancy and reproductive health needs are another neglected area of healthcare. Problems of pregnant inmates include lack of prenatal and postnatal care, inadequate education regarding childbirth and parenting, and little or no preparation for the mother's separation from the infant after delivery.

Estimates suggest that 25 to 60% of the female prison population require mental health services. Estimates further suggest over 60% of female jail inmates had symptoms of drug abuse, and over 30% had signs of alcohol dependence.[4]

Privatization

Nationally, a private corrections industry has matured, creating the potential to align the innovation and efficiencies inherent to competitive service delivery with the public interest of safely housing and reforming both juvenile and adult offenders. As the cost of correctional services continues to increase, many states and the federal government have turned to private correctional corporations to provide a wide range of services, extending from specialized services to entire institutional operations. Some of the most commonly privatized services in corrections include medical services, mental health services, staff training, vocational training, food services, canteen and commissary, and recreational services.

Inmate Litigation

Inmate litigation has been an increasing problem and concern for corrections for the last three decades. By the 1960s, it was clear the conditions of our correctional institutions and the reluctance on the part of government to provide the vision and resources to improve those conditions had brought corrections to a crisis. As a result, inmate access to the courts, under the guarantees of the Eighth Amendment, opened the doors to extensive inmate-generated litigation challenging all aspects of correctional operations.

The 1964 *Cooper v. Pate* decision cleared the way for considerable freedom of religion in prisons. Following this decision, Nation of Islam ministers were permitted to conduct services in Stateville Penitentiary in Illinois, enabling black Muslims to practice their faith. Other Supreme Court decisions, such as *Procunier v. Martinez* (1974) and *Wolff v. McDonnell* (1974), virtually abolished the censorship of mail by prison officials. Furthermore, in the *Wolff* decision, the court offered the opinion that although prisoners had "diminished rights," they could not be "wholly stripped of constitutional protections" and the due process of the law.

By 1995, 25% of suits filed in federal district court were brought by inmates. While the first set of prison reform cases were litigated, later generations of prison reform cases were settled by consent decree.[4]

Congress passed the *Prison Litigation Reform Act*. A primary objective of the Prison Litigation Reform Act is to reduce the burden imposed by prisoner litigation upon the federal courts and the state governments that defend against such lawsuits. Congress clearly intended to reduce judicial involvement in the improvement of prison conditions and to stop federal courts from providing more than the constitutional minimum "necessary to remedy the proven violation of federal rights."[5]

Though the value and impact of inmate-generated litigation can be debated for decades, what is clear is that early inmate litigation forced correctional reform in a manner that could not otherwise be achieved. Unfortunately, much of the current inmate litigation is counterproductive to correctional operations. Much of the new wave of inmate litigation is of little value and draws valuable resources from the public sector, which is responsible for responding to the court action.

Breaking the Cycle of Recidivism

Though we have discussed the impact of recidivism upon corrections, the transition of the offender from prison to the community is an important issue in the eyes of the correctional administrator. The reentry movement has been premised on the notion that a transition process is needed that addresses both the survival needs, such as food, housing, and employment, and skill-based services, such as treatment, literacy, and job training, to thwart the recycling of offenders from prison to the community and back to prison. Addressing both survival and skill-based services is considered essential to securing reintegration in light of the traditional issues that offenders confront once entering the community, such as insufficient services, societal barriers to employment, and housing.

Summary

Correctional administrators struggle to provide and maintain safe institutions that are operated cost-efficiently. So much more than just walls and cells, correctional facilities are living communities, each with its own identity and facing the challenges that are unique to the institution itself. Increasing populations and ever-raising costs require that new and innovative alternatives to traditional confinement be discovered. It is up to our current and future correctional administrators, legislators, and policy makers to work together to shape the future of corrections.

Vocabulary

Closed communities

Confinement

Prison Litigation Reform Act

Discussion Questions

1. What are some ways in which rehabilitation of inmates can be facilitated?

2. Why is funding such an important and difficult aspect of corrections?

3. What are some ways in which you think funding issues can, or should be, addressed?

4. Overcrowding is a problem among correctional institutions. What are the consequences of this?

5. What is the significance of *Estelle v. Gamble*?

6. In your opinion, what is the largest health problem among inmates in correctional institutions?

7. Do you think having privatized services in corrections is a positive or negative idea? Why?

Notes

1. *Drug use and dependence, state and federal prisoners, 2004.* (2006, October). NCJ 213530.

2. Price, C.A. (2006) Aging Inmate Population Study, North Carolina Department of Corrections Division of Prisons.

3. Human Rights Watch. (1996). *All too familiar: Sexual abuse of women in U.S. state prisons.* New York, NY: Human Rights Watch.

4. Prisons: Prisons for women—Problems and unmet needs in the contemporary women's prison. http:law.jrank.org/pages/1805/prisons-prisons-women-problems-unmet-needs-in-contempo-rary-women-s-prison.html (accessed March 15, 2011).

5. Baradaran-Robison, S. (2003). Kaleidoscopic consent decrees: School desegregation and prison reform consent decrees after the Prison Litigation Reform Act and Freeman-Dowell. *Brigham Young University Law Review*, Vol. 2003, No. 227.

Inmate Rights and Correctional Law

National Prison Project is dedicated to ensuring that our nation's prisons, jails, juvenile facilities and immigration detention centers comply with the Constitution, federal law, and international human rights principles, and to addressing the crisis of over-incarceration in the U.S.

—ACLU

Introduction

Inmates are usually not born in prison. They come to be residents there as a result of their violation of some law, statute, resolution, or ordinance. They not only had to violate this rule, but they had to be prosecuted for and convicted of this violation in order to be placed into the penal system by a court order called a sentence. So, everyone that is an inmate in the American prison system has had a trial, been found guilty, and was sent there by the courts. The convicted lose their freedom and some, but not all, of their rights under the law and the Constitution.

The American correctional system is a part of the overall American judicial and legal system. Thus, all correctional policies and correctional practices are covered by two basic controlling factors: the law and the U.S. Constitution. Some of the laws are statutory, and these laws usually govern the structure and organization of the department of corrections in each state. Much of the law that corrections officials have to deal with is called case law and is a result of rulings by the courts.

These legal rulings have evolved over time to paint a picture of what can or cannot be done by correctional officials in the operations of their correctional institutions. The rulings by the courts are usually based on the 1st, 4th, 5th 6th, 8th, and 14th Amendments of the U.S. Constitution (Table 10.1). The government's defenses, legal justifications, and claims of immunity are usually based on the 10th Amendment. Thus, a person wishing to understand correctional law and inmate rights should know these amendments and what they contain.

History of Correctional Law

In the study of prisoner rights one must first grasp the concept of civil death or *civiliter mortuus*. Under common and civil law, *civil death* referred to the loss of almost all civil rights by those who were convicted of a felony or were declared civilly dead by a government. Civil death was provided by statute in many states and involves the imposition of numerous disabilities, including the denial of the privilege to vote, to hold public office, and to obtain or retain many jobs and occupational licenses. Offenders could not enter into contracts and were often deprived of their right to engage in lawsuits. The spouse of the offender who was declared civilly dead could remarry in many states.

In an 1871 Virginia case (*Ruffin v. Commonwealth*), the courts found that a prisoner was a "slave of the state" and had no rights.[2] This type of penalty was reserved for those under sentence of death or serving a life term in some states. In others, the offender need only be a felon (i.e., Alabama or New York).[3] Upon release of the offender from confinement, civil death often continued unless legally relieved by a *writ of de libertatirus allococandis* by the courts.[4]

Since the convicted prisoner was separated from civil society not only physically but legally, the offenders had few, if any, rights for almost the first 100 years of the republic. The prisons were run by the states. The states were considered to be immune from lawsuits by their protection under the 10th Amendment of the Constitution (absolute immunity), and this is reflected in most state statutes. This immunity and the civil death of the prison inmates led to a so-called *hands-off doctrine* by the courts that lasted until the 1960s.[5]

Beginning in the 1960s the federal courts began to reexamine the hands-off doctrine and allow certain lawsuits against both the state and federal governments if the prisoner could demonstrate a

TABLE 10.1: CONSTITUTIONAL AMENDMENTS THAT AFFECT CORRECTIONS

Amendment	Text
1st	Congress shall make no law respecting an establishment of religion, or prohibiting the free exercise thereof; or abridging the freedom of speech, or of the press; or the right of the people peaceably to assemble, and to petition the Government for a redress of grievances.
4th	The right of the people to be secure in their persons, houses, papers, and effects, against unreasonable searches and seizures, shall not be violated, and no Warrants shall issue, but upon probable cause, supported by Oath or affirmation, and particularly describing the place to be searched, and the persons or things to be seized.
5th	No person shall be held to answer for a capital, or otherwise infamous crime, unless on a presentment or indictment of a Grand Jury, except in cases arising in the land or naval forces, or in the Militia, when in actual service in time of War or public danger; nor shall any person be subject for the same offence to be twice put in jeopardy of life or limb; nor shall be compelled in any criminal case to be a witness against himself, nor be deprived of life, liberty, or property, without due process of law; nor shall private property be taken for public use, without just compensation.
6th	In all criminal prosecutions, the accused shall enjoy the right to a speedy and public trial, by an impartial jury of the State and district wherein the crime shall have been committed, which district shall have been previously ascertained by law, and to be informed of the nature and cause of the accusation; to be confronted with the witnesses against him; to have compulsory process for obtaining witnesses in his favor, and to have the Assistance of Counsel for his defence.
8th	Excessive bail shall not be required, nor excessive fines imposed, nor cruel and unusual punishments inflicted.
10th	The powers not delegated to the United States by the Constitution, nor prohibited by it to the States, are reserved to the States respectively, or to the people.
14th, Section 1	The powers not delegated to the United States by the Constitution, nor prohibited by it to the States, are reserved to the States respectively, or to the people.[1]

constitutional violation. This led to modification by the courts of the absolute immunity standard and the adoption of qualified immunity for actions taken during the course of one's official duties. Lawsuits were now permitted against prison officials under the provisions of 42 USC 1983.[6]

The legal floodgates were now opened and a wave of inmate lawsuits began to inundate the courts across the United States. Inmate legal rights would become a major legal issue for corrections officials the next 50 years. That trend continues to this day.[7] Since 1976, the general standard of proof that the inmate must show is that the prison authorities acted with "deliberate indifference" to the inmate's legally protected rights or medical needs.[8]

Inmate Access to the Courts (First Amendment)

Even before the courts began to modify the hands-off doctrine, the courts demanded that inmates must be allowed unfettered access to the courts. Prior to 1941, in the state of Michigan, inmate petitions and pleadings to the courts had to be examined by prison officials for "accuracy and completeness." If they were correct, they were forwarded to the court; if not, they were returned to the inmate for correction. Keep in mind that in 1941, when this case was decided, the average person entering the U.S. army as a draftee had an eighth grade education.

The courts ruled that the inmate's petitions must be forwarded to the courts without examination or review, and that the courts would decide the merit of the inmate's legal pleading.[9] In a 1961 case from the Iowa State Penitentiary, the court ruled that legal filing fees by indigent prisoners were also waived by the courts (*in forma pauperis*) and the inmates were allowed to file *pro se* (without attorney) litigation.[10]

The next issue that the court spoke out on was: Could inmates use the services of a more literate or legally knowledgeable inmate to assist them in preparing their legal pleadings and working on their legal case before the courts? Most prisons had regulations against using these *jailhouse lawyers*, citing security and association reasons. In one Tennessee case (*Johnson v. Avery*) the appeals court even held that the practice of law should be limited to licensed attorneys. The Supreme Court noted that many inmates are illiterate and need assistance in preparing their legal papers, and that the fundamental access of prisoners to the courts could not be denied or obstructed. However, prisons could regulate whether or not the jailhouse lawyer would receive any compensation from the inmate and where these activities could be conducted. They could not, however, totally eliminate them.[11]

After 1977, correctional institutions were required to provide a law library and inmate access to the library so that the inmates could perfect their appeals. However, the size and content of these law libraries has been the subject of much debate. Inmates are not allowed unlimited access to the law library, and the amount of time spent there by inmates may be regulated by corrections authorities.[12]

Inmate Mail and Other Communications (First Amendment)

Inmate mail is a major source of contraband in a penal institution. Therefore, the prison authorities have a legitimate penalogical security interest in making sure contraband is not smuggled in to the inmates. While inmate mail may be regulated, examined, and the amounts of mail in the inmate's possession regulated, it cannot be totally prohibited.[7,13] As a general rule, outgoing inmate mail is not searched or censored without a legitimate reason.[14] An example of legitimate regulation of mail by prison authorities would include banning the receipt of materials by inmates that could aid an escape attempt or banning pornography for sex offenders. An inmate could not mail order a weapon or materials to build a weapon.[5,15] Inmates may also be prohibited in their receipt of mail from certain individuals or in sending mail to certain individuals (i.e., victims, witnesses, etc.).

Legal mail has a certain privileged status. Outgoing legal mail from inmates to the courts may not be censored, read, or refused delivery.[16] Incoming legal mail that is properly marked as legal mail coming from an attorney also enjoys certain privileges and may not be read or censored by prison authorities. However, in order to prevent smuggling or the receipt of contraband by inmates, prison authorities may require the inmate to open the legal mail in the presence of the prison officers for the sole purpose of determining if any contraband is contained in the envelope. Officers are forbidden to read the legal correspondence contained in the envelope.[17]

Prison officials may regulate inmate's communication by telephone. Most telephone calls that are placed by the inmate are collect calls and may be monitored by prison officials. Calls to attorneys are an exception to this rule and may not be monitored by prison officials as a general rule without a search warrant from the courts.

Religion (First Amendment)

For the most part, government usually does not get involved in religious matters. This has been a cornerstone of the First Amendment since 1789. However, in the 1960s some African Americans who followed Elijah Muhammad and the Nation of Islam (NOI) began to sue the prison systems for the right to have religious services, possess religious artifacts, pursue religious instruction, and receive a religious diet. The rulings by the various state courts were mixed. Prison officials cited security concerns and the involvement of various NOI members in gang and other criminal acts within the prisons.[5] However, many of the same concerns were expressed in the case of *Cruz v. Beto* (who claimed to be a Buddhist).

The Supreme Court ruled that the First Amendment protected all religions, not just the popular ones.[18] In 1972, this led to the Supreme Court ruling in *O'Lone v. Shabazz* that although the prisoners had a constitutional right to practice their religion (Muslim), the prison officials had a right to regulate that practice in furtherance of a legitimate penological objective.[19]

In 1993, Congress passed Public Law 103-141, the *Religious Freedom Restoration Act of 1993* (RFRA; 42 USC 2000bb). The law opened the floodgates to all sorts of inmate religious activity, some of which was of questionable religious value. Some white and black extremist groups began to meet and conduct their activities under the guise of religious meetings inside the institution. When the prison officials objected to the nonreligious portion of their activities, the inmates sued. The RFRA was declared unconstitutional in 1997.[20]

To correct the problems in the RFRA, in 2000 Congress passed the Religious Land Use and Institutionalized Persons Act (RLUIPA).[21] This required prison officials to use the least restrictive methods of supervision of religious groups in their custody unless the prison officials could demonstrate a compelling governmental interest for the restriction. In 2005, a Satanist, a Wiccan, two members of Asatru (Norse/Germanic paganism), and a member of Church of Jesus Christ Christian (white supremacist) religions sued the Ohio prison system for the right to practice their religions in the prison system. The court found that RLUIPA did not differentiate between various bona fide faiths. However, the court did recognize the institutional needs of order, discipline, and security.[22]

Most prisons provide a specialized religious diet when membership in a faith requires it (i.e., no pork for members of the Jewish or Islamic faiths). Other issues that have arisen revolve around personal appearance, name changes, access to clergy (and just who is qualified to act as clergy), and access to religious mail (especially when the religious group advocates hatred or violence against another group).[13]

Visitation and Association Rights of Inmates (First Amendment)

An inmate must have access to the courts. Therefore, legal visits are protected under *Procunier v. Martinez*.[14] Attorneys and their attendant paralegals and law students are allowed almost unlimited visitation with inmates to work on their cases.

The right of an inmate to contact or be interviewed by the news media has also been a subject of inmate suits. While total contact may not be prohibited, it may be severely regulated by correctional officials. Inmates do not have a right to face-to-face interviews on demand by the media or the inmate.[23] The courts have held that news organizations have no special "constitutional right of access to individual interviews with inmates beyond that afforded the general public."[24]

Prison officials have the right to regulate visits between inmates with friends and relatives. In-custody visits are usually either contact (where the inmate may be in the same room and even allowed to touch the visitor) or noncontact (where the visitor or the inmate are separated by glass and must speak over a telephone). The main penal concern is security and the passage of contraband. Prison officials often monitor these and other communications between prisoners and those on the outside (except legal communications with attorneys). Prison and jail officials may search incoming visitors and prohibit those who are under the influence of alcohol or drugs. Prison officials may also prohibit those visitors that misbehave while inside the institution.[23,25] Some states allow conjugal visits as an earned privilege for prisoners, but there is no constitutional right to such visits.[26]

Search, Seizure, and Inmate Privacy (Fourth Amendment)

With few exceptions, inmate privacy ends at the prison door. The law addresses two separate issues involving searches of persons and searches of cells. Looking at the issue of prison officials searching inmate cells, the court listed the institution's need for security and safety within the institution. In 1984, the Supreme Court found in the case of *Hudson v. Palmer*:

Notwithstanding our caution in approaching claims that the Fourth Amendment is inapplicable in a given context, we hold that society is not prepared to recognize as legitimate any subjective expectation of privacy that a prisoner might have in his prison cell and that, accordingly, the Fourth Amendment proscription against unreasonable searches does not apply within the confines of the prison cell. The recognition of privacy rights for prisoners in their individual cells simply cannot be reconciled with the concept of incarceration and the needs and objectives of penal institutions.[27]

Searches of the inmate's body are somewhat more complicated. Pat-down searches of clothed prisoners by same-sex officers has been held as constitutional. Cross-sex pat-down searches by an officer of the opposite sex have been approved by the courts in some cases, but in other cases they have been ruled to be inappropriate. In *Timm v. Gunter*, a male inmate complained about being pat searched by female correctional officers.[28]

Strip searches are another matter. Strip searches are generally confined to felony suspects/prisoners, or the officers must have probable cause to believe the inmate is in possession of contraband. The strip search must be conducted by same-sex officers and out of view of members of the opposite sex, except in emergencies.[29] The need for a body cavity search often elicits a higher standard and, depending on circumstances, may require a warrant.[30]

Inmate Discipline and Due Process (5th and 14th Amendments)

How do you keep discipline among those who by their very nature are rule breakers? This is the critical issue in dealing with inmate discipline cases. Inmate discipline often invokes claims of violations of the 5th and 14th Amendments by prison officials. The result of inmate disciplinary hearings can mean solitary confinement, loss of privileges, and loss of good time in many states. Inmates were even beaten in many states (including Arkansas and Mississippi) until the late 1960s.[31] Inmates are provided an inmate handbook in most institutions that outlines the institutional rules of the prison and, in some cases, the jail.

Out of the case law that has emerged from the courts on this issue, several rules have been imposed by the courts onto the jails and prisons. Inmates may not be punished by other inmates.[7] Inmates may only be punished for violating a specific rule or regulation. Inmates must be given notice (usually written) of what specific regulation they violated. Inmates may be entitled to a disciplinary hearing to determine if they in fact were guilty of violation of the rule in question. The standard of proof in disciplinary hearings is generally "some evidence" or *preponderance of evidence*. At a hearing, an inmate can call witnesses on his or her behalf. Inmates are not automatically entitled to counsel in institutional disciplinary hearings.[17,32]

Other Due Process Issues: Classification, Transfers, Personal Injuries, and Property Loss (5th and 14th Amendments)

Classification is a process that jail and prison officials use to determine the security custody status of inmates in their custody. Inmate classification is based on several factors: age of the offender, offense, special needs of the offender, security threat group (gang) affiliation, and so on. Classification is important to inmates because it can affect their housing assignments, institutions in which they are sent to serve their sentences, privileges within the institution, inmate work assignments, eligibility for participation inmate programs, and so on. In short, classification materially affects the conditions of inmate confinement or transfers.

Classification can change based upon inmate behavior. In 1975, the court declared in *Kelly v. Brewer* that the classification system used by the penal institution must be "rational and reasonable rather than arbitrary and capricious." Classifications should have the capability of being reviewed periodically.[33] Inmate transfers between institutions have been the subjects of numerous lawsuits. The courts have ruled that a prisoner is not entitled to due process before transfer, except when the inmate is being classified as mentally ill.[34]

Sometimes inmate property is lost or destroyed within the institution. Most states have a process that addresses that within the institution. Some inmates have chosen to sue the institution, rather than using the existing process for reimbursement. The Supreme Court has ruled that the inmate must use any existing process provided by the state to resolve his or her claim of property loss. However, if the state does not have a process, then the inmate may begin a tort action in the federal courts.[35]

Inmates who have suffered personal injuries have sued their captors and the institution. The key in these lawsuits seems to be the amount of negligence that an inmate can demonstrate occurred. The courts have ruled that simple negligence does not evoke the due process clause. However, the courts have also ruled that prison officials must take reasonable steps to protect inmates from injury or a known threat.[36]

Conditions of Imprisonment: Cruel and Unusual Punishment (Eighth Amendment)

When one considers cruel and unusual punishment under the Eighth Amendment, one must consider what was considered to be cruel and unusual in 1789 when the Constitution was signed. Whippings of inmates using a lash or bullwhip were not considered to be cruel and unusual. The U.S. military and naval forces routinely whipped convicted soldiers and sailors until the late 1870s.

In fact, Delaware still publically whipped convicted misdemeanants as late as 1962. The Arkansas state correctional system still whipped inmates as a disciplinary measure until the late 1960s. Mississippi DOC did the same until 1971.[31] The U.S. military and naval force routinely branded deserters and cowards with a branding iron on the face or forehead until the late 1870s. This was not considered to be cruel or unusual; in fact, it was considered to be merciful as opposed to the alternative, which was death by firing squad or hanging.

In the late 1960s the courts began to look at the conditions of confinement within the prisons. As mentioned above, the courts began to limit or ban corporal punishment of inmates, ban inmates punishing other inmates, and impose due process requirements on disciplinary procedures for inmates. Another area that the courts began to define was the use of solitary confinement, isolation, or administrative segregation by prison authorities. While the court did not prohibit the use of such measures, it began to restrict how they were used and for how long such measures could be used on an inmate.[37] The use of excessive force by prison staff against inmates can cause a claim of a constitutional violation.[47]

Prison overcrowding has been an issue for decades within the correctional community. Prison overcrowding can result in dangerous or inhumane living conditions for both the inmates and the prison staff. It boils down to the taxpayers and legislature demanding that more and more people are sentenced to confinement as a way to control crime. But on the other hand, the legislature (and because of how things are paid for, the taxpayers) wants to restrict budgets to pay for the incarceration of inmates. The various wars on drugs and mandatory sentences for even such simple crimes as driving while intoxicated have resulted in the massive overcrowding of most prison facilities.

The courts have ordered the states to build more prison bed space, find alternatives to incarceration, or release prisoners until they are within limits. The states have replied by doing all three at various times. None of the solutions are popular, and none fully solve the problem.[38]

Some of the most frequent arguments invoking the Eighth Amendment have centered around the death penalty. Most of the arguments have concentrated on sentencing issues in the courts and are not a part of the discussion in a corrections text. However, some arguments, such as death row conditions, are under the control of corrections officials. Death row inmates must be treated in a humane way right up to the time the state executes them.[39] The death penalty itself has been ruled to be constitutional.[5] However, many arguments about who is sentenced to death and how are valid for a courts or legal issues text because correctional officials have no control over those aspects and only can carry out the sentences of the courts.

Healthcare (Eighth Amendment)

The Supreme Court has ruled that the government must provide healthcare to the people that it has imprisoned. If prison officials act with deliberate indifference to an inmate's health needs, they may be sued.[40] However, this does not mean that inmates may receive medications (prescribed or their choice) on demand. The decision of what (if any) treatment is needed is left up to prison medical authorities. The prison authorities have a duty to take precautions in the case of inmates with infectious diseases and to try and prevent inmate suicides.

The issue of whether an inmate can be treated involuntarily has also been a subject of court attention. This issue has arisen in the treatment of the many mentally ill inmates within the correctional system, or if the inmate is unconscious or uncooperative. Because of the court's 1992 findings in *Riggins v. Nevada*, that a person has the constitutionally protected right to refuse medication (in this case it was antipsychotic drugs), a court order is usually required to administer medication for inmates who refuse or are uncooperative. Unconscious inmates are dealt with using existing medical protocols for those patients in similar circumstances on the outside of the penal system.[41] These issues are becoming more and more complicated due to aging inmates.

Female Inmates and Other Special Inmate Populations (14th Amendment)

Female inmates pose special problems within the prison system. These problems stem from the fact that there are fewer of them, fewer places to put them, and fewer programs available for them. This combined with special health needs that are in excess of the average male inmate population's (due to pregnancy, access to abortion care, a higher STD and addiction rate, a higher rate of prior sexual abuse, and a higher rate of mental illness) sometimes leads to a discrepancy on what is available to a male or female inmate. Changes in the sentencing laws and the results of the drug wars that began in the 1980s have flooded the correctional systems with female prisoners.[42]

With the advent of cross-gender supervision in the male institutions came the problem of cross-gender supervision of inmates in the female institutions. The courts have ruled that female inmates have a reasonable expectation of privacy not to be seen nude by officers of the opposite sex except in emergencies.[43] Classification problems arise in some female institutions because of overcrowding and lack of bed space.[44] Another issue arises in where to place transgendered inmates. Do they go in custody with their original sex or their new sex?[45]

The most frequent area of female inmate complaints and lawsuits is the lack of inmate programs for females compared to male inmates. This has arisen nationwide because of the number of male inmates incarcerated versus females. The courts have not yet ruled that male programs must be either closed or equalized with female programs. In fact, in *Archer v. Reno* the federal courts ruled there was no constitutional right to be rehabilitated, and the female inmates had no special right to be in any particular program.[46]

Inmate Labor

According to Mushlin, "Prisoners lack a constitutional right to choose whether to work." This is an exception contained in the 13th Amendment to the involuntary servitude clause. However, an inmate must be convicted of a crime before he or she can be forced to labor on behalf of the state or others.[13] Inmates may be disciplined for refusal to work, and they have no constitutional right to choose the particular job they are assigned. Inmates may be paid for their labor, but they are not covered under the minimum wage laws or the Fair Labor Standards Act. There are federal laws that restrict the use and interstate transport of prison-made goods.

Summary

Correctional facilities are the only hotel where the innkeeper (jail and prison official) has no control over the front or back doors. The courts decide who comes into the facility and who leaves (and when they can checkout). Prisoners must be treated fairly and humanely. This does not mean they (the prisoners) are necessarily happy about being there or the accommodations offered for their stay. Thus, lawsuits in a prison or jail are inevitable. Correctional officials must train their employees in the law of corrections, proper procedures to dealing with inmates, and inmate rights. Jail and prison officials have a defense of qualified immunity against lawsuits provided their actions were taken within clearly established constitutional law at the time of their actions. However, qualified immunity does not apply to intentional violations by correctional staff.[47]

Vocabulary

Civil death

Hands-off doctrine

Jailhouse lawyer

Preponderance of evidence

Religious Freedom Restoration Act of 1993

Discussion Questions

1. What is meant by the hands-off doctrine?

2. What constitutional amendments are most cited by prisoners claiming rights? What rights are associated with each of the amendments?

3. How do male inmates' rights compare to the rights of female inmates?

Notes

1. U.S. Constitution. Retrieved June 3, 2010, from http://www. archives.gov/exhibits/charters/bill_of_rights_transcript.html

2. *Quick v. Western Ry. of Alabama*, 207 Ala. 376; *Holmes v. King*, 216 Ala. 412; *Ruffin v. Commonwealth*, 62 Va. (21 Gratt.) 790 (1871).

3. Civil Death in New York State. Retrieved June 4, 2010, from http://civildeathinnewyorkstate.com/

4. Black, H. (1968). *Black's law dictionary* (4th ed.). St. Paul, MN: West.

5. Cripe, C., & Pearlman, M. (2005). *Legal aspects of correctional management*. Sudbury, MA: Jones and Bartlett.

6. 42 USC 1983. Retrieved June 4, 2010, from http://www.law. cornell.edu/uscode/html/uscode42/usc_sec_42_00001983----000-.html

7. Omodt, D. (1983). *Inmate's legal rights* (rev. ed.). Washington, DC: National Sheriff's Association.

8. Vaughn, M. (1993). *"Deliberate indifference": An analysis of Supreme Court standard in prison civil liability claims for medication distribution and inmate on inmate assault*. Huntsville, TX: Sam Houston University.

9. *Ex Parte Hull*, 312 U.S. 546 (1941).

10. *Smith v. Bennett*, 365 U.S. 708 (1961); *Lane v. Brown*, 372 U.S. 477 (1963).

11. *Johnson v. Avery*, 393 U.S. 483 (1969); *Cross v. Powers*, 328 F.Supp. 899 (W.D. Wisc. 1971); *Shaw v. Murphy*, 532 U.S. 223 (2001).

12. *Younger v. Gilmore*, 404 U.S. 15 (1971) (Per Curiam); *Bounds v. Smith*, 430 U.S. 817 (1977); *Lewis v. Casey*, 518 U.S. 343 (1996).

13. Mushlin, M. (2002). *Rights of prisoners* (Vols. 1–3, 3rd ed.). St. Paul, MN: Thompson/West.

14. *Procunier v. Martinex*, 416 U.S. 396 (1974); *Turner v. Safley*, 482 U.S. 78 (1987); *Procunier v. Navarette*, 434 U.S. 555 (1978).

15. *Thornburgh v. Abbott*, 490 U.S. 401 (1989).

16. *Carothers v. Follette*, 314 F.Supp. 1014 (S.D. N.Y. 1970).

17. *Wolff v. McDonnell*, 418 U.S. 539 (1974).

18. *Cruz v. Beto*, 405 U.S. 319 (1972).

19. *O'Lone v. Shabazz*, 482 U.S. 342 (1987).

20. *City of Boerne v. Flores*, 521 U.S. 507 (1997).

21. 42 USC 2000 cc-1.

22. *Cutter v. Wilkinson*, 544 U.S. 709 (2005).

23. *Pell V. Procunier*, 417 U.S. 817 (1974).

24. *Saxbe v. Washington Post Co.*, 417 U.S. 843 (1974).

25. *Block v. Rutherford*, 468 U.S. 576 (1984); *Kentucky Department of Corrections v. Thompson*, 490 U.S. 454 (1989); *Lanza V. New York*, 370 U.S. 139 (1962); *United States v. Hearst*, 563 F.2d 1331 (9th Cir. 1977).

26. *Payne v. District of Columbia*, 253 F.2d 867 (D.C. Cir. 1958); *Lyons v. Gilligan*, 382 F.Supp. 198 (N.D. Ohio, 1974).

27. *Hudson v. Palmer*, 468 U.S. 517 (1984).

28. *Bell v. Wolfish*, 441 U.S. 520 (1979); *Watson v. Jones*, 980 F.2d 1165 (8th Cir. 1992); *Timm v. Gunter*, 917 F.2d 1093 (8th Cir. 1990).

29. *Kennedy v. Los Angeles Police Department*, 901 F.2d 702 (9th Cir. 1989); *Goff v. Nix*, 803 F.2d 358 (8th Cir. 1968).

30. *People v. West*, 170 Cal. App. 3d 326 (5th Dist. 1985); *Michenfelder v. Sumner*, 860 F.2d 328 (9th Cir. 1988); *Zunker v. Bertrand*, 798 F.Supp. 1365 (E.D. Wis. 1992).

31. *Jackson v. O E Bishop Ernst*, 404 F.2d 571 (8th Cir, 1968); *Gates v. Collier*, 501 F.2d 1291 (5th Cir. 1972).

32. *Sandin v. Conner*, 515 U.S. 472 (1995); *Baxter v. Palmigiano*, 425 U.S. 308 (1976); *Superintendent v. Hill*, 472 U.S. 445 (1985).

33. *Kelly v. Brewer*, 525 F.2d 394 (8th Cir. 1975); *Doe v. Lally*, 467 F.Supp. 1339 (D. Md., 1979); *Farmer v. Brennan*, 511 U.S. 825 (1994); *Riley v. Johnson*, 528 F.Supp. 333 (E.D. Mich., 1981).

34. *Meachum v. Fano*, 427 U.S. 215 (1976); *Vitek v. Jones*, 445 U.S. 480 (1980); *Kansas v. Hendricks*, 521 U.S. 346 (1997); *Kansas v. Crane*, 534 U.S. 407 (2002).

35. *Parratt v. Taylor*, 451 U.S. 527 (1981).

36. *Daniels v. Williams*, 474 U.S. 327 (1986); *Davidson v. Cannon*, 474 U.S. 344 (1986).

37. *Wright v. McMann*, 387 F.2d 519 (2nd Cir., 1967); *Davis v. Lindsay*, 321 F.Supp. 1134 (S.D. N.Y. 1970).

38. *Bell v. Wolfish*, 441 U.S. 520 (1979); *Rhodes v. Chapman*, 452 U.S. 337 (1981); *Whitley v. Albers*, 475 U.S. 312 (1986); *Wilson v. Seiter*, 501 U.S. 294 (1991).

39. *In re Medley*, 134 U.S. 160 (1890); *Sinclair v. Henderson*, 331 F.Supp. 1123 (E.D. La. 1971).

40. *Estelle v. Gamble*, 429 U.S. 97 (1976); *West v. Atkins*, 487 U.S. 42 (1988).

41. *Washington v. Harper*, 494 U.S. 210 (1990); *Riggins v. Nevada*, 504 U.S. 127 (1992).

42. Bloom, B., Johnson, J., & Belzer, E. (2003, September/October). Effective management of female offenders: Applying research on gender-responsive correctional strategies to local jails. *American Jails*; *Gibson v. Matthews*, 926 F. 2d 532 (1991).

43. *Bowling v. Enomoto*, 514 F.Supp. 201 (N.D. Calif. 1981).

44. *Batton v. State Government of North Carolina*, 501 F.Supp. 1173 (E.D. N.C. 1980).

45. *Crosby v. Reynolds*, 763 F.Supp. 666 (D. Me. 1991); *Farmer v. Brennan*, 511 U.S. 825 (1994).

46. *Archer v. Reno*, 877 F.Supp. 372 (E.D. Ky. 1995).

47. *Clevenger v. Saxner*, 474 U.S. 193, 206 (1985); *Hope v. Pelzer*, 536 U.S. 730 (2002).

Victims' Rights

Unfortunately, new and important concerns for victims remain
mere beginnings, veritable drops in the bucket, when compared to
the needs. Victims still remain peripheral to the justice process.
In the legal process, victims represent footnotes to the crime.

—Howard Zehr

Introduction

While the crime victim is a vital part of the criminal justice system,
until the 1970s victims were rarely recognized in our nation's laws
and policies. Since then, victim services and victims' rights legislation have developed at the national and state levels. The *crime victim*
is anyone who is injured or killed due to a violation of the criminal
law.[1] A parent or guardian is considered the crime victim if the actual
victim is below 18 years of age or is incompetent. Similarly, a victim
may be family members and friends, if the actual victim is deceased
or incapacitated. The *National Crime Victimization Survey* (*NCVS*) is
the nation's primary source of information on criminal victimization.

Each year, data are obtained from a nationally representative
sample of 76,000 households comprising nearly 135,300 persons on
the frequency, characteristics, and consequences of criminal victimization in the United States. The NCVS provides the largest national
forum for victims to describe the impact of crime and characteristics
of violent offenders. According to the NCVS, in 2008 U.S. residents age
12 or older were victims of 21 million crimes. A little over 16 million
(76%) were victims of property crimes; 23% or 4.9 million involved

crimes of violence and 136,700 (1%) were personal thefts. Murders were the least frequent violent victimization, with approximately 6 murder victims per 100,000 persons in 2007.[2] This chapter discusses the history of the crime victims' movement in the United States, the various types of victims, the costs that crime victims suffer, and the role correctional agencies play in meeting victims' needs.

History of the Crime Victims' Movement in the United States

There are three major eras associated with the crime victims' movement: The *dark age*, *golden age*, and reemergence of the *victim age*.[3] The dark ages, or medieval time frame, was an era when victims were used simply as witnesses for arresting and prosecuting offenders. Their involvement ended at the conclusion of the trial, and they had no say in the sentencing process. During the golden age, victims acquired some rights, including a personal say in imposing punishments on apprehended offenders. The Code of Hammurabi developed in 1750 by the king of Babylon is an example of the golden age when the government assumed a duty to the crime victim. The code established certain obligations and objectives for the citizens of Babylon to follow. The government assumed the need to protect the weaker from the stronger. For instance, widows were to be protected from those who might exploit them, elder parents were protected from sons who would disown them, and lesser officials were protected from higher ones. Crime victims were to be made as whole as possible, and in turn, they were required to forgive vengeance against their offender. In reality, this code may have been the first victims' rights statute in history. Unfortunately, not all societies assumed a duty to the crime victim. Many began to neglect victims in their rush to punish the offender, with the result that victims' rights would not resurface until the twentieth century. During the 1950s and 1960s, the system clearly emphasized offender rehabilitation, giving little attention to the suffering of crime victims. However, by the mid-1970s, when jurisdictions initiated the first victim/witness assistance projects, the pendulum shifted gradually toward providing fewer rehabilitation services to convicted felons and more services to innocent crime victims and witnesses.

Beginning in the 1970s, the reemergence of the victim age produced a resurgence of efforts intended to assist crime victims. Throughout the past four decades, crime victims in the United States have observed a number of changes in their rights. The feminist movement of the 1960s laid the foundation for the initial victims' rights movement. Feminists argued for laws holding the criminal justice system responsible for reducing violence, especially in cases of rape and domestic assault.[3]

To garner support for their initiative, the State of California conducted the first national victims' survey in 1965. The survey results eventually legitimized the victims' rights movement during the 1970s. Criminal justice professionals began to recognize that insensitive treatment of victims and witnesses led to a lack of cooperation on the part of victims and witnesses and ultimately caused criminal prosecutions to fail. As a result, the Law Enforcement Assistance Administration (LEAA) established start-up funds for many states to develop victim/witness programs.[3]

The first victim assistance programs were created in prosecutors' offices in St. Louis, Missouri; San Francisco, California; and Washington, D.C., and were developed to overcome the emotional anxiety and trauma associated with testifying in court. The victim assistance programs encouraged witness cooperation in the filing of criminal charges, as well as testifying in court. The programs also provided secure and comfortable reception areas for witnesses waiting to testify in court, transportation services, and advocates to accompany witnesses to court to interpret court proceedings. In addition to victim assistance programs, the first victim impact statement was created by a Fresno County, California, probation officer to provide the sentencing judge with a list of victim injuries prior to sentencing. The National Organization for Victim Assistance (NOVA) was established in 1975 as a national advocacy and support group by citizen activists to expand victim services and increase recognition of victims' rights. More substantively, the first legislation mandating arrest in domestic violence cases was enacted in Oregon in 1975, and the National Coalition Against Sexual Assault (NCASA) was formed to promote services for sexual violence survivors.[3]

As momentum increased, the first Bill of Rights for crime victims was enacted in Wisconsin in 1980, and President Ronald Reagan commemorated National Victim Rights Week for the first time in 1981. Considered the Marshall Plan of the victims' movement, the *Victims of Crime Act* (VOCA) was passed in 1984. VOCA created the Crime Victims Fund as a nontaxpayer funding source for services to help victims cope with the trauma and aftermath of crime. The monies used to fund VOCA are generated from various federal criminal fines, forfeitures, assessments, and penalties. None of the money used by VOCA is derived from taxpayer appropriations. Although annual amounts have varied considerably, over $5 billion has been deposited in the VOCA account since its inception in 1985.[4] According to the National Coalition Against Domestic Violence and National Alliance to End Sexual Violence, all 50 states, the District of Columbia, Puerto Rico, and the Virgin Islands depend on Crime Victim Funds to assist more than 4 million crime victims each year.[5] All the money deposited into the Crime Victim Fund is used to support a variety of services to crime victims at the federal, state, and local levels. Most of the funds are distributed by formula grants to states that use those funds to provide financial support to local direct victim service providers, such as domestic violence shelters, rape crisis centers, and victim/witness assistance programs, as well as direct compensation to crime victims.[4]

The 1990s witnessed the passing of landmark federal legislation. One of the more noteworthy was the *Violence Against Women Act* (VAWA). At the time, VAWA was the most significant legislation in the victims' rights field since the creation of VOCA. This act doubled the maximum federal sentences for sex offenses and domestic violence and required that temporary restraining orders (TROs) be honored by all other jurisdictions. Domestic violence perpetrators with TROs were prohibited from possessing firearms. For the first time, information shared by domestic violence and rape victims with an advocate was considered to be privileged communication. This act also established the Office of Violence Against Women and doubled the available funding for domestic violence and rape counseling programs. Also, in 1996, Congress passed Megan's law, the *Community Notification Act*, as an amendment to the national Child Sexual Abuse Registry legislation. This law required that local communities be notified of the residential addresses of convicted sex offenders. In 1996, the Antiterrorism and Effective Death Penalty Act included the Mandatory Victims' Restitution Act, mandating limited types of restitution in all federal misdemeanor and felony cases. Compensation and victim assistance services for victims of terrorism both at home and abroad, including victims in the military, were expanded.[5]

An explosion of legislation occurred at the start of the new millennium. The *Trafficking Victims Protection Act of 2000* was enacted to combat the trafficking of persons, especially into the sex trade, slavery, and slavery-like conditions. The act provided for prevention, prosecution, and enforcement against traffickers and increased the protection, assistance, and mandatory restitution for victims. Similarly, the VAWA of 2000 provided for direct federal compensation to victims of international terrorism. This act improved and expanded the legal tools and programs addressing domestic violence, sexual assault, and stalking. It authorized new grant programs expanding both programs and research for sexual assault and domestic violence. Even the USA Patriot Act of 2001 addressed the needs and concerns of victims of terrorists' acts. The act allowed the Office for Victims of Crime (OVC) director to respond to both internal and external acts of terrorism against the United States. It established an antitesrrorism emergency reserve in the Crime Victims Fund and increased federal grants for state crime victim compensation benefits.[6]

The *PROTECT Act of 2003*, better known as the Amber Alert Law, created a national system, facilitating rapid law enforcement and community response to kidnapped or abducted children. AMBER is an acronym for America's Missing: Broadcast Emergency Response. In November 2008, the State of California approved Marcy's Law, the strongest and most constitutional victims' rights law in the United States. The law ensures that victims' rights are codified. As a result, victims of crimes in California, by law, must be treated with respect and dignity by the criminal justice system. Courts must consider the safety of victims and families when setting bail and release conditions, and family members are granted legal standing at bail hearings, pleas, trial, sentencing, and parole hearings.[7]

Between 1986 and 2003, the Office for Victims of Crime Act (VOCA) distributed over $1 billion in VOCA grant funds that were used for restitution payments. Since that period, victim compensation funds have continued to grow at a rapid rate. In 2009, President Obama signed into law House Resolution 1, the American Recovery and Reinvestment Act of 2009. In accordance with this act, more than $2.76 billion was designated for the Office of Justice Programs (OJP) to develop the nation's capacity to prevent and control crime, administer justice, and assist victims. The Recovery Act provides for $100 million in funding for victim compensation and assistance. Of that $100 million, $47.5 million in formula funding will be administered to state agencies that administer VOCA-funded crime victim compensation programs, and an additional $47.5 million in formula funding will be directed to state agencies that administer VOCA-funded crime victim assistance programs. It appears the federal government has made restitution a priority in sentencing procedures. As a result, offenders are required to accept financial and moral responsibility.[8]

Types of Victims

The National Crime Victimization Survey (NCVS) obtains offender information from the victims of crimes. The victim is asked to provide information on age, race, and gender of the offender. The victim is also asked about his or her relationship with the offender, whether the victim perceived that the offender was drunk or on drugs, and whether the offender was a gang member. For crimes committed by strangers, the victim may not be able to provide all of the information. For crimes in which a relative, friend, or acquaintance was the offender, the victim may provide more detailed information about the offender. Victims are encouraged to recall incidents involving relatives or other nonstrangers that may have been a crime and describe these incidents in the interview. Information about nonstranger crime still may be underreported in the survey since some victims may not feel comfortable providing such information, or victims may not perceive some events as crimes.

- According to *Criminal Victimization, 2008*, victims knew the offenders in about 5 in 10 violent crimes against men and 7 in 10 violent crimes against women. Offenders known to the victims were most often identified as friends or acquaintances, accounting for a similar percentage of violence against male (42%) and female (38%) victims. Strangers were responsible for about a third (36%) of all violent crimes measured by the NCVS in 2008. In contrast, intimate partners were responsible for 3% of all violence against males and 23% of all violence against females in 2008.

- In 2008 victims of violent crimes perceived their assailants to be gang members in 5% of crimes that occurred. Hispanics were more likely than non-Hispanics to report being victims of violent crimes committed by gang members, and gang members were more likely to victimize younger persons than older persons.

- Family violence accounted for 11% of all reported and unreported violence between 1998 and 2002. Roughly 22% of murders in 2002 were intrafamily murders. Of the nearly 500,000 men and women held in state prisons for a violent crime in 1997, 15% were serving time for a violent crime against a family member.[9]

The NCVS also provides information on characteristics of victims, including age, gender, marital status, household income, and hate crimes. For violent crimes (murder, rape, assault, and robbery) the characteristics are based upon the victim who experienced the crime. For property crimes (household burglary, motor vehicle theft, property theft) the characteristics are based upon the household respondent who provided information about these crimes for the household. Property crimes are defined as affecting the entire household.

Age

The history of children as victims is well documented and has evolved over centuries. In many early societies, children were viewed as the property of their parents, who were allowed to sell, kill, or exploit children at their discretion. Child welfare agencies did not originate in the United States until 1875 in New York, with the case of Mary Ellen Wilson, a child that had been neglected and physically abused by her caretakers. There were no legal means to protect Mary Ellen from the abuse, so her social worker pleaded with the president of the Society for the Prevention of Cruelty to Animals to advocate on her behalf. While she was eventually removed from the home, many believed Mary Ellen had to be viewed as an animal in order to be rescued. The case is significant because it stimulated the development of child welfare agencies.

The development of child protective services peaked in the late 1800s and early 1900s. Yet progress was only superficial. It was not until the mid-1900s that substantial developments were observed. In 1974, the Child Abuse Prevention and Treatment Act was passed to provide direct assistance to states for developing programs for children who are victims of abuse and neglect. Guardian *Ad Litem* and Court Appointed Special Advocates (CASA) are among more recent programs that have been designed to help children victims. The guardian *ad litem* and court appointed special advocate are both appointed by the judge and act as advocates for the child victim during judicial proceedings. The advocates are interested in the welfare of children and enable the children to have a voice in what happens to them in court.[3]

Teens and young adults experience the highest rates of violent crime. In 2008, persons in older age groups experienced lower violent victimization than persons in younger age groups. The FBI's Uniform Crime Reports show that in 2008, 88% of murder victims were age

18 or older. Of all murder victims, 24% were between the ages of 18 and 22.

The elderly, persons age 65 or older, generally experienced less violence and fewer property crimes than younger persons. In 2008, persons age 65 or older experienced 3.1 violent crimes per 1,000 persons. During that same period, members of elderly households experienced property crimes at a rate of 62.4 per 1,000 households. Persons age 50 or older had the lowest rates of violent crime, while persons age 12 to 24 had the highest rates.

Abuse of elders takes many different forms, frequently involving physical and emotional abuse, neglect or abandonment by caregivers, financial exploitation, or healthcare fraud and abuse. While the elderly, as a group, are less likely to be victims of all crimes, they have a higher probability of being a victim of a crime motivated by economic gain, such as robbery, personal and household larceny, and burglary. Most elderly people live on fixed incomes, making it difficult for them to recover financially.[10]

Numerous accounts of maltreatment led policy makers to pass a series of laws intended to protect the elderly victim. The passage of the federal Older Americans Act of 1965 (OAA) and the creation of the Vulnerable Elder Rights Protection Program in 1992 were instrumental in promoting states to enact laws addressing the needs and concerns of the elderly. The Vulnerable Elder Rights Protection Program legislation promoted advocacy efforts through ombudsmen offices; abuse, neglect, and exploitation prevention programs; and legal assistance on behalf of older Americans. It also offered federal funding incentives that made it possible for states to develop and maintain programs designed to assist the elderly. In most states, the first agency to respond to a report of elderly abuse is Adult Protective Services (APS). Its role is to investigate abuse cases, intervene, and offer services and advice. The power and scope of APS varies by state. However, every state has at least one toll-free elder abuse hotline or helpline for reporting elder abuse in the home, in the community, or in nursing homes and other long-term care facilities.

Gender

Violent crime rates have declined for both males and females since 1994. In 2008, males experienced higher victimization rates than females for all types of violent crime except rape/sexual assault. According to the *FBI's Uniform Crime Reports of 2007,* murder victims were overwhelmingly male (78%).

Intimate violence is a societal problem that has recently caught the attention of policy makers and service providers. The women's rights movement is credited with bringing domestic or intimate violence into the spotlight. Of all intimate violence victims, 85 to 95% are female. Intimate violence is the leading cause of injury to women, with over 1,200 women killed and nearly 500,000 stalked each year by an intimate partner.

Annual Household Income

In general, violent victimization rates were inversely related to household income; persons living in households with lower incomes generally had higher rates of violent crime. In 2008, the robbery rate for persons in households with annual incomes of less than $7,500 was 6 per 1,000 persons age 12 or older, compared to 1 per 1,000 persons in households with incomes of $75,000 or more. The aggravated assault rate for persons in households with annual incomes of less than $7,500 was 9 per 1,000 persons age 12 or older, compared to 2 per 1,000 persons in households with incomes of $75,000 or more.[2]

Marital Status

In 2008, divorced or separated persons and those never married experienced similar rates of overall violence. Their rates were significantly higher than those married or widowed. The robbery rate was 4 per 1,000 persons who had never married, and 1 per 1,000 married persons age 12 or older. Persons who never married experienced simple assault at a rate of 22 per 1,000 age 12 or older, compared to 6 per 1,000 for married persons, 4 per 1,000 widowed persons, and 22 per 1,000 divorced or separated persons.[2]

Hate Crimes

Hate crimes are directed at specific groups that have an identifiable characteristic. While these crimes may be motivated by race, religion, ethnicity, or sexual orientation, the FBI reported more than half of all hate crimes are based on race. According to the Bureau of Justice Statistics, hate crimes involve violence far more often than other crimes. The data showed 84% of hate crimes were violent, meaning they involved a sexual attack, robbery, assault, or murder. In contrast, just 23% of nonhate crimes involved violence. About one-third of the racially based crimes were antiblack crimes, and about

20% were antiwhite crimes. The Anti-Defamation League (ADL) has recommended model legislation for all states to use in developing their own hate crime laws. The purpose of hate crime laws is to deter bias-motivated criminal activity.

Today nearly every state and the federal government have laws requiring sentencing enhancements for offenders convicted of hate crimes. A defendant who has engaged in a criminal act because of bias will receive a harsher sentence upon conviction for a hate crime. The U.S. Supreme Court unanimously found that *penalty enhancement* hate crime statutes do not conflict with free speech rights because they do not punish an individual for exercising freedom of expression. Instead, the penalty enhancement statutes allow courts to consider motive when sentencing a criminal for conduct that is not protected by the First Amendment.

When it enacted the Hate Crimes Act of 2000, the New York State legislature found:

> Hate crimes do more than threaten the safety and welfare of all citizens. They inflict on victims incalculable physical and emotional damage and tear at the very fabric of free society. Crimes motivated by invidious hatred toward particular groups not only harm individual victims but send a powerful message of intolerance and discrimination to all members of the group to which the victim belongs. Hate crimes can and do intimidate and disrupt entire communities and vitiate the civility that is essential to healthy democratic processes.

Race

Serious violent crime rates declined in recent years for both blacks and whites. In 2008, the rate of violent victimization against blacks was 26 per 1,000 persons age 12 or older; for whites, 18 per 1,000; and for persons of other races or ethnic groups, 15 per 1,000. Blacks were victims of rape/sexual assault, robbery, and aggravated assault at rates higher than those for whites.

According to the FBI's Uniform Crime Reports, in 2006, about 50% of murder victims were black, 47% were white, and 3% were Asians, Pacific Islander, and Native Americans. Between 2002 and 2006, American Indians experienced violence at rates almost twice that of blacks, about 2½ times that of whites, and more than 5 times that of Asians.

The U.S. Department of Justice operates the *Community Relations Service (CRS)*, a specialized federal conciliation service available to state and local officials to help resolve and prevent racial and ethnic conflict, violence, and civil disorders. The CRS helps local officials and residents address and resolve conflict and violence that threaten community welfare. While CRS conciliators have no law enforcement authority and do not require solutions, they work closely with community stakeholders to identify the sources of violence and conflict and utilize specialized crisis management and violence reduction techniques that are tailored specifically for each community. The following represents an example of the interaction of the CRS with local law enforcement:

> In Anchorage, Alaska, after white youths videotaped themselves shooting Native Alaskans with paint balls, the CRS worked with community groups, citizens, as well as state and local officials to calm community concerns. In response to the incident, CRS trained Anchorage Police Department Academy recruits to increase their ability and skills when interacting with people of color. CRS provided officers with additional tools and conflict resolution skills. Participants were provided an overview of services of perspective organizations and shared strategies in strengthening police-minority community relations and methods of prevention and reduction of racial tensions.[11]

Sexual Orientation

In addition to race, sexual orientation is another target of hate crimes. Studies have suggested that hate-motivated violence, especially against homosexuals, is more extreme than other violence. Hate crimes motivated by sexual orientation compose 18% of the total. Given that the best studies indicate about 3% of the American population is homosexual, gays and lesbians are victimized at six times the proportionate rate. Among crimes motivated by sexual orientation bias, 56% were violent and 42% were property offenses. Simple or aggravated assault was the most serious offense recorded in 37% of these incidents, intimidation in 16%, and rape or sexual assault in 2%.

Research indicates 31% of gay youth were threatened or injured at school. These experiences have a devastating impact on the educational success and mental health of youth. Antigay prejudice affects straight youth, too. For every gay, lesbian, and bisexual youth being harassed, four straight students were harassed because they were perceived as being gay or lesbian.[12]

One of the nation's most famous sexually oriented hate crimes involved Matthew Shepard, who was only 21 years old when he was brutally murdered in October 1998, in the small college town of Laramie, Wyoming. Shortly after midnight on October 7, 1998, Shepard met Aaron McKinney and Russell Henderson at the Fireside Lounge in Laramie. McKinney and Henderson offered Shepard a ride in their car. After admitting he was gay, Shepard was robbed, tortured, and tied to a fence in a rural area and left to die. Still tied to the fence, Shepard was discovered 18 hours later by Aaron Kreifels, who initially mistook Shepard for a scarecrow. At the time of discovery, Shepard was still alive, but in a coma. Shepard suffered severe brain stem damage, which affected his body's ability to regulate vital functions. There were approximately a dozen lacerations around his head, face, and neck. His injuries were deemed too severe for doctors to operate. Shepard never regained consciousness, remaining on full life support until he was pronounced dead five days later. Henderson and McKinney were not charged with a hate crime, as no Wyoming criminal statute provided for such a charge. They were both charged with murder and originally pleaded the *gay panic defense*, arguing that they were driven to temporary insanity by alleged sexual advances by Shepard. Both were eventually convicted and sentenced to life in prison without the possibility of parole.

The nature of Matthew Shepard's murder led to requests for new legislation addressing hate crime, urged particularly by those who believed that Shepard was targeted on the basis of his sexual orientation. The Matthew Shepard Act passed on October 22, 2009, and was signed into law by President Barack Obama on October 28, 2009, as a rider to the National Defense Authorization Act for 2010 (H.R. 2647). This measure expanded the 1969 U.S. federal hate crime law to include crimes motivated by a victim's actual or perceived gender, sexual orientation, or gender identity.[13]

Costs That Crime Victims Suffer

The primary costs that victims suffer include medical expenses, mental health counseling, lost wages for victims unable to work because of crime-related injury, lost support for dependents of homicide victims, and funeral expenses.

Hospitals', doctors', and therapists' costs comprise well over half of the amounts of victim expenses. Lost wages and survivor support payments are the next largest expense category. In addition, a number of other costs include the following:

- Moving or relocation expenses, where the victim is in imminent physical danger, or if the move is medically necessary. For instance, a victim may suffer severe emotional trauma from a sex assault.
- Transportation to medical providers.
- Replacement services for work the victim is unable to perform because of crime-related injury (primarily child care and housekeeping).
- Crime scene cleanup, or the cost of securing a home or restoring it to its precrime condition.
- Rehabilitation, which may include physical therapy or job therapy.
- Modifications to home or vehicles for paralyzed victims.[14]

The Role Correctional Agencies Play in Meeting Victims' Needs

The court and government agencies meet victims' needs in three major areas. First, sentencing courts have broad discretion to order restitution as a condition of probation with the goal of fostering rehabilitation and protecting public safety. Next, states have established victim compensation funds to fund services to victims. Finally, state victim notification programs operate to provide victims with timely and reliable information about criminal cases and the custody status of offenders.

Restitution

There are two types of restitution: monetary and community service. *Monetary restitution* is defined as a financial payment by the offender to the victim for the harm resulting from the offense. The other type of restitution, popular among those sentenced to supervised probation, is *community service*, a condition of probation that requires an offender to perform unpaid labor, to pay a debt to society. Sentences

to community service stipulate that offenders must perform specified periods of uncompensated work for public or nonprofit agencies.
Orders for community service have gained considerable popularity
over the past 25 years in response to the increasing cost of incarceration, as well as the fact that it has been linked to a decrease in
recidivism rates, in which the offender completes a specified number
of hours. Both the monetary and community service forms of restitution encompass a sense of giving back or making amends for their
crimes. Furthermore, these forms of restitution permit punishment,
promote deterrence, and engage those who have a legitimate interest or stake in the offense and its resolution (victims, offenders, and
community members).[15]

The concept of restitution dates back to the Code of Hammurabi,
which required payment in kind to crime victims. This practice has
continued and is a well-established component of today's criminal
justice system in the United States. During the 1970s, there was
a renewed interest in providing methods into the criminal process
that required offenders to make restitution to their victims for losses
suffered as a result of their crimes. By 1990, all 50 states had implemented statutes regulating restitution. In most states, restitution
became a permissible condition of probation, although some states
made restitution a mandatory condition.[16] In recent years, the federal courts have broadened the concept of victim beyond direct victims of a crime. Restitution has been extended to parties such as
the Internal Revenue Service, insurance companies, and even own-
ers of cars used and damaged during kidnappings. In addition, the
federal courts have interpreted the restitution statutes to support a
wide range of amounts and types of restitution. Furthermore, the
establishment of the U.S. Courts National Fine Center, a centralized,
nationwide, computerized system for tracking and receiving restitution and fines, seeks to improve restitution compliance.[17]

Studies of adult offenders suggested that judges are more likely to
order restitution when the offender is better educated and gainfully
employed because these increase the likelihood that the offender will
pay the imposed restitution. Research focusing on adults also suggested that restitution collection rates are low. Collection rates for
restitution hover around 50%, and at the federal level, there is more
than $35 billion in unpaid fines. It has also been suggested that the
likelihood of payment may be increased if offenders are (1) told about
the importance of restitution, (2) given employment opportunities, (3)
closely supervised, and (4) allowed to pay in installments.[18]

Court-ordered monetary restitution and community service work are specifically a court sanction, with costs being born by the offender. These court functions imply the state is accepting some responsibility for not providing victims safety and security. Similarly, government compensation programs, such as federal and state crime victim funds, ensure reparation to victims.

Federal and State Crime Victims Funds

In 1995, deposits in the federal Crime Victims Fund reached a then high of more than $583 million, available for state crime victim compensation, local victim assistance programs, national training and technical assistance, and federal victim assistance. As a result of this increase in fund collections, state assistance grants in 1997 increased threefold over the previous year. In 1999, the fund deposits reached an all-time high of $985 million. As a result of significant fluctuations in annual fund deposits, Congress began capping the amount that could be obligated each year, with annual revenues above the cap stored in the fund balance to be used as a "rainy day fund" when revenues did not meet the cap. Congress also began using the fund to support federal victim services, including victim/witness coordinators in U.S. attorneys' offices, victim specialists in FBI field offices, and a federal victim notification system. The following programs and services are supported by money from the Crime Victims Fund:

- Children's Justice Act (to improve the investigation and prosecution of child abuse cases)
- Victim witness coordinators in U.S. attorneys' offices
- Victim assistance staff in FBI offices
- Federal Victim Notification System (VNS)
- Formula grants to state crime victim compensation programs
- Formula grants to states to support direct victim assistance services
- Discretionary grants by the Office for Victims of Crime (OVC) to support services to victims of federal crimes and national scope training and technical assistance[14]

The types and level of offender assessments mildly vary among the states. Many states require offenders to pay a standard penalty into a crime victim compensation fund, such as $50 per felony and $25 per

196 Introduction to Corrections

misdemeanor. Other states exact a certain percentage of the offender's fine or place a surcharge upon the fine and use it for compensation funding. Some states also generate income from wages inmates earn in prison industries.

While eligibility requirements vary by state, all programs have the same basic criteria. The victim generally must:

- Report the crime promptly to law enforcement. Many states have a 72-hour standard, but nearly all states have "good cause" exceptions applied liberally to children, incapacitated victims, and in other special circumstances.

- Cooperate with police and prosecutors in the investigation and prosecution of the case. Again, some states can make exceptions.

- Submit a timely application to the compensation program (generally one year from the date of the crime, though a number of states have longer time frames, and most can waive this requirement when necessary) and provide other information as requested by the program.

- Have a cost or loss not covered by insurance.

- Be innocent of criminal activity or significant misconduct that caused or contributed to the victim's injury or death.[14]

Federal and State Victim Notification Programs

Where possible, all victim information and notifications in criminal cases that have been accepted for prosecution from federal investigative agencies are made available (in both English and Spanish) by means of the Department of Justice's Victim Notification System (VNS). The Victim Notification System is a cooperative effort between the Federal Bureau of Investigation, the U.S. Postal Inspection Service, the U.S. Attorney's Office, the Federal Bureau of Prisons, and the Criminal Division. This free, computer-based system provides federal crime victims with information on scheduled court events, as well as the outcome of those court events. It also provides victims with information on the offender's custody status and release.

Victim Information and Notification Everyday (VINE) and the Statewide Automated Victim Information and Notification (SAVIN) system are *National Victim Notification Networks* that operate statewide in 41 states and in selected counties of 6 additional states. This service allows crime victims to obtain timely and reliable information about criminal cases and the custody status of offenders 24 hours a day. Crime victims, law enforcement officers, public safety officials, criminal justice and corrections professionals, and other concerned citizens can register for free notification by phone, email, or text message of changes in an offender's custody status. Figure 11.1 presents, as an example, a victim notification letter received by a bank robbery victim. The victim's name has been removed to protect her identity.

U.S. Department of Justice
United States Attorney's Office

Thomas F. Eagleton U.S. Courthouse 111 South 10th Street, Room 20.333 St. Louis, MO 63102	329 Broadway 2nd Floor Cape Girardeau, MO 63701
314-539-2200/Fax: 314-539-2309 Toll Free: 1-800-214-2690 TDD: 314-539-7690	573-334-3736/Fax: 573-335-2393 Toll Free: 1-888-787-6387 TDD: 573-332-1208

Victim Witness Assistance Unit   **Allison Stafford, Victim Witness Program Coordinator**

April 27, 2005

RE: Defendants: COREY D. LYONS, DEREK E. RIGGS, DAREME P. TIPLER, TORIA W. LAWRENCE

Pursuant to federal law, you are entitled to be notified of the court proceeding relating to the criminal litigation of this case. This letter is to inform you of the following:

USAO Number: 2004R00076, Court Docket Number: 1:04CR45 CDP

On May 3, 2004, the defendant, DAREME P. TIPLER, pled guilty to the charges listed below. As a result of the guilty plea, there will be no trial involving this defendant.

Number of Charges	Description of Charges	Disposition
1	Bank robbery and incidental crimes	Guilty
1	Use/carry of firearm during crime of violence/drug trafficking offense	Guilty

A sentencing hearing has been set for May 9, 2005 at 11:30 AM at CAPE in the case involving defendant(s): TORIA W. LAWRENCE. You are welcome to attend this proceeding although your attendance is not required by the court. If you plan on attending, please check with the VNS Call Center to verify the sentencing date and time. You may call this office the day before the scheduled hearing for the most current information on the date/time of this event.

Before a defendant is sentenced a Pre-sentence Investigation Report (PSR) is prepared by a U.S. Probation Officer and provided to the Judge for his/her use at sentencing. The PSR contains a section on victim impact. You may be contacted by the U.S. Probation Officer responsible for this report asking about victim impact information with respect to this crime. If you desire, you may contact the U.S. Probation Office directly at 314-244-9700.

A sentencing hearing has been set for May 10, 2005 at 09:00 AM at CAPE in the case involving defendant(s): DAREME P. TIPLER, DEREK E. RIGGS, COREY D. LYONS. You are welcome to attend this proceeding although your attendance is not required by the court. If you plan on attending, please check with the VNS Call Center to verify the sentencing date and time. You may call this office the day before the scheduled hearing for the most current information on the date/time of this event.

Figure 11.1 Victim notification letter. (*continued*)

Before a defendant is sentenced a Pre-sentence Investigation Report (PSR) is prepared by a U.S. Probation Officer and provided to the Judge for his/her use at sentencing. The PSR contains a section on victim impact. You may be contacted by the U.S. Probation Officer responsible for this report asking about victim impact information with respect to this crime. If you desire, you may contact the U.S. Probation Office directly at 314-244-9700.

The defendant, DAREME P. TIPLER, was sentenced by the court on February 14, 2005.

The Court ordered defendant DAREME P. TIPLER to serve the following term of imprisonment: 84 months

Upon release from confinement, the defendant shall be on supervised release for the following term: 3 years

The Victim Notification System (VNS) is designed to provide you with information regarding the case as it proceeds through the criminal justice system. You may use you Victim Identification Number (VIN), "629348", and Personal Identification Number (PIN), "7060", which has been assigned to you to telephone the VNS Call Center (1-866-DOJ-4YOU*) or (1-866-365-4968*), TDD/TTY users call 1-866-228-4619, and obtain the current status of the case. In addition, you may call the toll-free number and speak with an operator to update your contact information and/or change your decision about participation in the notification program. If you have other questions which involve this matter, please contact the office listed above.

Sincerely,

Allison Stafford

ALLISON STAFFORD
Victim Witness Program Coordinator

*For international callers, 1-502-213-2767.

Figure 11.1 (continued) Victim notification letter.

Summary

This chapter began by providing a working definition of the term *crime victim*. In recent years, there has been a strong emphasis on crime victims. This is perhaps due to the corresponding victims' rights movement as well as the emergence of the field of victimology. Likewise, there has been a desire for accountability among offenders and the government to ameliorate the plight of the crime victim. The crime victims' movement has witnessed three distinct eras; the dark age or age of indifference was where victims were expected to serve the public interest through service in legal matters. During the golden age the focus shifted to victims and witnesses as human beings with rights and privileges, and the government's responsibility to protect and compensate them. That focus waned as the medical model brought attention to the offender. The reemergence of the victim, the current era, is centered on the victim in terms of preventing future crimes as well as attending to the needs and rights of those hurt or impaired by criminal activity.

The chapter delineated the abundance of legal activity associated with the crime victims' movement in the United States. The chronological examination of the movement highlighted how crime victims' participation in the criminal justice system has changed dramatically over the years. The influence of advocacy groups and supporters has changed since the first victim assistance programs were created in prosecutors' offices to overcome the emotional anxiety and trauma associated with testifying in court. The Bill of Rights for crime victims, Community Notification Act, Trafficking Victims Protection Act of 2000, and Recovery Act of 2009 illustrate the nation's continued emphasis on crime victims.

An abundance of trends regarding victimization were introduced. This chapter focused on various groups of victims, such as women, children, and elderly. Specific examples of hate crimes, where the focus was on race and sexual orientation, were given.

A crime victim's search for restoration may never be complete, but criminal justice sanctions that are crime victim oriented can go a long way toward reaching this end. Today, programs try to provide some sense of restoration through sanctions that require offenders to pay restitution and compensation programs by the government. While many of these programs have been in operation for decades, it is only in the past two decades that they have received the priority and funds necessary to impact crime victims. The growth of these programs and the criminal justice system's responsiveness must continue if the crime victim is to achieve restoration of his or her former life.

Vocabulary

Community Notification Act

Community Relations Service (CRS)

Community service

Crime victim

Dark age

Gay panic defense

Golden age

Guardian *ad litem*

Hate crimes

Monetary restitution

National Crime Victimization Survey (NCVS)

National Victim Notification Networks

PROTECT Act of 2003

Trafficking Victims Protection Act of 2000

Victim age

Victims of Crime Act (VOCA)

Discussion Questions

1. Know the three major eras associated with the crime victims' movement. From a victim's point of view, what were the advantages of each?

2. Discuss the various types of crime victims. What can be done to change the pattern?

3. Identify the various costs that victims suffer. If you were a judge, what steps would you take to reduce the victim's distress?

4. Explain how court and government agencies meet victims' needs. What implications does the impact have for the effectiveness of the criminal justice system?

Notes

1. *Black's law dictionary* (7th ed.). (1999). St. Paul, MN: West.

2. Bureau of Justice Statistics. National Crime Victimization Survey. Retrieved May 27, 2010, from http://bjs.ojp.usdoj.gov/index.cfm?ty=dcdetail&iid=245

3. Jerin, R. A., & Moriarty, L. J. (1998). *Victims of crime: Issues, programs, and policies.* Chicago, IL: Nelson-Hall.

4. Victims of Crime Act. (2010). Retrieved April 11, 2010, from http://www.ncadv.org/files/VOCA.pdf

5. Matson, S., & Lieb, R. (1997). *Megan's law: A review of state and public policy: Federal legislation.* Olympia, WA: Washington State Institute for Public Policy.

6. Territo, L., & Kirkham, G. (2010). *International sex trafficking of women and children: Understanding the global epidemic.* Flushing, NY: Looseleaf Law Publications.

7. *The Protect Act and the First Amendment.* Retrieved May 29, 2010, from http://bjs.ojp.usdoj.gov/index.cfm?ty=dcdetail&iid=245

8. Office for Victims of Crime. (2009). *New directions from the field: Victim's rights and services for the 21st century.* Washington, DC: U.S. Department of Justice.

9. Rand, M. (2009, September). *Criminal victimization, 2008* (Bureau of Justice Statistics Bulletin, NCJ 227777). Retrieved May 29, 2010, from http://bjs.ojp.usdoj.gov/content/pub/pdf/cv08.pdf

10. Bachman, R. (1992). *Elderly victims* (Bureau of Justice Statistics Special Report). Washington, DC: U.S. Department of Justice.

11. Community Relations Service. Hate crime: The violence of intolerance. Retrieved May 28, 2010, from http://www.justice.gov/crs/pubs/crs_pub_hate_crime_bulletin_1201.htm

12. Sexual orientation hate crimes & discrimination. Retrieved May 29, 2010, from http://karisable.com/crhateso.htm

13. Loffreda, B. (2000). *Losing Matt Shepard.* New York, NY: Columbia University Press.

14. National Association of Crime Victims Compensation Boards. Crime victim compensation: An overview. Retrieved April 11, 2010, from http://www.nacvcb.org/articles/Overview_prn.html

15. Bazemore, G. (2005). Whom and how do we reintegrate? Finding community in restorative justice. *Criminology and Public Policy, 4*(1), 131–148.

16. Ruback, R. B., & Bergstrom, M. H. (2006). Economic sanctions in criminal justice: Purposes, effects, and implications. *Criminal Justice and Behavior, 33*(2), 242–273.

17. Tobolowsky, P. M. (1993). Restitution in the federal criminal justice system. *Judicature, 77*(2), 90–95.

18. Van Voorhis, P. (1985). Restitution outcome and probationers' assessments of restitution: The effects of moral development. *Criminal Justice and Behavior, 12,* 259–287.

Correctional Counseling

The whole business of promoting change is about doing. It isn't about wishing, though you will have a few wishes. It isn't about hoping, though your hopes will guide your actions. It is about doing, about acting positively to produce a desired result.

—Mark Homan

Introduction

Over 103,000 people are employed today in the capacity of probation and parole officer or correctional treatment specialist.[1] The need for correctional counseling at the federal, state, and local levels is projected to grow approximately 19% between 2008 and 2018 to meet larger prison populations as a product of longer prison sentences, which resulted from mandatory sentencing guidelines and reduced parole for inmates. Many states, however, are reconsidering mandatory sentencing guidelines in response to budget concerns. Consequently, states are considering rehabilitation and alternate forms of punishment, such as probation or parole, prompting a need for additional probation and parole officers and correctional treatment specialists. The range and complexity of the issues addressed by correctional counselors have extended far beyond what might have been envisioned a few years ago. For this reason, correctional counseling in the near future may look quite different, depending on one's particular perspective. This chapter is concerned with how correctional treatment strategies at the community and institutional levels are utilized to compassionately treat offenders' criminal lifestyles, attitudes, or behaviors.

Defining Correctional Treatment

Correctional treatment is generally defined as a process that is designed to target offenders' *criminogenic characteristics*, those that tend to generate crime or criminality. Some examples of offenders' criminogenic characteristics include dysfunctional attitudes, debilitating behaviors regarding employment, poor education, aberrant peers, destructive substance abuse, and unhealthy interpersonal relationships. More specifically, some researchers define correctional counseling with an emphasis on affecting recidivism. Clear, Cole, and Reisig, for example, believe counselors must identify offenders' criminogenic needs in order to focus their efforts on objectives that are likely to reduce recidivism rates.[2] Similarly, Hanser and Mire define correctional counseling as a concept that describes the "process of trained counselors helping offenders identify and incorporate better behavioral, psychological and emotional responses to life events that serve to improve their quality of life and reduce or eliminate their involvement in criminal activity."[3] And, Kratcoski described correctional counseling as "any planned and monitored program of activity that has the goal of rehabilitating or 'habilitating' the offender so that he or she will avoid criminal activity in the future."[4] Conversely, Schrink and Hamm described correctional counseling as programming that addresses offenders' imminent needs associated with incarceration or status on probation and parole and is only modestly concerned with recidivism.[5]

Institutional versus Community-Based Correctional Treatment Specialists

Before the scope of correctional treatment strategies can be examined, it is important to distinguish between two types of correctional treatment specialists, community based and institutional. Correctional treatment specialists working in community-based parole and probation agencies perform many of the same duties as their counterparts who work in correctional institutions. While they may be trained to provide individual counseling or group counseling, they often refer clients to community-based counselors and make collateral contacts with family and programs, such as local mental health centers, employment agencies, and housing centers. *Collateral contacts* involve contacts with people who have explicit knowledge of the clients' behaviors and compliance with supervision conditions.[6] Information gleaned from collateral contacts, observations at home and office visits, and results of risk/ need assessment instruments combine to assist the counselor in formulating appropriate treatment plans. Finally, correctional treatment specialists prepare progress reports for the sentencing judge and parole boards and are sometimes required to testify at probation or parole revocation hearings.

In jails and prisons, correctional treatment counselors monitor the progress of inmates. They may assess inmates' risks and needs by administering questionnaires and psychological tests. They also work with inmates, institutional probation officers, and other agencies to create parole and release plans. The institutional treatment specialists develop case reports, which discuss the inmate's history and likelihood of recidivism. The case reports contain treatment plans and are provided to the parole board when clients approach their eligibility dates. In addition, institutional correctional treatment specialists plan education and training programs to improve inmates' marketable job skills and provide them with counseling, either individually or in groups. It is common for institutional correctional treatment counselors to be required to testify at parole hearings. Finally, institutionally based correctional treatment specialists may be required to serve as custodial staff, when emergency situations arise.

Custodial Staff versus Correctional Treatment Staff

There is a conflict between custodial staff and correctional treatment staff that may impede the implementation of correctional treatment strategies. Correctional counselors are often caught in a role dichotomy, a conflict between advocates of treatment and rehabilitation and the maintainers of order and security. Disclosure is a major problem that confronts correctional treatment staff. Inmates must be advised that issues of confidentiality may be compromised if any information they reveal is believed to be relevant to the issue of security or safety. Correctional treatment counselors are mandated to disclose the concerned information to custodial staff. The offender, who willingly participates in any of the correctional treatment strategies, may be hesitant to fully commit to treatment if there is a fear that treatment-induced statements may be incriminating.

Security and safety for inmates and staff is perceived as the most significant role of custodial staff. They believe management and staff should view correctional counseling as a less important (secondary) correctional function. Researchers Hanser and Mire believe the primary reason for security being the paramount concern for any correctional facility stems from the fear of liability, both civil and criminal.[7] Liability is a concept that describes the process of being accountable or legally bound to ensure that one's basic rights are not violated. One of the convenient means of ensuring the safety of offenders, while avoiding liability, is through the maintenance of strict security measures. Those who support the custodial staff's role in corrections believe the concept of helping offenders learn to cope with social, educational, and vocational issues is secondary to the security of the facility. In contrast, correctional treatment counselors believe their services are of profound importance because they aim at reforming the offenders' behavior, which they believe ultimately enhances security.

Theoretical Counseling Perspectives

Correctional treatment strategies have been predicated on a variety of theoretical perspectives from the fields of psychology, criminology, and sociology. The strategies are an approach to counseling based on the offender's cognition and behavior, and each perspective contains elements that may be useful under specific conditions with particular offenders.

The *positivist perspective* argues offenders have certain characteristics that distinguish them from law-abiding people. In the early 1900s, criminologists believed criminals possessed certain biological traits that noncriminals did not have. A biological trait, such as a defective gene, was believed to have been inherited. Sociologists would state, "Criminals will always be criminals because they were born criminals." Attention later shifted from biological to psychological traits. Criminals were described as psychotic or mentally disturbed. The traits were believed to be a feature of the individual. Regardless of a change in society or culture, counselors assumed offenders would always be criminals. Today, positivist sociologists have mostly abandoned the biological and psychological traits to differentiate criminals from noncriminals. Social factors are frequently used to explain one's criminality. Instead of criminal behavior staying with an offender, new explanations hold that criminality is subject to change, in response to changes in the offender's society or culture.

Correctional treatment counselors, working in prisons or in the community, typically have years of training and experience in such fields as psychology, social work, public health, and sociology, among others that shape the theoretical approach they use as counselors. The real-world training counselors acquire from their experiences is necessary to apply theoretical perspectives and effectively work with offenders struggling with a variety of issues. The following section will address some theoretical perspectives and how they apply to violent crimes and alcohol- and drug-related crimes, two categories of offenses most often observed among community-based and institutional clients.

Violent Crimes

According to the Bureau of Justice Statistics, at year-end 2008, nearly half (42%) of the nation's 1.6 million federal and state prisoners were incarcerated for a violent offense.[8] Of the 4.3 million adults on probation or parole, 26% were on correctional supervision for a violent offense.[9] The external restraint theory and subculture of violence theories are two of several theoretical perspectives used by counselors to explain violent crimes such as murder and felonious assault. Another violent crime, rape, may be explained by psychological theory: sexual inadequacy, social psychological theory: sexual permissiveness, and feminist theory.

External Restraint Theory

The *external restraint theory* explains why some people who are extremely frustrated commit homicide. In 1954, Andrew Henry and James Short speculated the strength of external restraint is the amount of social control imposed on people so as to limit their freedom and range of behaviors.[10] According to the theory, people who suffer weak social controls, who have strong external restraints, are more inclined to commit murder because they can legitimately blame others for their frustration. More recent studies, however, suggest external restraint can lead to homicide only if a third variable, called external attribution of blame, is evident.[11] External attribution of blame is the act of blaming others, rather than oneself, for one's own frustration. Simply stated, positivist theorists believe excessive external restraint encourages people to blame others rather than themselves for their own problems in life, which in turn causes then to engage in physical violence against others.

Subculture of Violence Theory

The *subculture of violence theory* was developed by Marvin Wolfgang in 1958. He theorized that the subculture of violence is the basic cause of high homicide rates in poor neighborhoods. Wolfgang believed the subculture of violence accounts for why offenders do not define physical assaults as wrong or antisocial.[12] Violence becomes a part of the lifestyles of many who live in underprivileged areas. Offenders consider the use of violence a normal part of life, a means for survival. As a result, they experience little if any guilt for their violent behavior.

In addition to working with offenders who have been convicted of violent offenses such as murder or felonious assault, correctional counselors also have many rapists as clients. Attempts have been made to explain why some men are more likely than others to rape. Psychologists attribute rape to some psychological problem in the offender. Social psychological theory attributes rape to sexual permissiveness in society. Others rely on a feminist theory to view rape as an expression of gender inequality. The three theories are also positivist in nature because they focus on the causation of rape.

Psychological Theory: Sexual Inadequacy

Psychologists, psychiatrists, and psychoanalysts agree that rapists suffer from some personality defects or emotional disturbance. The professionals, however, disagree on what the specific psychological problem is. One explanation is that rapists suffer from feelings of sexual inadequacy.[13] *Sexual inadequacy* is a personality disorder that prohibits an individual from being able to relate successfully to women. The inadequacy drives the rapist to indulge in fantasy and then act out the fantasy by raping a woman. The psychological theory of sexual inadequacy is less applicable to acquaintance rapists. Those rapists are viewed as decidedly skilled in dealing with women. In 1985, Eugene Kanin described the date rapists in college as far more heterosexually successful than other male students: They have had more dates and more consensual sexual experiences than other male students.[14]

Social Psychological Theory: Sexual Permissiveness

In 1971, Duncan Chappell, a sociologist, asked why the rate of rape is higher in some societies than in others. Using social psychological theory, Chappell and his colleagues theorized that societies with higher rape rates are more *sexually permissive*. According to the theorists, the explanation lies in a concept of relative frustration. The concept holds that men become more frustrated if they are rejected by a woman in a sexually permissive society. On the other hand, if a man is rejected in a sexually restrictive society, his ego is protected by the rationalization that she only rejected him because society prevents her from accepting his sexual invitation.[15] The social atmosphere of sexual permissiveness, therefore, produces a great number of rapes because it generates more relative frustration by causing men to take a woman's rejection personally.

Feminist Theory

The *feminist theory* questions the social psychological theory's perception that the violent crime of rape is mostly sexually motivated. To feminists, rape is primarily motivated by the man's desire to dominate the woman because of gender inequality. Rape is viewed by feminist theorists as a means to intimidate women, keeping them in their place to maintain sexual authority. Peggy Sanday discovered that male dominance is a key feature of rape-prone societies, such as universities.[16] Simiarly, Schwartz and DeKeseredy found rape is high in colleges where masculinity and male dominance are highly valued.[17]

Correctional Treatment Strategies for Violent Offenders

Based upon the theoretical perspectives, correctional counselors recognize offenders are in need of interventions to regulate their emotions and violent behaviors. Because of the high concentration of violent offenders in institutions and on community supervision, it is not uncommon to see offenders mandated to anger management counseling. Specific techniques that are often used in an anger management course aid offenders in recognizing how they may fuel their own sense of rage through *irrational self-talk*, the internal dialogue that violent offenders use to build themselves up to an abusive incident. Offenders learn to identify negative thoughts and feelings as precursors to their explosiveness and violence. They are taught to identify these cues at an early stage and to intervene with opposing thoughts that will prevent their typical reaction. Through cognitive restructuring and other behavioral techniques, such as timeouts, the abuser can learn coping statements, relaxation techniques, and noncompetitive forms of physical exercise to reduce tension.

Cognitive restructuring with rapists requires them to identify and examine their rationalizations and how their distorted thinking is used to justify their violent behavior. One technique used with rapists is the use of role-play exercises. Group members play the role of someone related to the victim, and the correctional counselor plays the role of the rapist who uses distorted thinking to justify violent behavior. While offenders may have difficulty in identifying their own thinking errors, they are usually adept at noting the distorted thinking that occurs among other offenders. Another treatment strategy is called *covert sensitization*, whereby offenders are taught to anticipate the consequences of their actions. In most cases, rapists only focus on the immediate pleasure they expect to achieve when committing their crime. The goal of covert sensitization is to teach offenders to substitute thinking about possible negative consequences of committing rape rather than what is appealing about forcible rape.[18]

Alcohol and Drug Crimes

According to the Bureau of Justice Statistics, at year-end 2008, less than one-fifth (17%) of the nation's 1.6 million federal and state prisoners were incarcerated for an alcohol- or drug-related crime. In contrast, however, 37% of the 4.3 million adults on probation or parole were on correctional supervision for an alcohol- or drug-related crime. Psychologists, psychiatrists, and medical scientists agree that some offenders are genetically vulnerable or biologically predisposed to chemical dependency. Sociologists, on the other hand, point to environmental factors as contributing to offenders' alcohol- and drug-related crimes. The genetic and economic deprivation theories are two of several theoretical perspectives used by counselors to shape their theoretical counseling approaches.

Genetic Theory

A study by Blum et al.[18a] in the May 1990 issue of the *Journal of the American Medical Association* reported that the gene for the D2 dopamine receptor, the A1 allele, was significantly higher among chemically addicted individuals. The gene was found to deprive its carrier of the feeling of pleasure. According to Cloninger, people born with this defective gene are predisposed to use alcohol or some other drug, as a means of seeking the pleasure that genetically normal people can enjoy without drinking excessively. It appears that the A1 allele contributes to addicted behavior, but does not cause addiction.[19]

Both genetics and the environment influence the brain, which in turn affects the behavior of usage. Once an individual begins using psychotropic substances, such as cocaine or heroin, measurable changes in serotonin perpetuate the cycle of addiction. *Serotonin*, a neurotransmitter that regulates mood, appetite, sleep, and some cognitive functions, including memory and learning, has been connected to violence. Those with low serotonin levels, compared to those with normal levels, are more prone to aggression and violence. While there is a correlation between serotonin level and crime, there is not any clear evidence as to whether low serotonin levels have a direct impact on crime, or if they simply lessen impulse control. Addicted offenders often take greater risks or make irrational decisions to fulfill short-term gratification.[20]

Economic Deprivation Theory

Elliott Currie proposed the *economic deprivation theory*, which explains why impoverished individuals resort to drug usage or transactions in response to poverty-related social conditions. According to Currie, poor individuals are routinely denied avenues of achieving a sense of belonging, admiration, and respect. Within poor communities, a drug culture frequently exists that serves as a substitute source of admiration and respect. Drug use or sales help the individual cope with the cruel realities of poverty. Drugs can also provide a sense of structure or purpose to dysfunctional lives. Without steady employment or family life, the poor lack structure that others enjoy. The drug use and the challenges of drug distribution help alleviate the boredom and emptiness experienced by the poor. Finally, poor communities are often inundated with illicit drugs. The availability of drugs makes it easy for individuals to become dependent on drug use and sales, disregarding the criminal consequences.[21]

Correctional Treatment Strategies for Drug- and Alcohol-Related Crimes

Based upon the theoretical perspectives, correctional counselors recognize offenders are in need of interventions to regulate their behaviors associated with drug- and alcohol-related crimes. Cognitive behavioral therapy is a therapeutic modality that is often used with drug and alcohol offenders. The framework for cognitive behavioral therapy is based on the assumption that offenders' drug- and alcohol-related crimes are a result of improper or faulty cognitive structuring that generates self-defeating thoughts, which leads to criminal behaviors. In other words, offenders are not only taught more positive behaviors to replace their old ways of coping with life's problems, but also shown how to be more attuned to the thought processes that led them to choose negative actions in the past. Three programs in general are used in both institutions and the community: Thinking for a Change, Relapse Prevention Therapy, and In Custody Drug Treatment Program.

- *Thinking for a Change* is a cognitive-based intervention program that focuses on the here and now. Programming requires offenders to evaluate their current situations and what decisions they have made. Offenders eventually make connections between their thinking and their offending. It is an intervention program that is empowering for offenders because it allows them to learn about themselves in an interesting and productive way. Both correctional treatment providers and offenders clearly see that the offender is in charge of his or her thinking, and that is the key to behavior change.[22]

- *Relapse Prevention Therapy* was originally designed as a maintenance program for use following the treatment of addictive behaviors, although it is also used as a stand-alone treatment program. It is a behavioral self-control program designed to teach individuals who are trying to maintain changes in their behavior how to anticipate and cope with the problem of relapse. Like other cognitive behavioral therapies, the therapy combines behavioral and cognitive interventions in an overall approach that emphasizes self-management and rejects labeling clients with traits like "alcoholic" or "drug addict."[23]

- *In-Custody Drug Treatment Program* (ICDTP) is designed for parolees who are failing in the community so they can begin their recovery, while still on parole. ICDTP classes are held in county jail facilities while parolees serve 60 days. After the completion of the in-custody phase of the program, participants are required to complete 30 days of residential aftercare in the community. In addition, 60 days of voluntary aftercare is provided upon release from ICDTP. This program gives parolees an understanding of substance abuse and recovery using a behavioral self-control type curriculum.[24]

Counselors may also use *aversion therapy* to reduce or eliminate drug- and alcohol-related crimes. Aversion therapy is a form of behavior therapy in which an aversive (causing a strong feeling of dislike or disgust) stimulus is linked with the criminal behavior in order to reduce or eliminate that behavior. A variety of aversive stimuli have been used as part of this approach, including chemical and pharmacological stimulants such as Antabuse. Antabuse is a stimulant prescribed to help people who want to quit drinking by causing a negative reaction if the person drinks while he or she is taking the drug. Foul odors and loud noises have also been employed as aversive stimuli, somewhat less frequently.

The theoretical perspectives discussed in this section represent a small sample of the vast spectrum of theoretical perspectives available to correctional counselors to explain and treat violent and alcohol- and drug-related crimes. The perspectives provide insight into the offenders' criminal behavior, but the true value of the perspectives lies in the quality of the counseling that is correlated with the depth of one's understanding.

Group versus Individual Counseling

Humans often need and thrive on interaction with others. Offenders meet their needs through interactions with correctional counselors. There is no ideal mechanism for delivering treatment services. Counseling, however, is normally delivered in either group or individual counseling sessions. The following segment addresses advantages and disadvantages for individual or group counseling. In the end, it is up to the offender which one serves him or her best.

Advantages of Individual Counseling

There are multiple advantages of an offender participating in individual counseling as opposed to group counseling. First, during individual counseling sessions, the counselor and client are free to work on a one-on-one basis, able to concentrate on the offender's specific needs. The counselor is not distracted by other offenders, so it is easier for the counselor to really listen to the offender and apply the most appropriate treatment approaches. In individual sessions, the client's thoughts and behaviors may not be distorted or influenced by other offenders. As a result, the client has the power to change his life for the better based on the choices he makes, not on choices influenced by other offenders. In addition, he can control his level of commitment. His willingness to work on his treatment plan dictates how successful he will be in developing new behaviors. Finally, it is much easier to ensure confidentiality, both a legal and ethical issue, when working on a one-on-one basis.

Disadvantages of Individual Therapy

The major disadvantage of individual therapy rests with the cost. If the offender resides in the community, correctional counseling can be very expensive, and thus cost-prohibitive. In a prison or jail, the correctional counselor is one of the most sought after staff members. State and federal prison administrators have limited funds to hire an adequate amount of counselors to satisfy the demand for individual therapy. Another disadvantage to individual therapy is that the client may not be able to generate multiple perspectives and ideas from the counselor. Frequently, a counselor's theoretical orientation and technique do not serve the client well.

Individual Treatment Programs

A number of individual techniques are used within the prison and in community-based counseling programs. Insight-based therapy and behavior therapy are two of the most common individual techniques.

Insight-based therapy helps clients develop the understanding and personal resources needed to start lasting change. Insight-based therapy is designed to help offenders alleviate and heal from depression, anxiety, social problems, addictions, loss, and chronic life conditions. Each individual session is devoted to creating a caring process of insightful reflections that generate new perspectives and promise. Through attentive and honest dialogue between the client and counselor, offenders develop the strength, understanding, and confidence needed to affect positive change.[25]

Behavior therapy is another form of individual treatment built on the assumption that desirable behaviors that are rewarded immediately will increase, and undesirable behaviors that are not rewarded or punished will lessen or be eliminated. Positive reinforcers include attention, praise, and privileges. Negative reinforcers include threats, confinement, and ridicule. Correctional counselors use behavior modification in individual sessions by awarding privileges to inmates as they become more accepting of the prison rules and procedures and as they demonstrate positive attitudes.[26]

Advantages of Group Counseling

Group counseling provides members with the opportunities to learn with and from peers and to be able to understand one's own patterns of thoughts and behaviors, as well as those of others. Whether in prison or in the community, group correctional counseling is very confrontational. Group members are expected to recognize and confront offenders' manipulations and rationalizations. By confronting others, the offenders can understand their own versions of those same manipulations and rationalizations. Other members of the group may see attitudes and behavior patterns that are restraining and difficult for the offender to see in his or her self. Another advantage of group counseling is that a group of offenders, who feel free to share their thoughts, creates a very powerful sense of community. A group is an opportunity to receive genuine support, honest feedback, and useful alternatives from peers. It also enables members to learn from multiple perspectives. Group therapy is an excellent way to bridge the gap between the theoretical concepts offered by counselors and the practical circumstances of the offender's developmental experiences. Finally, group counseling costs less for each member of the group, and more offenders can receive counseling in groups than on an individual basis.

Disadvantages of Group Counseling

Group counseling has some disadvantages. There is a concern that offenders may conform to the views of others and engage in actions that are not authentic. Offenders possessing a strong desire to be accepted by the group may have a difficult time forming or articulating their own opinions. This disadvantage is referred to as *group think*, a dangerous phenomenon in which members conform to attitudes and views expressed in a group that may not be their own.[27] For offenders who have a difficult time speaking in front of others, group counseling can be very intimidating. Finally, offenders have expressed dissatisfaction with the counselor's ability to keep the group focused. Because it is common to have offenders in groups who are motivated to attend for nontherapeutic reasons, members can become easily distracted and disruptive to the sessions.

Group Treatment Programs

A number of group treatment techniques are used within the prison and in community-based counseling programs. Twelve-step and therapeutic communities are two of the most common group treatment programs.

Several twelve-step programs are offered to offenders in prisons and in the community. Alcoholics Anonymous (AA), one of the most widely known group treatment programs, was founded in 1935. The only requirement for joining AA is the sincere desire to stop drinking. Once joining AA, members chose another AA member as a sponsor. The sponsors are also recovering alcoholics who lend support to others as they complete 12 chronological steps. The treatment involves attending a series of meetings where other alcoholics share their experiences with alcohol abuse. Because of the success of AA as a group treatment program, additional 12-step programs have emerged to address problems other than alcoholism. Other 12-step programs found in correctional counseling include Narcotics Anonymous, Al-Anon Family Groups, Gamblers Anonymous, and Adult Children of Alcoholics.

Therapeutic communities are group treatment programs designed to give offenders an opportunity to increase levels of individual and social responsibility. Interactions with other offenders are an important component of therapeutic community programs. Offenders learn acceptable behaviors and develop more effective social skills through daily community meetings and work assignments. Daily interactions are used to cultivate a sense of community and *mutual self-help.* Under the mutual self-help concept, individuals assume responsibility for the recovery, personal growth, and right living of their peers in order to maintain their own recovery.[28]

Self-Help Correctional Programs

Self-help programs exist in prisons and in community-based correctional programs. Self-help groups are encouraged to help offenders assume responsibility for their own rehabilitation. Some self-help programs commonly offered include Toastmasters, Jaycees, Positive Mental Attitude, and various religious programs.

Toastmasters

Many U.S. prisons now have active Toastmasters clubs, where inmates learn the same public speaking and leadership skills they would in the outside world. Inmates learn how to operate in a "normal" setting: presiding over meetings, making presentations, and perhaps most importantly, standing up in front of a group and speaking. Some judges now include mandatory membership in Toastmasters as part of an offender's sentence, believing that participating in the group helps the offender develop the necessary social skills to integrate into legitimate society upon release.

> Toastmasters has given those interested in our maximum security population an organization to join that promotes positive goals such as improving self-worth, self-esteem, basic life skills, and friendly competition. We have found that when an inmate gets truly involved with a positive organization such as Toastmasters, this inmate becomes a better inmate with little or no disciplinary problems. Then, by his own actions, becomes a positive force who promotes positive attitudes and behavior to his peers. (Warden Burl Cain, Angola Prison, Louisiana)[29]

Jaycees

One of the largest self-help groups in the nation, Jaycee chapters in the community sponsor programs in institutions to promote *civic engagement*. Civic engagement involves individual and group service projects designed to identify and address issues of public concern. Members organize blood drives for leukemia victims, send money to children in underdeveloped countries, and plant trees in prison courtyards. One chapter even raised $2,500 to buy a used fire truck for an impoverished Indian reservation in Nebraska. In North Carolina, Jaycee inmates toured nearby schools to warn students of the dangers of drugs, and inmate Jaycees in Washington state and Maryland have successfully lobbied prison reform bills through the state legislatures.[30]

Positive Mental Attitude (PMA)

Positive Mental Attitude is a self-help program created by W. Clement Stone in which the central idea is that an offender can improve his or her position in life through optimistic thinking. PMA implies that an offender sincerely wants to find and execute ways to win, or find a desirable outcome, regardless of the circumstances.[31]

The Thresholds Program

Offered by the Catholic Charities of the Archdiocese of Atlanta, Inc., the Thresholds program is an Atlanta-based six-week self-help program designed to help soon-to-be released prisoners integrate feelings and emotions related to problem solving. Although offered by a Catholic archdiocese, the nondenominational Thresholds utilizes faith-based volunteers who lead small classes and personal mentoring sessions at selected correctional facilities or halfway houses.[32]

Miracles Prisoner Ministry (MPM)

As a nondenominational self-help program, MPM ministers to all faiths. The program freely offers a diversity of religious reading materials and offers on-site spiritual training classes for prisoners. A yearlong spiritual recovery correspondence course is also offered to those in need of a more structured religious program. In order for prisoners to fill an ever-growing gap in their spiritual lives, MPM volunteers believe that inmates must learn to depend on their higher power. The higher power may be referred to as such or, more specifically, as their Creator, Source, Supreme Architect, Single Source of Reality, or simply, God.[33]

National Islamic Prison Foundation (NIPF)

Another self-help religious program, NIPF is funded by Saudi Arabian resources. NIPF and two dozen interconnected groups form a nationwide network of prison-based programs, claiming to convert 135,000 prisoners a year. Al Qaeda training manuals emphasize that non-Muslim prisoners should be targeted for religious conversion, since their bitterness toward the government makes them easy targets. Each year, this organization ships more than 20,000 Qurans and other Islamic publications to U.S. prisons. During their prison stays, prisoners (potential Muslim converts) are told by NIPF that when they are freed, they will be able to find food and shelter as well as assistance in finding employment, in virtually any mosque or Islamic center.

Christian Women's Prison Outreach Ministries

The Christian Women's Prison Outreach Ministries is a resource for female prisoners committed to building good character and emotional health. Their focus is to provide Bible studies and living skills training for women in prisons. This volunteer organization believes offender rehabilitation is achieved through (1) reconciliation, drawing others into a closer relationship with Christ; (2) restoration, reestablishing emotional health and building good Christian character; and (3) regeneration, encouraging and equipping women to be fruitful servants in God's kingdom.[34]

Summary

Correctional counseling at both the institutional and community levels is necessary for successful treatment, rehabilitation, and reintegration. There are a wide variety of options available to correctional treatment providers, including overriding paradigms and theories, behavior-specific programs, individual versus group counseling, government-sponsored versus private programs, and secular versus nonsecular programs. Ultimately, the decision will rest with the organization/institution and the individual preferences of the counselors themselves. Students should consider completing an internship to become better acquainted with current correctional treatment strategies.

Vocabulary

Aversion therapy

Behavior therapy

Collateral contacts

Covert sensitization

Criminogenic characteristics

Economic deprivation theory

External restraint theory

Feminist theory

Genetic theory

Group think

Insight-based therapy

Irrational self-talk

Mutual self-help

Positivist perspective

Psychological theory: Sexual inadequacy

Serotonin

Social psychological theory: Sexual permissiveness

Subculture of violence theory

Discussion Questions

1. What are the differences between institutional and community-based correctional treatment specialists?

2. How do conflicts between custodial staff and correctional treatment staff impede the implementation of correctional treatment strategies?

3. Know the various theoretical perspectives that guide correctional treatment strategies. Based upon the theoretical perspectives, how do treatment strategies address violent and chemically dependent offenders?

4. What are the advantages and disadvantages for individual and group counseling?

5. Identify the different self-help correctional programs. In what ways do the programs help offenders assume responsibility for their own rehabilitation?

Notes

1. Bureau of Labor Statistics. (2010). *Occupational outlook handbook, 2010–11 edition. Probation officers and correctional treatment specialists.* Retrieved March 15, 2010, from http://www.bls.gov/oco/ocos265.htm

2. Clear, T. R., Cole, G. F., & Reisig, M. D. (2011). *American corrections* (9th ed.). Belmont, CA: Wadsworth.

3. Hanser, R. D., & Mire, S. (2011). *Correctional counseling.* Boston, MA: Prentice Hall.

4. Kratcoski, P. C. (1989). *Correctional counseling and treatment.* Long Grove, IL: Waveland Press.

5. Schrink, J., & Hamm, M. S. (1989). Misconceptions concerning correctional counseling. *Journal of Offender Counseling, Services & Rehabilitation, 14*(1), 133–148.

6. Hanser, R. D. (2010). *Community corrections.* Thousand Oaks, CA: Sage.

7. Hanser, R. D., & Mire, S. (2011). *Correctional counseling.* Boston, MA: Prentice Hall.

8. Sabol, W., West, H. C., & Cooper, M. (2008). *Prisoners in 2008* (Bureau of Justice Statistics NCJ 228417). Retrieved March 17, 2010, from http://bjs.ojp.usdoj.gov/content/pub/pdf/p08.pdf

9. Bonczar, T. P., & Glaze, L. E. (2008). *Probation and parole in the United States, 2007* (Bureau of Justice Statistics NCJ 224707). Retrieved March 17, 2010, from http://bjs.ojp.usdoj.gov/index.cfm?ty=pbdetail&iid=1099

10. Henry, A., & Short, J. (1954). *Suicide and homicide.* New York, NY: Free Press.

11. Unnithan, P., Huff-Corzine, L., Corzine, J., & Whitt, H. (1994). *The currents of lethal violence: An integrated model of suicide and homicide.* Albany, NY: State University of New York Press.

12. Wolfgang, A. E. (1958). *Patterns in criminal homicide.* Philadelphia, PA: University of Pennsylvania Press.

13. Groth, N., & Birnbaum, J. (1979). *Men who rape.* New York, NY: Plenum.

14. Kannin, E. J. (1985). Date rapists: Differential sexual socialization and relative deprivation. *Archives of Sexual Behavior, 14,* 219–231.

15. Chappell, D., Geis, G., Schafer, S., & Siegel, L. (1971). Forcible rape: A comparative study of offenses known to the police in Boston and Los Angeles. In M. M. Henslin (ed.), *Studies in the sociology of sex.* New York, NY: Appleton-Century-Crofts.

16. Sanday, P. R. (1981). The socio-cultural context of rape: A cross-cultural study. *Journal of Social Issues, 37,* 5–27.

17. Schwartz, M. D., & DeKeseredy, W. S. (1997). *Sexual assault on the college campus: The role of male peer support.* Thousand Oaks, CA: Sage.

18. Aylwin, A., Reddon, J., & Burke, A. (2005). Sexual fantasies of adolescent male sex offenders in residential treatment: A descriptive study. *Archives of Sexual Behavior, 34*(2), 231–239.

18a. Blum, K., Noble, E. P., Sheridan, P. J., Montgomery, A., Ritchie, T., Jagadeeswaran, P., Nogami, H., Briggs, A. H., Chen, J. B. (1990) Allelic association of human dopamine D2 receptor gene in alcholism. *Journal of the American Medical Association,* 18, 263 (15) 2055–2060.

19. Cloninger, C. R. (1991). D2 dopamine receptor gene is associated but not linked with alcoholism. *JAMA* 266(13), 1833–1834.

20. Patzelt, J. (2006). Drug addiction: Which comes first—brain or behavior—and does it matter? Retrieved March 17, 2010, at http://serendip.brynmawr.edu/bb/neuro/neuro06/web1/jpatzelt.html

21. Currie, E. (1993). *Reckoning: Drugs, the cities, and the American future.* New York, NY: Hill and Wang.

22. Thinking for a change. Retrieved March 19, 2010, at www.nicic.gov/T4C

23. Parks, G. A., & Marlat, G. A. (2000). Relapse prevention therapy: A cognitive-behavioral approach. *The National Psychiatrist.* Retrieved March 18, 2010, from http://www.nationalpsychologist.com/articles/art_v9n5_3.htm

24. In Custody Drug Treatment Program, Division of Addiction and Recovery Services (DARS). Retrieved March 20, 2010, from http://www.cdcr.ca.gov/Divisions_Boards/Adult_Programs/DARS.html

25. Hanser, R. D., & Mire, S. (2011). *Correctional counseling.* Boston, MA: Prentice Hall.

26. Geller, S. E., Hamlin, P. H., & Kennedy, T. D. (2007). Behavior modification in a prison. *Criminal Justice and Behavior, 4*(1), 11–43. DOI: 10.1177/009385487700400102.

27. Robbins, S. P. (2005). *Organizational behavior* (11th ed.). Upper Saddle River, NJ: Pearson.

28. Pelissier, B., Motivans, M., & Rounds-Bryant, J. L. (2005). Substance abuse treatment outcomes: A multi-site study of male and female prison programs. *Journal of Offender Rehabilitation, 41*(2), 57–80.

29. Taking flight. Why and how to start prison Toastmasters club. Retrieved March 24, 2010, from http://www.takingflight.org/starting_club.htm

30. The law: Jaycees in prison. Retrieved March 24, 2010, from http://www.time.com/time/magazine/article/0,9171,910004,00.html

31. Positive Mental Attitude. (2006). *The Register, 7*(8), 3–7.

32. De Long, C. F. (1998). Changes in prisoner perceptions of control over life situations as a result of learning decision-making skills. Retrieved March 24, 2010, from http://www.ncjrs.gov/App/Publications/abstract.aspx?ID=56360

33. Miracles Prisoner Ministries. Retrieved March 24, 2010, from http://www.miraclesprisonerministry.org/

34. Christian Women's Prison Outreach Ministries. Retrieved March 24, 2010, from http://gardenpath.org/gp/index.php

Capital Punishment

Society has erected the gallows at the end of the lane instead of guideposts and direction boards at the beginning.

—Edward Bulwer-Lytton

Introduction

One of the most controversial issues in the United States is *capital punishment* or, as it is commonly known, the death penalty. Public opinion as to the need for capital punishment finds the nation divided.

Capital punishment is the ultimate penalty; once imposed, the convicted is executed. World history is filled with examples of the use of capital punishment, but by the middle of the twentieth century, nation after nation moved away from capital punish as a necessary criminal sanction, replacing it with long periods of confinement, to include life sentences with no possibility for release.

By 2010, 139 nations abolished capital punishment in law or practice, and the majority of those retaining the sentence use it sparingly. The United States is one of those nations that retained the death penalty, but even in the United States, capital punishment is not accepted in all jurisdictions.[7]

In the United States, the decision to include capital punishment as a judicial sanction is within the authority of the various legislative branches of the states and the federal government. Not surprising, state legislatures are divided on the value and need for the death penalty, though most state legislatures have chosen to retain capital punishment for the most serious crimes.

Though most jurisdictions in the United States have capital punishment within their criminal codes, in reality, the penalty itself is not often applied, nor do we see evidence that capital punishment serves as a deterrent to the criminal behavior of others.

Methods of Execution Used in the United States

Five methods of execution have been used in the United States: lethal injection, electrocution, lethal gas, hanging, and firing squad. Methods of execution have been technology driven. Hanging and the limited use of the firing squad were replaced in many jurisdictions by the more "humane" methods of lethal gas and electrocution. By the end of the twentieth century, lethal injection was the method of execution used by most jurisdictions in the nation.

History of the Death Penalty in the United States

Europeans establishing settlements in North America were well familiar with the concept of capital punishment, witnessing the death penalty as a common criminal sanction throughout Europe for centuries. The Jamestown colony in Virginia was the site of the first execution in colonial America. In 1608, Captain George Kendall was executed by firing squad after conviction for treason against the English crown. Though Kendall would be the first such execution, he would not be the last, with over 13,000 executions in America following over the next 400 years.

Across the colonies and then into the new United States, capital punishment was a possible sentence for a wide variety of crimes. In those early days, the execution itself would become a public event, drawing crowds of spectators.

Though crime in colonial America was not extensive or complex by the standards of today, the need existed within society to impose sanctions, and some of those criminal sanctions included execution for the most severe crimes. Throughout the colonies, laws were enacted defining criminal behavior, opening the door for arrest, convictions, and criminal sanctions. Corporal punishment was typically used for minor offenses; long-term confinement was not viewed as a reasonable option.

Colonial leaders witnessed their early criminal codes evolve. In 1612, Virginia governor Sir Thomas Dale enacted the divine, moral, and martial laws, which provided the death penalty for even minor offenses, such as stealing grapes, killing chickens, and trading with the Native Americans.[1]

In Massachusetts between 1692 and 1693, one of the most infamous uses of capital punishment occurred with the Salem witch trials. Accused and convicted on the wave of public hysteria, over 200 were accused of witchcraft-related offenses, with 19 of those convicted executed by hanging.

Over the next century, the colonies and then the states of the new nation developed their own identities, and with them their criminal codes and criminal sanctions. Upon the conclusion of the American Revolution, the new United States moved from a confederation to a constitutionally based republic. Quickly attached to the new Constitution were 10 amendments now known as the Bill of Rights.

The Bill of Rights were formal "guarantees" viewed important enough to connect to the Constitution, with the intent of ensuring liberties within the nation to its citizens. Within the Bill of Rights is the Eighth Amendment, which includes a prohibition of the imposition of cruel and unusual punishments. This amendment has been pointed to by critics of capital punishment, suggesting that the death penalty should be prohibited in the United States based upon their interpretation of this amendment.

Further Evolution of the Death Penalty in the United States

In the late 1700s and early 1800s prisons in the United States began to emerge. Confinement began replacing the corporal and capital punishment that was frequently publically administered. An early movement commenced to eliminate capital punishment in some states. During this period, five states abolished the death penalty for all crimes except murder. By the 1820s, the nation witnessed the majority of northern states restricting capital punishment for murder.

The most frequently used method of execution across the United States was hanging, but by the 1880s, discussions were occurring suggesting that electrocution might well be a more effective and humane form of execution. In the late 1880s, New York State established a committee to determine a new, more humane system of execution to replace hanging, and acting upon the work of the committee, New York became the first state to adopt electrocution as an execution method in 1888.

The first person to be executed by electrocution was William Kemmler. Kemmler, a convicted murderer, was executed in the electric chair in New York's Auburn Prison on August 6, 1890. Following the lead of New York, many states adopted the electric chair as a method of execution.

Over the next 40 years, the majority of states across the nation adopted electrocution as their method of execution, and with it corrections added a new chapter in its history. Electric chairs (Figure 13.1) gained their own identities, such as "Old Sparky," which was the nickname for the chairs in states such as Arkansas, Florida, New York, Oklahoma, Ohio, West Virginia, South Carolina, Louisiana, Illinois, and Kentucky. In Alabama, the electric chair was known as the "Yellow Mamma." Texas's Old Sparky was used to execute 361 inmates between 1924 and 1964.

Old Sparky: Texas Prison Museum

Mississippi utilized a traveling electric chair that was moved from county to county within the state to execute those condemned. Other states established execution areas within their correctional facilities, frequently with death row inmates housed just steps away from the execution chamber.

In 1924, technology again influenced methods of execution when Nevada became the first state to adopt lethal gas as an execution method. That year Nevada executed convicted murderer Gee Jon. Lethal gas was, as electrocution before, seen to be more humane and efficient than both hanging and electrocution.

Figure 13.1 Electric chair. (From http://www.deathpenaltyinfo.org.)

The crime wave of the 1920s and 1930s forced a reexamination of crime and the responses to criminal behavior in the United States. Commencing in 1930, the federal government began officially collecting and maintaining statistics pertaining to crime. Drawing from those statistics pertaining to capital punishment in the United States, we see that from 1930 until 1967, 3,859 persons were executed under civil jurisdiction in the United States.

The Move to Eliminate Capital Punishment

By the 1960s, the social changes in the United States reached into the justice system, and capital punishment became a topic of major discussion in public, legislative, and judicial areas. Several cases drew the attention of the various courts in the nation challenging the legality of capital punishment. In 1972, the U.S. Supreme Court agreed to review the case *Furman v. Georgia*. The issue in the Georgia case pertained to a state statute giving the jury complete discretion to decide death or life imprisonment upon conviction of murder. The U.S. Supreme Court ruled this statute unconstitutional, finding in a 5 to 4 plurality opinion that the death penalty was applied in Georgia in a "freakish and wanton" manner due to unguided jury discretion.

The practical effect of this decision by the Supreme Court was to strike down existing statutes in all states, removing approximately 629 inmates from death row. More than 600 of these death row inmates had their death sentences lifted as a result of *Furman*. But the court did not prohibit the death penalty itself. Many state legislatures altered their criminal statutes in a manner that would satisfy the Supreme Court's objections to arbitrary imposition of death sentences. Most states adopted a *bifurcated trial*, or two-part trial involving a guilt phase and a penalty phase. During the penalty phase, jurors and judges are advised of facts that may mitigate or aggravate the circumstances of the crime.

In 1976, the U.S. Supreme Court again addressed capital punishment when it ruled in *Gregg v. Georgia* and *Jurek v. Texas* that a death sentence is not a per se violation of the Eighth Amendment. The court stated that where the jury is given guided discretion through *aggravating* and *mitigating circumstances* focusing on the particularized nature of the crime and the character of the offender, the death penalty no longer violates the Eighth Amendment in application. This decision opened the door for a new era in capital punishment in the United States.

In 1977 capital punishment captured national attention when convicted Utah murderer Gary Gilmore waived his judicial appeals and pushed for execution. As a result of his efforts, the Gilmore execution was scheduled and he became the first person executed in the United States in almost 10 years. The execution of Gilmore opened the door for further executions.

Death Penalty in the United States after Gilmore

After the Gilmore execution, states and the federal government again examined their stand on capital punishment. For those jurisdictions that chose to retain capital punishment, new execution protocols were developed to ensure appropriate checks and balances were established, and lethal injection assumed the most accepted method of execution in the nation.

Other issues related to capital punishment were addressed after the Gilmore case. The mental status and age of the offender came into question by the various courts and state legislatures. In 2002, in the case *Atkins v. Virginia*, justices ruled that executing mentally retarded criminals violated the Constitution's ban on cruel and unusual punishment. Writing for the majority, Justice John Paul Stevens stated a "national consensus" against executing a killer who may lack the intelligence to fully understand his crime.[2]

Capital punishment was back as a criminal sanction in the United States. Following the Gilmore execution until 2010, over 1,200 executions were conducted in the United States. Figure 13.2 illustrates how the number of executions has dropped in the past three decades.

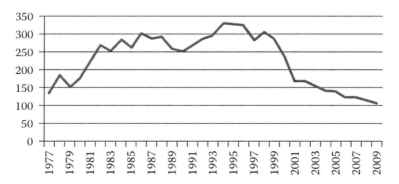

Figure 13.2 U.S. death sentences. (From http://www.deathpenalty-info.org.)

The drop in executions may be explained by the fact that some states have abolished the death penalty, while others have declared *moratoriums*, or periods of delay. Regardless, there is evidence that suggests juries look for alternatives to the death penalty.

Execution and Gender

Though the vast majority of those who have received capital punishment in the United States have been male, women have also been executed in the nation. Historically, women have rarely been subjected to the death penalty in the United States. The primary reason for this is that women have not committed the types of crimes with the levels of violence that we have seen committed by men. From the first woman executed in the United States, Jane Champion, who was hanged in James City, Virginia, in 1632, to the present, women have constituted only about 3% of U.S. executions, with less than 600 women executed of the over 13,000 executions that have been conducted in the nation.[3] As of June 30, 2009, there were 53 women on death row, which constitutes 1.6% of the total death row population of about 3,297 persons.

The first woman to be executed in the electric chair was Martha M. Place, executed at the New York Penitentiary at Sing Sing Prison on March 20, 1899. Several cases involving female offenders have captured national attention. Some of the more famous cases include Ethel Rosenberg, who was executed with her husband after conviction of espionage in 1953; Karla Faye Tucker, who was executed in Texas in 1998; and the serial killer Aileen Wuornos, who was executed in Florida in 2002.

Capital Punishment: Jurisdictional View

Federal Death Penalty

From what can be determined from existing records, the federal government utilized hanging, electrocution, and the gas chamber to execute 340 individuals between 1790 and 1963, not including military executions. The majority of federal executions occurred after convictions not only for murder or crimes resulting in murder, but also for piracy, rape, rioting, kidnapping, and spying and espionage. Also not included in those 340 executions are 34 individuals, including 2 women, executed under federal jurisdiction in the District of Columbia between 1927 and 1963.

From 1963 to 2001, no federal executions took place. Since 2001, three prisoners have been executed. The federal death penalty can be enacted in any state or territory of the United States, even in states that do not have the death penalty.

Federal prisoners are typically executed by lethal injection, pursuant to 28 CFR Part 26. In 1988, a federal death penalty statute was enacted for murders committed in the course of drug trafficking activities. However, for offenses under the Violent Crime Control and Law Enforcement Act of 1994, the method is that of the state in which the conviction took place, pursuant to 18 USC 3596. Additionally, in 1994, the federal death penalty expanded to include some 60 different offenses, including murder of certain government officials, kidnapping resulting in death, murder for hire, fatal drive-by shootings, sexual abuse crimes resulting in death, carjacking resulting in death, as well as certain crimes not resulting in death, including the running of large-scale drug enterprises.[4]

In 1999 the federal government completed a lethal injection execution chamber at the U.S. Penitentiary at Terre Haute, Indiana, where federal inmates under death sentence are housed.

Terrorism, to include the Oklahoma City bombing and the attacks upon the United States in 2001, also impacted the nation's view of federal capital punishment. Domestic terrorist Timothy McVeigh, convicted of the Oklahoma City bombing, was executed in 2001.

In 2009, U.S. Attorney General Eric Holder announced that five men being held in Guantanamo prison in connection with the September 11, 2001, attack on the World Trade Center will face trial in federal court in New York City: Khalid Shaikh Mohammed, Ali Abd al-Aziz Ali, Walid bin Attash, Mustafa Ahmed al-Hawsawi, and Ramzi bin al-Shibh. These defendants could face the federal death penalty.

The use of the federal death penalty on Native American reservations has been left to the discretion of the tribal governments. Almost all the tribes have opted not to use the federal death penalty.

Military Capital Punishment

U.S. military personnel have historically been subject to criminal penalties, to include capital punishment. Currently, not only is the conduct of military personnel covered by the federal, state, or international statutes of the location where they serve, but they are also subject to the military criminal code, known as the Uniform Code of Military Justice.

A recent amendment to the Uniform Code of Military Justice offers a new alternative to the death penalty. For crimes that occurred on or after November 17, 1997, a sentence of life without the possibility of parole is now possible. Prior to this legislation, those service members serving a life sentence would be eligible for parole after serving 10 years.[5]

Though no military executions have been carried out since 1961, as of January 2008, nine men are on military death row, which is maintained at the U.S. Disciplinary Barracks at Ft. Leavenworth in Kansas, where the lethal injection execution chamber is located.[6]

The Uniform Code of Military Justice provides the death penalty as a possible punishment for 15 offenses (10 USC Sections 886–934), many of which must occur during a time of war. All those currently on the military's death row were convicted of premeditated murder or felony murder. The president has the power to commute a death sentence, and no service member can be executed unless the president personally confirms the death penalty.

The *Military Commissions Act (MCA) of 2006*, which established special military commissions for detainees held at Guantanamo Bay, provides for the death penalty for certain offenses. Some Guantanamo prisoners may face capital charges under this act, while others are being moved to the United States to face capital charges in federal court.

State-Level Capital Punishment

As stated earlier, state legislatures have the authority to determine, through legislation, the capital punishment policy of their state (Figure 13.3). Though most states do have legislation allowing capital punishment as a judicial sentencing option, most states rarely use the penalty. Those states that do have capital punishment have adopted lethal injection as the method used when required. In each state, a sentence of capital punishment is automatically and extensively reviewed within the judicial appeal process. State governors also have the authority, as the chief executive in the states, to commute the penalty from death.

In 2000, Illinois governor George H. Ryan gained national attention when he issued a moratorium on executions in his state. In 2003, just before he left office, Governor Ryan commuted to life in prison

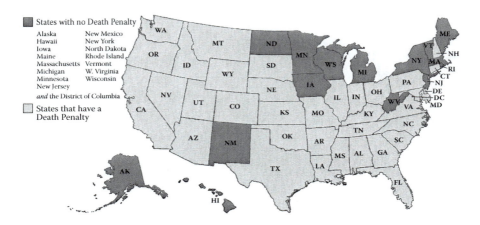

Figure 13.3

the death sentences of the 167 Illinois inmates at the time in his state. The actions of Governor Ryan, as would be expected, sparked extensive debate on the need for capital punishment. This should be expanded. It should especially discuss Governor Ryan receiving a Nobel Peace Prize, mostly because the wrongful convictions that were presented by the Northwestern University School of Law drew international attention to mistakes.

What we do see with the death penalty is that it is just one element in the justice system that inspires an emotional debate. Though we do not see evidence that the death penalty, if used, directly impacts the level of violent crime in a state, we do see that in the states that retain the sentence, major segments of the population feel the penalty to be not only important, but necessary.

Issues in Capital Punishment

What Crimes Bring a Sentence of Capital Punishment?

In the United States, the majority of executions are related to homicide convictions, but not all homicides result in capital punishment. This has been one of the major issues related to use of capital punishment. The possibility of execution after conviction of homicide remains very low in the United States. Some of the major issues related to the sentence include the following.

Sentencing

The death penalty in the United States is reserved for those crimes that are viewed by our society as the most unacceptable, which has typically been seen as homicide. But not all homicides result in a sentence of death. This is one of the most interesting aspects of the penalty. As an example, one of the earliest sentences to spark capital punishment debate was the Chicago case known as Leopold and Loeb. In 1924, these young men murdered 14-year-old Bobby Franks, essentially to see what it was like to commit a homicide. Cold blooded in nature, the crime was one of the earliest in the nation to be covered nationally by radio. Clarence Darrow, their defense attorney, attacked the death penalty as appropriate. His arguments attacked capital punishment as retributive; he argued criminal sanctions should focus upon rehabilitative. Leopold and Loeb avoided capital punishment.

In Kansas, Dennis Rader, the serial killer known as the BTK killer, who was responsible for a reign of terror in the Wichita area in the 1970s, was not subjected to the possibility of capital punishment. Decades after his murder spree, a break in the investigation led to Rader's arrest and conviction. Legislation in Kansas pertaining to the death penalty did not allow capital punishment as a sentencing option in his case, even though he may have been the worst serial killer seen within the state.

Texas has long been viewed as the state that most frequently employs capital punishment. Opponents of the penalty point to Texas and its rate of homicide as an example of the lack of a deterrent effect capital punishment has upon crime. This argument is not entirely fair in that there are countless factors influencing criminal behavior, the decision to commit crime, and the overall criminal rate in a jurisdiction, other than just the fear of punishment upon conviction.

Juveniles and the Death Penalty

The constitutionality of executing persons for crimes committed when they were under the age of 18 is an issue that the Supreme Court has evaluated in several cases since the death penalty was reinstated in 1976. In *Thompson v. Oklahoma* (1988), the court recognized that the age of the offender was an important consideration when trying to determine how the individual should be punished. The court endorsed the proposition that less culpability should attach to a crime committed by a juvenile than to a comparable crime committed by an adult.[7] In a 2005 decision called *Roper v. Simmons*, the Supreme Court of the United States ruled that the execution of people who were under 18 at the time of their crimes violates the federal constitutional guarantee against cruel and unusual punishments.[7] From 1976 until 2005, when the *Roper* case impacted capital punishment of juvenile offenders, 22 individuals were executed who had committed their crimes while juveniles. Of those 22, 13 of those executions occurred in Texas.

Of the 73 offenders under sentence of death on December 31, 2000, for crimes committed at age 17 or younger, 55 were age 17 at the time of their offense and the remaining 18 were 16. Nearly half of these offenders (33 of 73) were not juveniles at the time of their offense—they were legally adults because they were older than their state's upper age of original juvenile court jurisdiction. The majority of these (26 of 33) were 17-year-olds from Texas, where original juvenile court jurisdiction ends at age 16. The youngest of these 73 offenders was 19 years old as of December 31, 2000, the oldest was 42, and the average age was 25. As of year-end 2000, an average of 5½ years had passed since the offender's initial death sentence.[8]

The *Roper* opinion drew upon a 2002 decision by the court holding that the execution of persons with mental retardation is unconstitutional: In both decisions, the court reasoned that these special groups of offenders are less culpable than adult offenders with no intellectual impairment who committed the same crimes. By a vote of 5 to 4, the U.S. Supreme Court held in *Roper v. Simmons* (2005) that the Eighth Amendment forbids the execution of offenders who were under the age of 18 when their crimes were committed. In making its decision, the court considered both the national consensus that existed against the practice and testimony of professional medical and psychological organizations citing new evidence of delayed brain maturation that impacts culpability determinations for juveniles. The court's ruling in *Roper v. Simmons* affected 72 juvenile offenders in 12 states.[7]

Impact upon the Staff and Families

Little has been discussed on the issue of the impact of the death penalty upon the staff and families of both the victims and the executed individual. Dr. Donald A. Cabana, former warden of the Mississippi State Penitentiary and commissioner of Corrections for Mississippi, shared insight on the impact of the death penalty being imposed on those involved in his work in *Death at Midnight: Confessions of an*

Executioner.[9] Dr. Cabana, as warden, was responsible for conducting several executions. He discussed in his work the psychological impact on those involved in conducting the execution. For many of the staff, in systems such as Mississippi, many of those involved with the actual execution have interacted with the person to be convicted for years. In spite of all efforts to remain objective and professional, it is very difficult, if not impossible, to not be emotionally impacted by involvement in the process. In some states, inmates sentenced for execution are housed in institutions separate from the institution where they will be executed. This is done in an attempt to reduce personal involvement of the staff responsible to conduct the execution with the inmate.

For the families, execution is never simple. Many family members of victims express how the execution did not bring to closure the pain of the crime as anticipated. For the families of the person executed, the emotions range widely.

Summary

Though we are not sure of the actual number, it is estimated that over 13,000 people have been executed as a result of a judicial sentence in America since the first execution in Virginia in 1608.

The death penalty will remain a lightning rod for debate in the American criminal justice system. The public is also divided as to its value and appropriateness. Arguments in favor of or against its use can be well made on either side of the issue, but what we do know is that capital punishment has not proven to be a deterrent for crime.

Vocabulary

Aggravating circumstances

Bifurcated trial

Capital punishment

Furman v. Georgia

Gregg v. Georgia

Jurek v. Texas

Military Commissions Act of 2006

Mitigating circumstances

Moratorium

Roper v. Simmons

Thompson v. Oklahoma

Discussion Questions

1. Know the history of capital punishment in the United States.

2. What major Supreme Court decisions have had the most significant impact on capital punishment legislation? What have been their impacts?

3. What was the Supreme Court's rationalization for banning juvenile executions?

4. Distinguish between mitigating and aggravating circumstances.

Notes

1. Introduction to the death penalty. Retrieved May 30, 2010, from http://www.deathpenaltyinfo.org/part-i-history-death-penalty#IntroductionoftheDeathPenalty

2. Totenberg, N. (2005, March 2). Supreme Court ends death penalty for juveniles. National Public Radio. Retrieved June 8, 2010, from http://www.npr.org/templates/story/story.php?storyId=4518051

3. Women and the death penalty. (n.d.). Death Penalty Information Center. Retrieved June 8, 2010, from http://www.deathpenalty-info.org/women-and-death-penalty

4. Federal death penalty. Retrieved May 30, 2010, from http://www.amnestyusa.org/death-penalty/death-penalty-facts/federal-death-penalty/page.do?id=1101082

5. Capital punishment: An act of justice, or a cruel twist of "humanity"? Retrieved June 7, 2010, from http://www.fictionpress.com/s/2778024/1/Capital_Punishment

6. The US military death penalty. Retrieved May 30, 2010, from http://www.deathpenaltyinfo.org/us-military-death-penalty

7. Capital punishment in context: The death penalty for juveniles. (n.d.). Retrieved June 8, 2010, from http://www.capitalpunishmentincontext.org/issues/juveniles

8. Juvenile offenders and victims: National report series. Retrieved June 3, 2010, from http://www.ncjrs.gov/pdffiles1/ojjdp/202885.pdf

9. Cabana, D. A. (1996). *Death at midnight: Confessions of an executioner.* Northeastern University Press, Boston, MA.

Juvenile Corrections

The United States of America does not have a juvenile justice system. Rather, it has 51 separate systems.

—**National Center for Juvenile Justice**

There is no such thing as a bad boy.

—**Father Flanagan**

Introduction

In the United States we typically view three segments of our population, the youth, elderly, and special needs citizens, as those most vulnerable and most in need of protection. For these three groups, efforts have been made to create and maintain various programs to provide services to respond to their needs. Of these three populations, the youth provide special challenges for the criminal justice system.

Across the nation, communities remain concerned about juveniles and their involvement in criminal behavior. This concern focuses on two major issues: (1) the obvious impact of the crimes themselves, both petty and serious offenses, and (2) the concern that the juvenile offender of today will become the adult offender of tomorrow.

Even the simplest investigation into the background of adult offenders reveals that for many, their criminal history extends into their youth. Not uncommonly, we find adult offenders accumulated extensive juvenile records, suggesting criminal activity in their youth served as a springboard to their lives as adult offenders.

Juvenile Crime

There are countless reasons why a youth becomes involved in criminal activity, and there is no indication that juvenile crime will ever disappear from our society. What we do know is juvenile crime and the response to that criminal activity will continue to be a challenge in our communities, states, and nation. The pressing question within our society related to the juvenile offender is simply: Are there effective strategies that can be found to improve our response to the issues related to youths who have come in contact with the criminal justice system?

Each part of the nation finds its own juvenile challenge. Some jurisdictions experience few juvenile offenses, while others deal with a significant amount of serious juvenile criminal activity, including juvenile involvement in violent, urban gangs. Every jurisdiction struggles to meet the service needs that must be provided to juveniles as required by law.

Who Is the Juvenile Offender?

Although most of the cases in the juvenile court system involve children and youth between the ages of 10 and 18, the upper age of eligibility is determined by the juvenile law of each state. Most states try *juvenile crime* cases in juvenile court when the offender is younger than 18; a few states have younger cutoffs. Alternatively, in cases of *status offense* (juvenile offenses that would not be a crime if committed by an adult), many states extend jurisdiction through the age of 20. In some states, a sentence obtained from a juvenile court cannot extend beyond the individual's 18th birthday.

The nation is extremely concerned about the rise in juvenile crime. Youth violence, gang activity, and drugs have all influenced increased youth delinquency and criminal activity. In some cities, juveniles are major factors in the increase in homicide rates, auto theft, home burglary, assault, sale and use of drugs, armed robbery, and aggravated burglary.

Most of the juveniles in the juvenile justice system, especially the violent offenders, are males. This population in custody is also typically male, with minority youths making up the majority in residential placement. As an example, in 2009, males represented half of the juvenile population, but were involved in approximately three-quarters of juvenile arrests and delinquency cases processed in juvenile court. Males represented 87% of juveniles in residential placement.

Most juvenile offenders are "older" juveniles. While 16- and 17-year-olds constitute approximately 25% of the youth population ages 10 to 17, they account for nearly 50% of arrests of youth under age 18, nearly 40% of delinquency court cases, and more than 50% of juveniles in residential placement.[1]

The Juvenile System

Since the first efforts to separate the youthful offender from the adult offender, a comprehensive juvenile justice system has evolved. The foundation of the juvenile system is the notion of *parens patriae*, the power of the state to act on behalf of the child and provide care and protection equivalent to that of a parent. Under the *parens patriae* philosophy, the juvenile process or procedures are informal and nonadversarial. They are designed *for* the offenders rather than against them. For example, in the juvenile system a *petition* instead of a *complaint* is filed, and offenders are *detained* instead of *arrested*. Courts make findings of *adjudication* instead of *convictions*, and offenders receive *dispositions* instead of *sentences*. Though there are differences in each jurisdiction in personality and procedure, the components of the juvenile justice system can be generally divided for discussion into the following six main phases or stages.

Juvenile Intake and Assessment

Juvenile intake and assessment programs/centers serve as the gatekeepers of the juvenile system, providing service to juvenile offenders or children in need taken in the custody of law enforcement. Juvenile *intake* and assessment centers receive and perform diagnostic services for troubled minors, including risk assessment, prior history investigations, and treatment recommendations, and determine initial treatment strategies of the juveniles.[2] This assessment helps determine what community-based services may be appropriate for the youth and family, as well as determine if the youth can be returned home or if placement is appropriate, pending a subsequent court hearing.

Social Investigation

Typically, a juvenile probation officer is tasked with examining the juvenile's family, education, history of delinquency, and so on, for the juvenile court. Some investigations are supplemented by reports from child advocates or court-appointed social workers. This investigation is very important in providing the court with a more efficient insight and understanding of the youth himself or herself.

Fact-Finding Hearing

A juvenile appears before a judge who reviews the complaint and the social investigation. Special juvenile drug courts have been established in some locations to facilitate the evaluation and adjudication of alcohol and other drug (AOD)-related offenses. Assessment, paired with the possibility of diversion at an early stage in the juvenile justice process, appears to be successful in some cases in deterring a juvenile's further involvement in the system. Diversion programs typically allow a juvenile to complete certain requirements in lieu of being processed for adjudication. Diversion programs generally fall under the category of early intervention in that a juvenile's behavior is not yet serious enough to merit formal entry into the juvenile justice system. This period offers a crucial time in which to provide interventions with the potential to successfully move high-risk adolescents away from more serious substance abusing or delinquency behaviors.

Adjudication

The first juvenile court law in the United States came into effect in Illinois on July 1, 1899, when the Chicago Juvenile Court first opened its doors to the public. It was not a sudden invention by a single reformer, but was the result of agitation by two groups of women reformers during the 1890s, the Chicago Woman's Club and the Hull House Community.[3] The establishment of this court, one of the earliest social welfare reforms of the Progressive Era, represented a major change in the way in which the law dealt with wayward children.[4] By 1925, all but two states had established some form of juvenile court, and it would be 1950 before all states had established juvenile courts.[3] From this beginning, those who pushed for the separation of adult and juvenile courts have viewed the juvenile system as a caring parent as opposed to a punishing judge. While the juvenile system retains elements of the adult system, to include confinement, the primary focus is on rehabilitation of the youthful offender.

Disposition

If the juvenile is determined to be delinquent, a hearing is held where the judge decides case disposition. Judges may choose to impose any of a series of graduated sanctions upon the juvenile, to include release with a warning, community supervision, or commitment to a specialized treatment or detention facility, such as a training school, boot camp, or community residential facility,[5] based upon the severity of the conduct. Juvenile correctional facilities are the most restrictive placements for juvenile offenders and are intended to protect public safety as well as providing programs that develop accountability and skill development for juvenile offenders. The graduated sanctions continuum concept utilizes two broad intervention tracks: supervision options and treatment options. Judges consider both as essential aspects of any judicial adjudication and sentencing methodology. In about half of the states, the presence of prior convictions may lead to the exclusion of a youth from the jurisdiction of the juvenile court, or provide that a prosecutor may file the case directly in the criminal court if there are prior convictions in the juvenile court. This should always be done with great care.

Continuing Care

After the juvenile has completed the court's recommendations, he or she is often released to the supervision of a variety of continuing care providers. Provider services include counseling, school dropout prevention, structured social activities, and so on, each with the desire to influence the youth from future criminal activity. Opportunities to change are available, but as we see with the rate of juvenile recidivism, it is ultimately up to the youth to change.

Balanced and Restorative Justice and the Juvenile Offender

The justice system is in a continual state of change, with new ideas and concepts constantly being introduced. Popular today, applied to both the adult and juvenile offender, is the concept of *balanced and restorative justice* (BARJ). Balanced and restorative justice includes three components: accountability for conduct, competency development, and community safety. Accountability expects that when an offense occurs, the offender incurs an obligation. The objective under accountability is to restore the victim, to the greatest extent possible, to his or her precrime status. This may include financial status along with emotional and physical well-being. Competency development is a rehabilitative goal that expects the juvenile offender should be more capable of living productively and responsibly within the community when he or she leaves the system than when he or she entered. Community safety is a public safety goal that emphasizes the fundamental right of all citizens to both be and feel safe from crime. This model suggests that any response to youth crime must strike a balance between the needs of victims, offenders, and their personal responsibility to themselves and their community.

Juvenile Corrections: A Historical Glance

The strategies to respond to juvenile criminal activity have been under continual change since the first efforts were made to influence a positive change in the lives of the youthful offender. Juvenile crime, juvenile justice, and juvenile adjudication are directly linked to juvenile corrections. It is of value to briefly examine the evolution of juvenile corrections in the United States.

The Early Years

During colonial times, youths were often jailed with adults when their only "crime" was they had been abandoned and had turned to petty crime to survive. Difficult economic times, death of parents, and the lack of a social welfare support network resulted in many youths falling into the justice system of the day. The need in the early 1800s to develop solutions for juvenile neglect, abandonment, and crime was obvious in larger, urban areas. Various social groups, including fraternal and religious organizations, embraced juvenile issues and took steps to formulate alternatives to traditional confinement with adults.

In New York, the Society for the Prevention of Pauperism worked to develop solutions to many of the issues pertaining to juveniles. Their efforts resulted in what became known as the New York *House of Refuge.* In 1824, the New York State Legislature incorporated the Managers of the Society for the Reformation of Juvenile Delinquents in the City of New York, and then enacted a state statute authorizing courts statewide to commit juveniles convicted of crimes or adjudicated as vagrants to the New York House of Refuge. The reformatory opened on January 1, 1825, with six boys and three girls. Over the next 10 years, about 1,678 juveniles were admitted to the facility. The New York House of Refuge is recognized as the first juvenile reformatory in the nation and served as an example followed by many states over the next several decades.

Efforts to remove the juveniles from the adult inmate population increased in the northeast, where states began establishing houses of refuge. Between the 1830s and the 1840s approximately 50 houses of refuge were constructed and opened, with most for male offenders. These houses of refuge ranged in size, holding anywhere between 90 and 1,000 youths who had either committed an offense or were in danger of getting into trouble. Orphans were also confined to these institutions. Most residents lived there for a period of 6 weeks to 24 months. Though the House of Refuge was a great step from confinement with adult offenders, there is nothing to suggest the conditions in these facilities were easy. Soon, other ideas emerged in regard to the confinement and training of youths that fell into the custody of the various states.

Two features distinguished the New York institution from the juvenile facilities functioning in Britain at the time. First, youth in the United States were committed for vagrancy in addition to petty crimes. Second, youths could be sentenced to a specific time period or committed indefinitely; the House of Refuge *exercised* authority over inmates throughout their minority years (Figure 14.1).

The Reformatory Movement and the Cottage System

Soon after the creation of the first House of Refuge, discussion occurred focusing on the development of "reformatory or training schools" where youths could be placed, trained in a vocation, and released as productive citizens. The first reform school in the nation was established in Westboro, Massachusetts, in 1847 and was soon followed by others.[3] These facilities were similar to the House of Refuge except that they stressed a longer period of education and training, with a very heavy emphasis upon vocational training in either the industrial or agricultural arts. As with the houses of refuge, conditions were difficult, frequently overcrowded, and the use

Figure 14.1 An 1825 lithograph of the New York House of Refuge, located at Broadway and 23rd Street. This building is believed to be the city's first juvenile detention facility, housing both delinquent boys and girls. (From New York Historical Society, negative 20820.)

of cruelty and violence for disciplining was common. By 1900, 65 juvenile reformatories were in operation in the United States. Almost every state outside of the South had established a training school. For over the next century, reform schools operated across the nation. By the 1970s, many questioned the value of the remaining facilities. Pressured by changes in the accepted approaches to juvenile confinement, decreasing budgets, and the increasing application of federal constitutional rights to juveniles, many states chose to transform or close their state industrial/training schools.[6]

Another step in the evolution of juvenile confinement, education, and training was the introduction of the cottage system. The cottage system was introduced in 1854, and offered residents housing in separate buildings, usually no more than 20 to 40 per cottage. Unlike the typical house of refuge, which housed all the juveniles in one building with very limited support staff, the cottage system attempted to create and sustain a family type model.

As with many of the approaches to juvenile confinement, juvenile cottages were typically linked to extensive vocational educational efforts, to include agriculture and basic apprenticeships. The cottage system, as with the reform school, often used the labor of the youths to assist in offsetting the cost of operating the facilities.[7] In these facilities, early efforts at classification occurred, attempting the separation of juveniles based upon the danger they posed to themselves and others.

Treatment Movement

The most significant change that took place in the twentieth century, as related to the institutionalization of juveniles, was the idea of treatment. Instead of just institutionalizing a juvenile, facilities began to develop treatment plans to address behavioral issues. Today, the idea of developing a treatment plan for a juvenile under judicial sanctions is commonplace.

Juvenile Institutions, Detention, and Residential Confinement

From the jail, to the various houses of refuge, to the training schools, to the cottages, to the prisons, there has and remains a need to have institutions capable of confining the youthful offender. As the use of adult facilities for housing juveniles diminished over the last three decades, the need to develop and operate other facilities for juveniles increased. Depending on the seriousness of their offenses, juveniles may be confined for a short or long term. Short-term confinement facilities include jails, detention facilities, shelter care facilities, and community residential facilities. Long-term confinement facilities include boot camps, reception and diagnostic facilities, ranches and forestry camps, and training schools.

Reception and Diagnostic Centers

Reception and diagnostic centers are both publicly and privately administered. The purpose of these centers is to determine which treatment school best suits the adjudicated juvenile. When a juvenile is placed in a reception and diagnostic center, the juvenile receives a psychiatric evaluation. A social worker also completes a case study to determine the best course of action for the youth. Other evaluations include a physical and dental examination. All of these evaluations together take an average length of 30 days. Once complete, the youth is transferred to the facility that has been determined to be the most appropriate.

Juvenile Correctional Facility

Juvenile correctional facilities are the most restrictive placements for juvenile offenders and are intended to protect public safety as well as providing programs that develop accountability and skill development for juvenile offenders. They will range in size and focus of operation from jurisdiction to jurisdiction.

Jails

Up through the mid-1980s, it was very common to find juveniles confined within adult jails, though typically in separate cell blocks. In many of those jails, the juveniles were viewed in a manner similar to that of the female inmate, small in population and a burden or afterthought to the overall operation of the facility. Changes in juvenile confinement in adult facilities were occurring, even though many of those changes were slow. In the 1980s and 1990s the numbers of youths in jails declined due in part to the Juvenile Justice and Delinquency Prevention Act of 1973, which set forth standards to govern the confinement of youths in adult facilities. In 1980, Congress amended the act, requiring all juveniles to be removed from adult jails by 1985. In fact, juveniles must at all times be separated from adult offenders by both sight and sound. As a result, police and correctional officers have an obligation to ensure that a detained juvenile offender is not in the presence of or in a position to hear an adult offender. These changes led to a reexamination of short-term juvenile confinement and the increased need for detention centers.

Detention Centers and Attention Home

The primary purpose of *detention centers*, also known as juvenile halls, is to provide a place to detain juveniles, rather than placing them in jail. In 1991 there were a reported 363 detention centers. Juvenile detention centers are typically administered by the court, with the average length of stay in a juvenile detention center being about two weeks. An alternative to the detention center is the *attention home*. The purpose of attention homes is to provide juveniles attention rather than detention. In these facilities juveniles interact with residents and staff.

As with adult corrections, the private sector is involved in juvenile corrections, providing services ranging from support activities, such as contract counseling or food service, to conducting operations for an entire facility. Clarence M. Kelley, Inc., founded by a former director of the Federal Bureau of Investigation, has contracted operations of various juvenile facilities for more than a decade with success.

Sheltered Care Facilities and Community Residential Facilities

Sheltered care facilities are nonsecure facilities that are designed to house juveniles on a short-term basis, typically overnight or for a few days. Sheltered care facilities offer a more open environment where residents are often permitted to go home on the weekends and out on field trips. According to 1991 statistics, a total of about 750 shelters were in operation in the United States. *Community residential facilities* are nonsecure residential programs that house juvenile offenders in court-ordered custody as either a juvenile offender or child in need of care.

Juvenile Boot Camps

The search for innovative, cost-effective approaches to juvenile corrections has been ongoing. In the 1980s, the idea of using a regimented corrections model known as *boot camp* emerged as what appeared to be a promising alternative to traditional confinement, targeting first-time, nonviolent offenders. Initial results from adult boot camps suggested positive value, with the belief in many correctional and governmental circles being that the recidivism rate of those that completed boot camp was no worse than that of those released after traditional confinement. Within the field of corrections, the results of these early examinations of boot camp suggested promise.

In the early 1980s, experiments with juvenile boot camps began. The motivation behind the boots camps was threefold. First, boot camps were felt to have a shock value as short incarceration programs. The idea was to expose the offender to enough shock and intimidation for incarceration to serve as a deterrent, and not confine so long that the offender starts to institutionalize. These programs usually exclude youths who have committed sexual offenses, armed robberies, and violent offenses. Second, boot camps are structured on a military model incorporating discipline, physical training, and hard labor in their program structure. For many of the first-time offenders confined, their lives have been noticeably absent of discipline and exposure to employment. Third, reducing recidivism is seen as a primary goal.

Many of the youths placed in booth camps have failed with lesser sentences such as probation. As of 1999, there were approximately 50 boot camps in 10 states. The longest operating program in the United States opened in 1985 and is located in Orleans Parish, Louisiana.

Ranches and Forestry Camps

Other options in some jurisdictions for youth confinement are *ranches* and *forestry camps*. Based upon the belief that at-risk youths can benefit from the outdoor experience, youths who have committed minor offenses may be given the sentence of serving at a ranch or forestry camp. These facilities are minimum security institutions and offer youths the ability to work in the camp or ranch while obtaining treatment. As of 1992 there were 64 forestry camps in the United States.

Independent Living

As it applies to the juvenile offender population, independent living is the state of a juvenile offender living on his or her own without the direct supervision or financial support of a parent or guardian. These juvenile offenders have transitioned from foster care or group living environments and may be utilizing community support services as a young adult in the community.

Case Management and Supervision

Juvenile Case Management and Case Supervision Plan

Case management describes a wide range of juvenile services. It requires skills to assess the problems that bring juvenile offenders and their families to the attention of the state and to meet their needs so that public safety is addressed. Juvenile offenders are held accountable for their behavior with the expectation that they learn the social and cognitive skills necessary to become law-abiding, productive members of society.

This work is done by the community supervision officers, who are responsible for conducting assessments, developing a case plan with the juvenile offender, integrating the juvenile offender's family and other significant parties in the community, contracting for services that address the concerns outlined in the case plan, and providing supervision and monitoring of the juvenile offender's behavior and progress in the program.

The purpose of case planning is the development of a strategy assisting the juvenile by identifying specific treatment targets.

Treatments focus on thinking, beliefs, behaviors, and skills the youth needs to develop into a productive, noncriminal member of society. Supervision plans are created between the juvenile offender, parent/guardian(s), supervision officer, and any other parties that identify the risks and needs of the juvenile offender and family. The plan then addresses appropriate activities, services, and treatments to successfully address identified risks and needs, ultimately setting a course for the completion of a period of supervision.

Juvenile Justice Issues

Mental Health, Alcohol, Drugs, and the Juvenile Offender

Many of the 2 million children and adolescents arrested each year in the nation have a mental health disorder, which includes learning disabilities and psychiatric challenges. Some estimates suggest as many as 70% of youth in the system are affected with a mental disorder, and one in five suffer from a mental illness so severe as to impair their ability to function as a young person and grow into a responsible adult.[8] Four of every five children and teen arrestees in state juvenile justice systems are under the influence of alcohol or drugs while committing their crimes, test positive for drugs, are arrested for committing an alcohol or drug offense, admit having substance abuse and addiction problems, or share some combination of these characteristics. It is not surprising that many of these end up falling into the juvenile justice system.

Rights and the Juvenile Offender

For years, the youthful offender fell into a gray area of the justice system. The due process rights extended to juveniles differed from the rights afforded adults. *In re Gault*, 387 U.S. 1 (1967), was a landmark U.S. Supreme Court decision that established that under the 14th Amendment, juveniles accused of crimes in a delinquency proceeding must be accorded many of the same due process rights as adults, such as the right to timely notification of charges, the right to confront witnesses, the right against self-incrimination, and the right to counsel. The ruling was the result of an evaluation of Arizona's decision to confine Gerald Francis Gault, a 15-year-old who had been placed in detention for making an obscene call to a neighbor while under probation. The Arizona juvenile court had decided to place him in the State Industrial School until he became an adult (age 21) or was "discharged by due process of law."

In 1968 Congress passed the *Juvenile Delinquency Prevention and Control Act*. The act was designed to encourage states to develop plans and programs that would work on a community level to discourage juvenile delinquency. The programs, once drafted and approved, would receive federal funding. The Juvenile Delinquency Prevention and Control Act was a precursor to the extensive Juvenile Justice and Delinquency Prevention Act that replaced it in 1974.

By 1974, the nation had directed attention toward preventing juvenile delinquency, deinstitutionalizing youth already in the system, and keeping juvenile offenders separate from adult offenders. The Juvenile Justice and Delinquency Prevention Act of 1974 created the Office of Juvenile Justice and Delinquency Prevention (OJJDP), the Runaway Youth Program, and the National Institute for Juvenile Justice and Delinquency Prevention (NIJJDP).

Kent v. United States (1966) is a famous court case involving juveniles and their rights regarding a waiver of jurisdiction. The *waiver of jurisdiction* is basically the decision to allow a juvenile to be tried as an adult in criminal court. The court's decision was there must always be a hearing in the matter of waiver of jurisdiction, and there must always be assistance of counsel in a hearing of waiver of jurisdiction. If the judge determines that a waiver of transfer is the right answer, there must be a statement of facts based on a full investigation, including a statement of the judge's reasons for the waiver.

The Debate and Some of the Solutions

Kansas is a good example of the debate that occurred in the last decades of the twentieth century pertaining to juvenile justice. In Kansas, the debate centered on who should have administrative authority over those juvenile offenders that fall under the jurisdiction of the state. The Kansas Department of Corrections, which had authority over adult state-level offenders, did not see the additional responsibility of juvenile justice to be within a mission set they could effectively accomplish. On the other side of the debate, the Kansas Department of Social Services no longer believed they could serve the juvenile mission effectively. After much debate, the decision was made to form a new agency with the mission of the administration of juvenile justice.

The Kansas Juvenile Justice Authority (JJA) is a cabinet-level criminal justice agency that began operating on July 1, 1997. Individuals as young as 10 and as old as 17 may be adjudicated as juvenile offenders and ordered into the custody of the commissioner of Juvenile Justice. The JJA may retain custody of a juvenile offender in a juvenile correctional facility to the age of 22½ and in the community to the age of 23.

Juvenile Probation, Parole, and Aftercare

John Augustus is considered the father of probation. In 1843, he broadened his efforts in adult probation to children when he took responsibility for two girls, ages 8 and 10, and an 11-year-old boy, all of whom had been accused of stealing. By 1846, he had taken on the supervision of about 30 children, ranging from 9 to 16 years of age.[9] Augustus's efforts opened the door for juvenile probation across the nation.

By 1869, the Massachusetts legislature required a state agent to be present if court actions might result in the placement of a child in a reformatory, thus providing a model for modern caseworkers. The agents were to search for other placement, protect the child's interests, investigate the case before trial, and supervise the plan for the child after disposition. Massachusetts passed the first probation statute in 1878 mandating an official state probation system with salaried probation officers.[10]

Juvenile probation, parole, and aftercare work to assist the youthful offender in the community to ensure public safety and full compliance with court orders and conditions of his or her conditional release. Within juvenile community-based supervision is what is referred to as *Juvenile Intensive Supervision Probation (JISP)*. JISP serves youth sentenced by the court to a term of probation, assesses the youth's risk and needs, develops a supervision plan to address those needs, engages the youth and family, assists the youth and family to access community-based services, monitors the youth's adherence to court-ordered probation conditions, and provides updates to the court concerning the youth's supervision. Both adult and juvenile probation programs may utilize intensive social control approaches and close monitoring. Monitoring techniques may include electronic monitoring, urine monitoring, and monitoring through personal visits and telephone calls.

Juvenile parole seeks to hold parolees accountable for their behavior while simultaneously maximizing opportunities to engage each parolee in a reentry process that facilitates family reunification, furthers the parolee's education, and leads to the development of marketable skills, normative skills, such as self-disciplined, positive, goal-directed behavior, and moral values that will enable him or her to become a productive, contributing member of the community.

Aftercare is the period of supervision or treatment of a juvenile offender who has been returned to the community from a confinement or treatment facility. It is also the status or program membership of a juvenile offender who has been committed to a treatment or confinement facility, conditionally released from the facility, and placed in a supervisory or treatment program.

Life without Parole for Juveniles

While *Roper v. Simmons* was addressed in Chapter 13, on capital punishment, the issue of life without parole for juveniles is closely linked to the practice of the death penalty for juveniles. Amnesty International and Human Rights Watch estimate that there have been more than 2,200 prisoners in the United States sentenced to spend the rest of their lives in prison for the crimes they committed as children. However, Justice Anthony M. Kennedy reported in 2010 there were only 129 juveniles currently serving nonparole life sentences for nonhomicide crimes, 77 in Florida and the rest scattered among only 10 states.

In May 2010, the U.S. Supreme Court ruled in *Graham v. Florida* that their ruling in *Roper v. Simmons*, which had abolished the death penalty for juvenile offenders, also applies to sentences of life without the possibility of parole. Thus, only juveniles who are convicted of homicide may receive a sentence of life without parole.

Interstate Compact on Juveniles

An interstate compact on juveniles is an agreement between states governing children in court-ordered custody and placed in foster care in another state. These agreements regulate the interstate transfer of supervision of juvenile offenders and the return of absconders/runaways from state to state. The agreements also ensure public protection and provide juvenile offenders with accountability and needed services.

Federal Juvenile Population

Federal juveniles are a special population with special designation needs. Each juvenile is placed in a facility that provides the appropriate level of programming and security. The Federal Bureau of Prisons contracts for facilities to house juveniles in areas where services are needed. These facilities provide programs and services specifically for juvenile offenders and serve to keep the offenders out of the adult populations of Federal Bureau of Prisons facilities. Several factors are considered when making placements, such as age, offense, length of commitment, and mental and physical health.

Historically, the federal juvenile population has consisted predominantly of Native American males with an extensive history of drug or alcohol use/abuse and violent behavior. These juveniles tend to be older in age, generally between 17 and 20 years, and are typically sentenced for sex-related offenses. Federal law does not provide aftercare supervision for Federal Bureau of Prisons custody cases following release from residential programs.

Summary

Juvenile justice has evolved from a system that primarily provided custodial care to a comprehensive service delivery system that provides for a range of programs and services designed to address the needs of the diverse population served. There is no one strategy that can be used to solve the juvenile crime problem in all jurisdictions; therefore, we see each jurisdiction dealing with its juvenile justice issues in its own way. There are countless reasons for juvenile crime, and even for the most experienced juvenile justice professional, the diversity of juvenile justice-related issues never ceases to amaze.

Vocabulary

Adjudication

Aftercare

Arrested

Attention home

Boot camp

Balanced and restorative justice (BARJ)

Community residential facility

Complaint

Convictions

Detained

Detention centers

Disposition

Forestry camps

Graham v. Florida

House of Refuge

Intake

In re Gault

Juvenile correctional facilities

Juvenile crime

Juvenile Delinquency Prevention and Control Act

Juvenile Intensive Supervision Probation (JISP)

Kent v. United States

Parens patriae

Petition

Ranches

Roper v. Simmons

Sheltered care facilities

Status offense

Waiver of jurisdiction

Discussion Questions

1. Should the juvenile justice system be similar to the adult justice system. What issues should be similar? Where should there be differences?

2. What is the historical development of the juvenile court system? Discuss the U.S. Supreme Court cases that have given juveniles more due process rights.

3. How has the *In re Gault* decision influenced the juvenile court system?

4. What impact have juvenile boot camps had on reducing recidivism?

5. In addition to the alternative juvenile probation programs discussed in the chapter, what other programs may be effective in reducing juvenile crime?

Notes

1. *Juvenile offenders and victims: National report series.* (2004, June). Retrieved June 3, 2010, from http://www.ncjrs.gov/pdf-files1/ojjdp/202885.pdf

2. MTG Management Consultants, LLC. (1998, February). Kansas Juvenile Justice Authority Information System strategic plan. Retrieved June 11, 2010, from http://jjis.state.ks.us/download-ables/jjisneed.pdf

3. Carmen, R., & Trulson, C. (2006). *Juvenile justice.* Thomas Wadsworth.

4. Clapp, E. J. (n.d.). The Chicago juvenile court movement. Retrieved June 17, 2010, from http://www.le.ac.uk/hi/teach-ing/papers/clapp1.html

5. Schonberg, S. K. (1993). *Guidelines for the treatment of alcohol- and other drug-abusing adolescents* (Treatment Improvement Protocol (TIP) Series 4). Rockville, MD: U.S. Department of Health and Human Services, Substance Abuse and Mental Health Services Administration.

6. Bartollas, C. (1997). *Juvenile delinquency.* Boston, MA: Allyn and Bacon.

7. Barrows, S. J. (1900). *The reformatory system in the United States: Reports prepared for the International Prison Commission.* Washington, DC: U.S. Government Printing Office.

8. Skowyra, K. R., & Cocozza, J. J. (2006, January). *Blueprint for change: A comprehensive model for the identification and treatment of youth with mental health needs in contact with the juvenile justice system National Center for Mental Health and Juvenile Justice* (draft, p. ix). Washington, DC: National Center for Mental Health and Juvenile Justice.

9. Binder, A., Geis, G., & Bruce, D. D. (1997). *Juvenile delinquency: Historical, cultural and legal perspectives.* Cincinnati, OH: Anderson.

10. National Center for Juvenile Justice. (1991). *Desktop guide to good juvenile probation practice.* Pittsburgh, PA.

Index